MW01610983

"The modern Jew
is the product of
the Talmud."

—RABBI ISAAC M. WISE

From the Temple to the Talmud

Exploring Judaic Origins, History, Folklore & Tribal Traditions

From the Temple to the Talmud
Exploring Judaic Origins, History, Folklore & Tribal Traditions

By Dr. Harrell Rhome
Copyright 2011 by Dr. Harrell Rhome & The Barnes Review

Published by:
THE BARNES REVIEW
P.O. Box 15877
Washington, D.C. 20003

ISBN# 978-0-9846312-8-5

Ordering more copies:
Order more copies of *From the Temple to the Talmud* (softcover, 261 pages, $25 plus $5 S&H) from THE BARNES REVIEW, P.O. Box 15877, Washington, D.C. 20003. TBR subscribers may take 10% off the list price. Call 1-877-773-9077 toll free to charge copies to Visa, MasterCard, AmEx or Discover. See more books and videos online at www.barnesreview.com.

Subscriptions:
A subscription to THE BARNES REVIEW historical magazine is $46 for one year (six issues) and $78 for two years (12 issues) inside the U.S. Outside the U.S: Canada/Mexico: $65 per year. All other nations: $80 per year sent via air mail. Send payment with request to TBR, P.O. Box 15877, Washington, D.C. 20003. Call 1-877-773-9077 toll free to charge to major credit cards. Order online at www.barnesreview.com. See a special subscription offer at the back of this volume or call toll free number above and ask for best current subscription offer.

Reproduction Policy:
Portions of this publication may be reproduced without prior permission in critical reviews and other papers if credit is given to author, book title is listed and full contact information and subscription information are given for publisher as shown above.

Cover image:
The cover image is a portion of the epic painting *The Destruction of the Temple at Jerusalem*, crafted by Nicolas Poussin in 1637.

From the Temple to the Talmud

Exploring Judaic Origins, History, Folklore & Tribal Traditions

By Harrell Rhome, M.Div., Ph.D.

Published by The Barnes Review 2011

This book is DEDICATED to
Captain Sir Richard Francis Burton

Knight Commander of St. Michael and St. George—K.C.M.G.
Fellow of the Royal Geographical Society—F.R.G.S.
1821-1890

W hile in deep-cover disguise and speaking fluent Arabic, Sir Richard Burton Burton knew and showed respect for Islamic rites and traditions. No one thought he was anything other than another devout Muslim fulfilling his lifelong dream, participating in the holy hajj (pilgrimage). He risked death again to visit the forbidden city of Harar, Ethiopia, where previous European visitors were tortured and beheaded. Burton was already experienced at this. In the 1840s as a British military intelligence agent, he moved all about India in disguise, speaking the local dialects so well he was never detected.

Burton was not just a brave and adventuresome man. This alone would never have been enough. He had a natural gift of languages, speaking and writing over 25 major tongues and numerous dialects (bringing the total to over 40). For his extraordinary and distinguished army service (captain and combat veteran in India; front-line observer and adviser in the Crimean War), his explorations and discoveries in Africa and other lands, his later career in the British Consular Service, and not the least for his literary contributions (his steamy *Kama Sutra* translation notwithstanding), he was knighted by Queen Victoria in 1886 in the Order of St. Michael and St. George. Burton was a respected, longtime member, lecturer and fellow of the Royal Geographical Society and the British Association for the Advancement of Science, along with numerous other memberships and honors. In 1890, he expired of natural causes at the age of 69. His wife, Lady Isabel Arundell Burton, was author of *Inner Life of Syria* and other books.

Burton is shown dressed in mufti as an Afghan Pathan Muslim pilgrim during his notable 1853 covert visits in Arabia, where he visited both major Islamic holy sites, Mecca and Medina. If detected as an infidel, a mob would have torn him into small bits within the blink of an eye.

Lady Isabel followed him in death in 1896. Burton was responsible for more than 40 books and over 30 translations. His last and most controversial volume, *The Jew, the Gypsy and El Islam,* was posthumously published in 1898.

My book is dedicated to this man of honor and integrity, a veritable vast reservoir of knowledge on a host of subjects and languages that still amazes us well over a century later. Richard Burton was a truly brash, brave and brilliant explorer boldly seeking truth. He not only found it, but courageously shared it with others.

At right: Sir Richard Burton is shown at right dressed in mufti as an Afghan Pathan Muslim pilgrim during his notable 1853 covert visits in Arabia, where he visited both major Islamic holy sites, Mecca and Medina. If detected as an infidel, a mob would have torn him into small bits within the blink of an eye.

—Dr. Harrell Rhome
September 2011

Table of Contents

Low relief image in metal shows a Jewish religious figure reading from a holy book, possibly the Talmud or the Torah.

Beginning an Exploratory Journey

"He who dares not offend cannot be honest." —Tom Paine.

This book presents little-known facts about the cultural history and traditions of the Judaic (Jewish) peoples with an introduction to some unique literary sources, both old and new. This book will probably be called anti-Judaic and maybe anti-Christian. The true religion of any objective writer should be critical thinking, and it is in this spirit and style that I approach this project. Before reading further, you must consider a couple of things. This book contains death threats. No, not from your author, but from this very strange collection of literature we propose to explore. According to its practices and protocols, non-chosen ones are absolutely forbidden to study any of this. As you read on, you'll discover something else. Some of the most revealing, indeed some of the most shocking things said about Judaic religion and culture are written by Judaics themselves. Read on and see if you don't agree.

Socrates said: "The beginning of wisdom is the definition of terms."

The modern religion called Judaism is Talmudism. It was never, ever the religion of the ancient Israelites, nor are today's "Jews" the "people of the bible."

Before understanding any parts of the larger scheme of world history, gentiles, especially Christians, must grasp basic facts. For the purposes of this exposition, and because they are familiar to many readers, I draw your attention to the stories told in the Gospels. Let's be clear about the cast of characters. Who are the main players? Talmudism is the doctrine of the cult of scribes and Pharisees who, as portrayed in the New Testament, opposed Jesus, a young Palestinian revolutionary and would-be reformer of the Hebrew religion of the day. They actively conspired against him, eventually succeeding in causing his death. What he first and foremost opposed, most vehemently, was the doctrine of the scribes and lawyers, a compendium of controversial oral and written commentary that grew and grew over the years. In Hebrew it is called L_M_D, Lamud or Lamad, derived from the verb for to learn; meaning the instruction, the teaching or Talmud; the formerly oral tradition. The texts are written in either the Hebrew script or Aramaic, the later development of the language. The term halakha is often used, referring to both the biblical and the oral law codes and the interpretation thereof. In many ways, Judaism is a codified legal system as much as it is a religion.

To connect with the Old Testament in order to distract and deceive Christians, the rabbis tell us that the Talmud began with Moses on Mt. Sinai; thus there was not only the written law, but the oral tradition as well. But in truth, the Talmud came straight from Babylon, brought back into Palestine hundreds of years later by Judeo-Persians. The Old Testament clearly reflects the influence of the Zoroastrian religion, especially in the Book of Genesis. Talmudism was later co-opted and kidnapped by the Khazar convert Jews of the eighth century. Talmudism has little to do with the Old Testament except exploiting it as a system of rules and regulations providing "legal loopholes" and "escape clauses" to evade and avoid the Law said to have been given to them by god. Of course, all of this must be subject to the interpretations of the rabbinical caste.

The Talmudists are essentially saying that the Tennakh (or Tanakh) is not enough. "Tennakh" is a Hebrew acronym for Torah, Nevi'im (prophets) and Ketuvim, ("writings"), essentially what we refer to as the Old Testament. After many centuries and thousands of pages, LaMud, the Teaching or the Tradition, has itself become the real scriptures of the people known as Judaics. Not only that, there is an even more secretive oral tradition, seldom ever known about by outsiders or by ordinary believers. Moreover, the real god of Judaism is not the peripatetic YaHWeH/JeHoVaH/YaHu, a deity they appropriated from Egypt, and especially not the Father God spoken of by Jesus. The self-chosen ones, of course, appear to mostly worship themselves and their traditions. Here is your first "scripture verse" from the Talmud: "The messiah is without metaphor the Jewish people." Kethuboth 111a.

Prior to moving on and before emails and letters start flying my way, a further word is in order. In no way do I think that "all the Jews" believe all the things featured in this book. Indeed, as you'll see, some of the Talmudic texts and ritual practices are quite fanatical and shocking. I well know that many Judaists (the proper

English word for a practitioner of Judaism) repudiate such extremism. The more important point is that a goodly number of practicing Judaists at least sometimes ask for rabbinical advice, which is based on religious tradition. The basic question goes something like this: "Rabbi, what should a good Jew do in this or that situation?" Over the many centuries, the teachings of the Talmud have stood foursquare and foremost for knowledge about the proper beliefs and practices, providing all that is required to be a good Jew in the eyes of the synagogue. Again, I realize that the more radical texts and themes are avoided by the rabbis and largely unknown by the laity, but the "Spirit of the Law," the essence of the Talmud, colors their advice. This is as it should be. Muslims turn to their imams and the Koran, Christians consult their pastors and the bible, and Jews seek advice from their rabbis and the Talmud. Of course, there are many exceptions among Judaic folk as you will soon see. Hence, my target audience is not just "gentiles." If truth be told, many Judaists and people of Judaic heritage may not be all that familiar with the material we survey either. Get ready for some surprises.

Some of this information may upset readers. It is the difficult and somewhat disturbing task of the biblical Revisionist to deconstruct and demythologize some of the most popular and successful items of legend and lore. We are chipping away at a wall of obfuscation and lies that is thousands of years old. Even some of the most cynical persons have their favorite bible stories, told to them as youngsters. Deconstructing these dear and precious ideas is not an easy task, and not only that, it is one that is dismaying and irritating to many sincere Christians, Muslims and Judaics, but it is crucial if the searcher is to have the slightest chance of finding jewels of truth among the detritus of eons.

Are you ready to continue our exploratory expedition into the jungle of Judaic legends and lore? We've already come across a valuable find, so don't forget. It is essential to our quest. You must pick it up and put in your pocket right now, before moving to the next stop on our map.

The modern religion called Judaism is Talmudism. It was never, ever the religion of the ancient Israelites, nor are today's "Jews" the "people of the bible."

Ishtar, also known as Ashtaroth, the Queen of the Night. Old Babylonian, about 1700 B.C. From the British Museum.

CHAPTER 2

What Was the Ancient Hebrew Religion?

E arly on in this project, before moving directly into the Talmudic texts, I saw the need to answer basic questions as to the actual nature of the religion portrayed in the Old Testament. This is a project in biblical Revisionism that is crucial in several ways. First of all, it is important to know the truth about a period of the ancient past which still impacts us today. Second, the Old Testament bible stories are declared to be actual history as well as divinely inspired literature, from god himself, no less. All three Semitic religions (Judaism, Christianity and Islam) say this. Hence they are rooted in this material. Consider this for a moment. What if it is not true? What if it has other origins? Not only would this affect billions of believers, it impacts current events and geopolitics. The troublesome state of Israel is not only predicated on the alleged history of the Holocaust, but its land claims are quite solidly entrenched in the Old Testament bible stories. The political expansionist movement called Zionism glommed onto what is essentially a tradition of folklore and astrological symbolism to justify their seizure and occupation of Palestine.

Gerald Massey said in *Lectures*, published as a private edition c. 1900: "These and other matters pertaining to the astronomical allegory and the natural genesis of mythology were pre-extant in Egypt, and had been carried out over the world untold ages before a Palestinian Jew had ever trod the Earth."

George B. Vetter, in *Magic and Religion*, 1958, p. 403, writes: "Judaism? It is an all too obvious product of the Mesopotamian and Babylonian and Canaanite culture complexes."

The facts about bible origins are not a new revelation. This has been talked about and written about for a long time, but is largely ignored by the Powers That Be. A few hundred years ago, you might have faced death for your beliefs in both Catholic and Protestant realms. In some fundamentalist Muslim countries, the same thing can happen today. But, for the most part, these ideas are just ignored. Of course, tens of billions of dollars are generated by various religions. To say that the bible is theology, but not history, is a dangerous proposition.

And again from Massey: "It is not the ancient legends that tell us lies. The men who created them did not deal falsely with us by nature. All the falsity lies in their having been falsified through ignorantly mistaking mythology for divine revelation and allegory for historic truth."

Join with me now for an alternative explanation of the bible stories mistaken for history.

Hebrew Egyptian Origins

To avoid lengthily citing the works of a host of scholars and writers, suffice it to say that much of the ancient Hebrew-Habiru religious ethos and mythos, indeed all its gods (and goddesses), came from Egypt. The study called astrotheology teaches us that the origins of all religions come from ancient humans who studied and observed the heavenly bodies, the sun, moon and stars. This is portrayed particularly well in the 2008 documentary movie production, Zeitgeist as well as in, among others, the writings of D. M. Murdock (Acharya S).

In addition to Godfrey Higgins, Gerald Massey, Sir Richard Burton and more than a few other classic authors, researcher and metaphysician E. Valentia Straiton (in *Celestial Ship of the North*, 1927) informs us greatly as to the true and actual beginnings:

"The Jewish glyph and the Hebrew language are not original, but borrowed from the Egyptian and are considered sacred. Hebrew is composed of hieroglyphs, symbols and myths of the Egyptians and their gods. The imagery, allegory and divinities found in old Hebrew writings are Egyptian and appertain to the Typhorian cult. The Jewish "new" departure and developments were made out of the oldest of materials, originally made in Egypt, but converted into the historical by the Jews.

"Celsus says, 'The Jews were a tribe of Egyptians who revolted from the established religion.' Their Jehovah can be traced to the Great Mother. . . .

"The most high god of the Jews, El, Eloi, Elohim (plural), and Shadai, coexisted with Jehovah. The Hebrew El was the male supreme deity. El is also the Child. . . . He is also called the Lord of Hosts or Angels and was the greatest of all the gods, goddesses or divinities of the primal Seven in heaven, Jehovah, the Mother of the Seven Great Stars. The god of the Jews was frequently written in the Pentateuch as She, but was changed to He after the divinity had changed sex. . . .

"The names of Jehovah-Elohim are derived from the two words each of which is male-female; Jehovah, a compound or Jah, male, and Hovah or Eve, female. Numerically Jehovah is the diameter of the circle and Elohim the circumference. Jehovah-Elohim was the Mother of the Seven elementary gods, combined in one divinity, the one constellation.

"A seven-fold god is mythological, whether Jehovah or Iao-Sabaoth. Sevekh, the seven-fold, Ea with the seven arms, Ra with his seven souls, the Hindu Agni with the seven arms, the Gnostic Chnubis with his seven rays, the Dragon with his seven heads, and El of the seventh planet, and many others, were the vehicles of many imaginings, and finally became converted into gods in relation to celestial phenomena, when 'the gods were seen in their ideas as stars, and all their signs, and the stars were numbered with all the gods in them.' (Hermes Trismegistus)."

The "Seven Stars" or the "Seven Planets" as they were called, are the most visible heavenly bodies: the Sun, the Moon, Mercury, Venus, Mars, Jupiter and Saturn. Over the eons, these became the "Seven elementary gods," the various astrologically personified figures seen in all the primeval religions, including the Habiru-Hebrew tribes of Egypt.

Gerald Massey says: "The only satisfactory ethnological designation for a people like the Hebrews must be derived from a religion that had its rootage in mythology."

As we see, the Hebrews did not invent monotheism as claimed; far from it. Even Martin Luther, a skilled translator, sometimes let theology override his scholarship, such as in his limited translation of various words used for god, some of which are plural, others emphasizing feminine/goddess attributes. In truth, monotheism came from many sources, but especially from Pharaoh Akhenaton in Egypt. As we know, the Habiru-Hebrew wandering tribes learned a lot there, so they would surely have picked this up as well, to become an essential element in their later religious repertoire.

German writer F. Roderich-Stoltheim, in *The Riddle of the Jew's Success*, Leipzig, Hammer Verlag, 1927, pp. 69-70, comments on this at length:

"The contention that the Hebrews invented monotheism—the one god doctrine—belongs to the domain of thoughtless phrases, all the more as most ancient Jewish documents recognize a whole line of gods, such as Elohim, El-Schaddai, El-Elyon, Adorai, Zabaoth, Jahwe etc.

"It was first of all Luther's translation—which was frequently extremely free—of these names by the universal designation 'God the Lord,' which is responsible for this semblance of Jewish monotheism.

"Moreover, it has been sufficiently established for many decades that the Jewish god has nothing to do with the Christian Father-in-Heaven, or the universal Father of the Germanic nations. Jahwe. . . is the exclusive tribal god of the Hebrews: He has absolutely no desire to be the god of other peoples, for he persecutes the latter with unappeasable hatred, and assigns to his favorite the task of annihilating the remaining nations, or as Luther translates: 'to devour them'."

And from a website we learn: "The Temple in Jerusalem or the Holy Temple (Hebrew: *Bet HaMikdash*) was built in ancient Jerusalem in c. 10th century B.C. and subsequently rebuilt several times. It was the center of Israelite Jewish worship, primarily for the offering of sacrifices known as the korbanot. It was located on

Jerusalem's Temple Mount. It was the center of ancient Judaism and has remained as a focal point for Jewish services over the millennia." http://www.islamic-architecture.info/WA-IS/WA-IS-003.htm

Rites and Rituals of the Temple

As to the specific innermost beliefs, mysteries, rites and rituals of the Temple, apart from the copious, cruel and bloody animal sacrifices, we know very little more. Of course one need not read all that far into the Old Testament to realize that human sacrifice is also a part of their archetypal heritage. Not surprisingly, their nomadic experiences came with the desert tribes from Egypt all the way to Canaan, which they attacked and appropriated, and then to the Jerusalem Temple. What things came with them? In the desert, they carried the so-called Ark of the Covenant. Essentially this was what we might call "god in a box," where the mysterious Yahweh was either supposed to reside or at least speak from within. This is literally and symbolically how their deity accompanied them on nomadic journeys. Interestingly, both the seaborne Ark of Noah and the box Ark of the Covenant have similar symbolism and meaning. Blavatsky (*Isis Unveiled*, Vol. II, p. 444, tells us more with reference to what this "holiest of holies" was really about:

"In all traditions of the Deluge the Ark was made to contain the Sea of Life, which in various miraculous ways was always saved for future generations. This germ of all living things was necessary for the repeopling of the earth. It represented the survival of life, and the supremacy of spirit over matter, through the conflict of the opposing powers of nature."

She continues:

"The Ark, oblong in shape, was used as the 'Sacrificial Chalice' by the priests in the worship of the goddesses who represented the generative powers of nature. . . . The Talmud books say that Noah was himself the dove (spirit), thus identifying him more with the Chaldean Nouah. Baal is represented with the wings of a dove, and the Samaritans worshiped, on Mount Gezerim, the image of a dove."

Eminent explorer, ethnographer and linguist Sir Richard Burton (in *The Jew, the Gypsy and El Islam*, 1898) speaks of Egyptian and even earlier Indian origins:

". . . [A]nd the Hebrews, who claimed the most ancient as well as the noblest of pedigrees, could not tell the tale of their origin as a nation without elevating its simple estate by a hundred fables, and embellishing it with signs and marvels and wonders tending to the honor of the Chosen People. . . . In one point the Lawgiver [Moses] miscalculated his powers. He had proposed making of his Hebrew followers a race of pure theists, a kingdom of priests . . . but the Hebrew mind was thoroughly unfitted to receive pure truth. . . .

"Deeply imbued with the tenacious superstitions of the Nile, the stiff-necked race had become irritable rather than strong under the painful training of the desert. . . . [N]one had the eyes to look steadfastly upon the unveiled light of Revelation emanating from their leader and lawgiver. Finding after his return from temporary seclusion . . . his chosen people worshipping a metal calf, the god Apis, and playing—in other words, a scene of Egyptian debauchery—Moses broke in wrath the first Table of the Law. . . .

"Moses returned with a code (Exodus 34) better fitted to the sickly and diseased condition of the Hebrew soul. Of this the proportion of the ritual to the moral is as 10 to two. It is a priestly system, a faith of feasts and sacrifices, of holy days and ceremonies purposely assimilated to those idolatries of Egypt with which the minds of the people were familiar but secured to the worship of Jehovah their god. The Lawgiver no longer disdained to borrow from symbolical religion, especially in the ceremonial worship, which at first he appears to have avoided.

"The ark and the tabernacle were old types among the Egyptians, memorials of their Northern migration. The Urim and Thummim (Ra and Thenei) were the Sun and personified Justice—Light and Truth. The Elohim were Kneph and Pthah, the presiding spirit and the creative intellect of the Supreme. The Spirit of God that moved upon the face of the waters is again the deity Kneph. The silence with which Jehovah was to be adored appears to be an idea borrowed from Amon Ra, the Unutterable Word, similar to the Hindu 'Aum,' which must never be spoken. . . .

"The Tree of Life [central to the Kabala], whose fruit made gods of those who tasted it, was a mere symbol, long before the day of Moses, incorporated in the Indian and Egyptian mythologies. It survived in the Christian's early belief, and has even left its traces in the Tuba or Paradisiacal tree of El Islam. The cosmogony of Moses may be traced to the same origin."

As to what was actually done deep in the interior recesses of the Temple, the bloody and cruel sacrifice of animals may have been all the priests and deep adepts dared to show the ordinary worshippers. We must conclude that the innermost esoteric Hebrew beliefs and rituals were polytheistic and pagan in nature, conflicting greatly with the prevailing Judeo-Christian mythology. Other rituals rooted in Egypt would have been acted out, and serpent adoration and healing by serpents was widespread. Beyond this, I see no productive reason to speculate further, but if you must, read more in the Old Testament about various horrors, ethnic cleansings, torture and other assorted atrocities, and decide for yourself what even more sinister secrets the Temple inner sanctum might have contained. When we take a closer look, we see that the bible contains very little about the real doctrines and dogma of the Hebrew priests and adepts, who knew the truth about the origin of their beliefs and practices. The Torah books, from Egypt, really did not mean all that much.

Did an Ancient "Q Document," a "Proto-Talmud," Exist?

Valentia Straiton states: "Philo, the most industrious and devout Jew of his race, recognizing the true nature of all sacred writings, treats the Pentateuch as allegorized and symbolical. . . . The Pentateuch was written on papyrus by a scribe's pen from the ancient hieroglyphics, which were carved in stone. It is known that the Pentateuch arose out of the older primitive documents by means of a supplementary one. The real Hebrew bible was a secret volume, unknown to the masses, and is far more ancient than the Septuagint."

The Septuagint, of course, is the Koine Greek version of the Hebrew texts, translated between the third and first centuries B.C. It is still considered to be a useful rendering of the known and extant Hebrew scriptures of the day, including some books not included in the later Old Testament and Apocrypha. However, it seems that more than this was involved in preserving the secret traditions and lore, some of which were later taken into the Talmud and Kabala. As did Rudolf Bultmann about the Christian gospels, both Miss Straiton and I postulate that a "Q," a quelle, a source, a foundation document in common, must have existed. This "secret supplementary volume" as she describes it would have included both the oral and the already-written traditions, with commentary. Among other things, this preserved the original polytheistic Egyptian pagan legends and lore. We could call this a Proto-Talmud from eons ago, compiled by the Hebrew-Habiru priests, levites and scribes, intended only for the inner circle of Elders, adepts and properly initiated "chosen ones."

To claim, as do the three Semitic religions, that the mostly astrologically based mythos found in the Judeo-Christian bible (and the later Koran) is a factual account is not a seriously sustainable position. At its very best, the bible (indeed, any religious writing) should first and foremost be seen as theology, not history. What is more, to create and locate a nation-state based on myths and misrepresentations is a fallacy and a flaw. Many books and articles have been, could be, should be, and will be written on all these matters, but what you have here sufficiently presents a reasonable and honest alternative explanation of the bible legends and lore. You can take it from here. Search the Internet. Use your library. There are mountains of material. To bring this to a close, now you know just about as much as anyone else does concerning the rather murky, mystical, mysterious and elusive ancient Hebrew religious beliefs and practices. As a matter of fact, you probably know more.

CHAPTER 3

Exploring the Origins & Evolution of the Hebrew Language

ebrew is a most misunderstood linguistic topic. Gerald Massey, Valentia Straiton and others tell us that the most ancient form of the letters originally came from Egyptian hieroglyphs as the Hebrew/Habiru were a wandering Egypto-Semitic tribe. Godfrey Higgins's *Anacalypsis* tells us the people and the language first arose in ancient India (the Oude tribe), later migrating to Egypt and other lands. Regardless of its earliest beginnings, the later forms of Hebrew definitely have other origins. The older form decayed into a liturgical dialect by New Testament times.

Uninformed people sometimes tell you that Jesus spoke Hebrew. He did not. According to the New Testament, he read liturgical Hebrew in the synagogues, but neither he nor anyone else in those days used it in their everyday life. The patois of the people was Aramaic, and many spoke Greek, the lingua franca of the day in the eastern Roman empire. Old Hebrew evolved into Aramaic, which even today is still spoken in some small Syrian villages, mostly among Christians. Aramaic is used as a liturgical language among the Maronite Christians in Cyprus. Syriac, a dialect of Aramaic, is still used among Christians in the Syrian Orthodox Church of India.

The ancient Hebrew text of the Tennakh was preserved by a special cadre of rabbis called the Masoretes. They worked for centuries, getting it just like they wanted, and did not complete their work until very early medieval times, later influencing new Protestant translations of the Old Testament, including that of Martin Luther and the later translators of the King James version. The Aleppo Codex dates from c. A.D. 930, and represents the completion of their work. It was written on parchment in the Palestinian town of Tiberias by the scribe Shlomo Ben Boya'a, and still exists in parts after narrowly escaping destruction in Syria in 1947. Muslim mobs protesting against the newly founded state of Israel burned the synagogue where it had been stored. Wisely, the congregation anticipated this, preserving the ancient codices by distributing them among the members. Since then, most of it has been reassembled. The third-century B.C. Greek Septuagint, with some books not included in the bible, was translated from even earlier Hebrew manuscripts, apart from the Masoretic texts. When St. Jerome produced his Latin Vulgate Bible in the late A.D. 300s, he used the Septuagint as well as other Hebrew sources. In the Catholic tradition, Jerome is the patron saint of translators.

All these Hebrew manuscripts were in the older form, without the modern vowel points. The language is supposed to be virtually unreadable without the diacritical marks, added and interpreted, of course, by the rabbinical caste. Changing the vowel points can alter the entire meaning of a text. Ancient Hebrew is said to be like Sanskrit, a primordial root language. The most ancient versions probably are, but not all scholars agree about the later forms of the Hebrew script. As an aside, Godfrey Higgins's Anacalypsis says ancient Arabic is the older form of the earliest Semitic tongues.

Are Ancient Hebrew and Greek Related?

I present this subsection only as an interesting and quite fascinating hypothesis. Moreover, it seems to be rather ignored and perhaps even suppressed. This story, however, is rather complex and linguistically challenging. Nonetheless, I briefly present this as a valid alternative theory as to the actual origin of Hebrew. You may find it quite compelling. A noted linguistic scholar, Joseph Yahuda wrote a small volume called *Hebrew Is Greek* in 1982, but it has now largely disappeared, even from libraries. In summer 2009, a copy showed up for $1,295. Why has this obscure book either gone away or become rare and expensive? Hopefully, what is presented here may challenge some linguistically talented individuals to do more research.

Along with ancient Hebrew and Arabic, Greek is also an eons-old idiom. Could Hebrew and Greek be linguistically related in some way? Let's start with the basics. How do the alphabets begin? Alpha, Beta, Gamma and Delta; Aleph Bet, Gimel and Dalet. Daring Judaic researcher Joseph Yehuda (*Hebrew Is Greek*, pp. 6, 17) proposes a unique and challenging theory:

"A large number of Talmudic words were borrowed from the Greek. . . . Jewish scholars have learned Greek in order to gain direct access to the Septuagint and the works of Josephus and the better to understand the Talmud. Biblical Hebrew is Greek and the Hebrews are Asiatic Greeks. In fact, the outcome of my laborious, extensive and elaborate research may be summed up in a brief sentence: Hebrew is Greek with a mask on."

Was Joseph Yahuda yet another Judaic writer who decided to reveal some controversial ideas? If Hebrew really came from ancient Greek, would this affect its status as a holy and sacred language, supposedly spoken and understood by god? Among other things, that would contradict the Talmud. See what Greek reviewer Konstantinos Efstathios-Georganas says about Yahuda's now-rare and hard-to-find book:

"Yahuda. . . manages to prove with scientific accuracy that both Hebrew and Arabic are Greek in origin. This revelation broke a 3,000-year-old misconception. Having great knowledge of Hebrew, Arabic, French and English, as well as knowing the Old Testament and half the Koran by heart, Yahuda studied the translation of the Septuagint and Homer. He made a detailed comparison of these languages over the course of 30 years. . . .

"The work of J. Yahuda. . . documents the Greekness of the Hebrew language. Realizing the importance of his discovery, Yahuda has worked hard to elevate his people by attempting to prove a relationship with the Greeks. He convincingly demonstrates that 90% of all Hebrew and Arabic words are Greek, and, had he continued his research, would have proved this for 100% of the language. Not only are the words Greek, but the various symbols that are internationally recognized as Hebrew, are, according to this well-documented study, also Greek." (Source: http://www.democraticunderground.com/discuss/duboard.php?az=show_mesg&forum=209&topic_id=747&mesg_id=747.)

Please review the following charts.

(1) The early Greek alphabet is shown.

(2) Here, the Koine Greek of New Testament times, then the modern form.

transliteration	Koine	Modern	Name
a	Λ	Αα	Alpha
b	Β	Ββ	Beta
g	Γ	Γγ	Gamma
d	Δ	Δδ	Delta
e	Є	Εε	Epsilon
z	Ζ	Ζζ	Zeta
ê, E	Η	Ηη	Eta
th	Θ	Θθ	Theta
i	Ι	Ιι	Iota
k	Κ	Κκ	Kappa
l	Λ	Λλ	Lambda
m	Μ	Μμ	Mu
n	Ν	Νν	Nu
x	Ξ	Ξξ	Xi
o	Ο	Οο	Omicron
p	Π	Ππ	Pi
r	Ρ	Ρρ	Rho
s	C	Σσ	Sigma
t	Τ	Ττ	Tau
u	Υ	Υυ	Upsilon
f, ph	Φ	Φφ	Phi
ch	Χ	Χχ	Chi
ps	Ψ	Ψψ	Psi
ô, O	Ѡ	Ωω	Omega

(3) This is followed by the Hebrew letters, where we see that some consonants can also be vowels. Recall this and perhaps look again when we explore what Godfrey Higgins says about the modern-day Hebrew vowel points.

1	2	3	4	5	6	7
Order	Sign	Name	Literal Meaning	Ancient Script	Latin	Pronunciation
1	א	Aleph	Ox	⋉	A	Silent glottal stop, like the "-" in "a-ha"
2	ב	Bet	House	◁	B	ב (with a dot): B as in Bet ב (without a dot): V as in Vet
3	ג	Gimel	Camel	∧	C	G as in Gift
4	ד	Dalet	Door	△	D	D as in Door
5	ה	Hey	Behold	⋠	E	H as in Hey
6	ו	Vav	Nail	Y	F	V as in Vine. It also represents the vowels "u" as in "flute" (ו) and "o" as in "hole" (ו).
7	ז	Zayin	Weapon	Z	Z	Z as in Zechariah
8	ח	Chet	Fence	目	H	Ch as in Bach
9	ט	Tet	Twist, Serpent	⊗		T as in Turn
10	י	Yod	Hand	⋎	I,J	Y as in Yes. It also represents the vowels "i" as in machine and "ey" as in "they."
11	ך כ	Kaph	Palm of Hand	⋎	K	כ (with a dot): K as in King כ (without a dot): Ch as in Bach
12	ל	Lamed	Staff, Ox Goad	L	L	L as in Learn
13	ם מ	Mem	Water	⋈	M	M as in Memory
14	ן נ	Nun	Fish	⋏	N	N as in Now
15	ס	Samek	Support	≢		S as in Support
16	ע	Ayin	Eye	○	O	It is supposed to be formed in the back of the throat like a gulp, but is usually silent.
17	ף פ	Pey	Mouth	⊃	P	פ (with a dot): P as in Power פ (without a dot): Ph as in Phone
18	ץ צ	Tzaddi	Fish Hook	⋔		Ts as in Sits
19	ק	Quph	Eye of Needle	Ⴓ	Q	C as in Cry (more guttural than Kaph)
20	ר	Resh	Head	◁	R	R as in Rush
21	ש	Shin	Tooth	W	S	ש (with a dot above right): Sh as in Shine ש (with a dot above left): S as in Sun
22	ת	Tav	Mark, Sign Cross	X †	T	ת (with a dot): T as in Time ת (without a dot): Th as in Theme

(4) The last chart is quite informative and fascinating, showing related Semitic alphabets, including Hieratic Egyptian. The most ancient cultural and linguistic roots of the Habiru-Hebrew migratory tribal groups are in Egypt.

HEBREW NAMES OF LETTERS.	1. HIERATIC EGYPTIAN.	2. ANCIENT PHŒNICIAN.	3. MOABITIC.	4. OLD HEBREW.	5. OLD HEBREW. (Rock Inscriptions.)	6. SQUARE HEBREW.
Aleph	ζ	⊀Ⴙ⊀	Ϝ	ℵ	≮	א
Beth	⟋	99	9	9	9	ב
Gimel	⟨	7 /		⟍		ג
Daleth	⟋	◁◥	△	٩	◁	ד
He	Ⅲ	⋣⟡⋣	⋣	⋣	⋣	ה
Vav	⟍	٩٩	⟁	⟁	⟁↑	ו
Zayin	⟋	I2⟋	I	⟊ ⟊	⟉	ז
Cheth	θ	8Ⴙ⟊Ⴙ	⟊	8		ח
Teth	⟍	⊕⊕				ט
Yodh	⟋	⟋⟍⟋	⟋	⟍	⟋	י
Kaph	٩	٩⟍⟋	⟋	⟍	٩	כ ך
Lamedh	⟋	6⟍	6	⟋	⟋	ל
Mem	3	⟋ ⟋	⟍	⟍⟋	⟍	מ ם
Nun	7	٩⟍٩	⟋	⟋	⟋ ⟋	נ ן
Samekh	⟋	⟍⟊⟊⟋⟋	⟊	⟍	⟍	ס
Ayin		O	O	▽	△ O	ע
Pe	⟋	٩٩٩	⟋		⟋	פ ף
Tsadhe	⟋	⟋⟍	⟋	⟍⟍	⟍	צ ץ
Koph	⟍	٩٩φ	φ	P	↑	ק
Resh	9	٩⟍	⟍	Q	٩	ר
Shin	⟋	W	W	⟍	W	ש
Tav	6	+X	X	X	+	ת

From the charts we see several linguistic links and pathways among the tongues of the ancient world. While my Koine Greek from seminary years is pretty rusty, I finally located Mr. Yahuda's book so I could take a look. It doesn't take long to see that he was a master scholar of both tongues. So then, Greek may indeed be the mother tongue of the ancient Semitic world.

Hebrew, the Chosen Tongue of God?

While Hebrew is obviously very ancient, it is wrongly given a place of great prominence, mostly because of the Judaic books called the Old Testament. As with related issues, well-meaning but mistaken Christians, especially their "biblical scholars," are the ones who primarily perpetrate this mythology. Naturally, the Judaic religion promotes this errant view to support their misidentification as a chosen people with a special language. Wherever Hebrew actually arose, the three Semitic religions (Judaism, Christianity and Islam) basically say that god—among other things, also called Yahu, Yehovah, Jahveh, Jah-Hovah (a bisexual deity), Allah, El, El Shaddai, Elohim (plural), Jah, Iau, Ieue or whomever—spoke ancient Hebrew to Moses on Mt. Sinai. Even if you believed that, so what? One could just as easily say that through the Virgin Mary at Fatima in 1917 God spoke Portuguese, so we shouldn't use Hebrew anymore.

On the other hand, and exactly as we would expect, the teachings of the Talmud say that the Hebrew language is divinely blessed, just like the people who speak it. Prof. Dr. Johannes Eisenmenger translates from the Hebrew in his voluminous 1700 work *Endecktes Judenthum* ("Jewry Unveiled"):

"In the treatise Shalsheleth Hakkabala, we have the following passage. . . . Three angels are said to receive the prayers of the Israelites, and to make garlands of them. . . . Behold. These three who make the garlands, do not attempt to make garlands of any other prayers but only of such as are formed in the Hebrew tongue; those prayers that are admired in other languages, nay even in the Syriac and Chaldaic; although the holy scripture honors the same, when frequently something is mentioned in the Law, the Prophets, and the Hagiographis, in the Syriac language, they regard it not.

"By how much less will they be regardless of the prayers, which are done in any of the rest of the languages that have not been thought worthy of any notice, or honored to be mentioned in the Law?" English translation, Vol. II, 1742, p. 90ff.

English? Latin? Thai? Spanish? Sanskrit? Chinese? All the others? Just forget about it. Don't even bother praying. You are not among the chosen ones, and you do not speak the blessed tongue. Of this, there is no doubt. The Talmud tells us so.

Changing the Hebrew Language: Understanding the Added Vowel Points

This is from a remarkable and challenging work by Godfrey Higgins entitled *Anacalypsis: An Attempt to Draw Aside the Veil of the Saitic Isis; or, An Inquiry into the Origin of Languages, Nations and Religions* (London: 1836; reprinted 1992, A&B Books). The following is taken from an appendix in the print edition. For some reason this is not found in the online versions, so we have a rather unique source. Mr. Higgins wrote to the editor of *The Classical Journal*, a scholarly publication of the day. He says what we see in the more modern rendition of Hebrew has little to do with the language of long ago:

"The Hebrew language, as it is found in the copies of the Pentateuch used in the synagogues, consists of twenty-two letters, but is devoid of the marks which are known by the name of vowel points. The present Jews. . . maintain that these points are of the greatest antiquity; some asserting them to be as old as Ezra. . . .

"On the contrary, it has been the opinion of most learned men in modern times, that they have not only adopted as authority, but invented, since the time of Christ, that they were invented in the dark ages by the Jews, in order to enable them to give such meaning and pronunciation to the text as they saw proper, and further to enable them, on once having given it that meaning and pronunciation, to keep them from all ages in future. The object for which they were invented is evident from the circumstance, that they not only added a system of new vowels to the language, but they contrived to abolish the old ones, and render them silent and useless as vowels, and convert them, when joined to the new letters, into consonants. Had the object of the Jews in inventing the points been merely to fix the pronunciation, they would not have done away with the old vowels, but only added some points to them. But this would not have served their purpose, and convert them into consonants. The sacred books made use of by the Jews in their synagogues, have ever been, and still are, without the vowel points. . . .

"The ancient cabalists draw none of the mysteries from the vowel points, but all from the letters; which is an argument either that these vowel points were not in use in their time, or else were not then looked on as an authentic part of the sacred text; for had they been so, these triflers would certainly have drawn mysteries from the one as well as from the other, as the later cabalists have done.

"Neither the Mishna, nor the Gemara [the main divisions of the Talmud], either that of Jerusalem or that of Babylon, do make any mention of these vowel points. . . . And although. . . Jerome and Origen were well skilled in the Hebrew language, yet in none of their writings do they speak the least of them.

"It is a certain truth, and of which there is no doubt, that this law which Moses set before the Israelites was plain, without points, and without accents, and without any distinction of verses, even as we see it at this day; and according to the opinion of the cabalistic doctors, the whole law was one verse, yea, and there are some that say as one word."

Higgins reminds us of some important facts. The Hebrew manuscripts that were translated into the Old Testament books not only had no vowel points, they had no punctuation at all and very little, if any, spacing. Thus, there were no verses and chapters, little or no space between words, hence no sentences or paragraphs. The various divisions of chapter and verse, along with the book titles, were all added by the translators and theologians, closely guided by the Vatican.

Beyond that, some Judaic mystics tell us that the whole Torah, each and every Hebrew letter, forms a single word that is the name of god. Of course, even if it is, they don't know how to pronounce it, a true Kabalistic conundrum. The well made 1998 movie, Pi, vividly portrays a Kabalistic numerological cult seeking the name of god using, among other things, state of the art computer programs. As to the vowel points, Mr. Higgins concludes:

"The Samaritan Pentateuch, as well as the Chaldee paraphrases. . . were all without the points. . . . I apprehend that when the Hebrew became a dead language, the points were invented by degrees to enable the masters in the schools to instruct their pupils, and after some time they began to have authority given them by the rabbis. . . . "We learn that all the rabbinical authors were unpointed at the time, and that all their other books were originally without them; that in some editions points were put in them, but the best editions without them. . . ." (*Anacalypsis*, Vol. I, Appendix, pp. 840-43.)

As we know, all languages evolve and change over time, sometimes radically. Think of Old English and today's jumbled jargons. But, the most significant changes in Hebrew were deliberate and calculated to boost the power and influence of the Talmudists.

The rabbinical caste has always used their mastery and control of the language to reinforce their cultural and religious dominance over the Judaic religion, hence over the Judaic people. Obviously, this is quite effective. The Talmudic traditions are based on deception and duplicity, assigning secret codes and hidden mystical meanings to the letters, which in Hebrew are also numbers. Then, only the Kabalistic Rebbes, Tzaddics and Chachams can understand and, of course, manipulatively interpret for the faithful, ever and always boosting their personal power and prestige.

Truth be known, Hebrew is a very old and honorable language, with several possible origins and influences, including Egypt, India, the Phoenicians, other Semitic tribes, and other early culture centers. But no matter where it came from, it has been used, abused and misused by all three Semitic religions in their various and numerous attempts to establish their supremacy and dominance. To achieve this, they have to continually convince the credulous faithful of the legitimacy of the bible stories mistaken for history. The problems started when "god" (aka Yahu, Yahweh, bisexual Jah-Hovah, et al.), a deity out of an Egypto-Semitic lineage, supposedly spoke Hebrew to a highborn Egyptian fellow called Moses on top of a mountain in a desolate Egyptian desert. Apparently, his people didn't think too highly of all this. While old Musa/Moshe was on top of the mountain, talking to his god(s), his tribesmen quickly built their own Egyptian version of a Taurus the Bull egocentric idol, a god of pure gold, dancing around in Egypto-Habiru revelry and debauchery.

Summary and Conclusion

As we know, the bible is rich with Babylonian, Persian, Indian, sub-Saharan African, Chaldean, Canaanite and, of course, Egyptian lore. But whether translated into English, Swahili, Hopi or Hindi, at their very best, the Hebrew bible stories are theology, not history. That these tales are crucial to three closely held religious faiths for hundreds of millions of sincere believers is really not the point—not at all. As far as I am concerned, that is perfectly acceptable—as long as they don't try to forcibly impose it on the rest of us.

Under coldly logical lenses, the bible stories are mostly exaggerated Judaic fables, lurid legends and folktales, particularly the major ones such as the Exodus. Not only has the structure, and ultimately the meaning, of the Hebraic language been altered and adulterated, the collection of Old Testament stories it tells has been radically redacted, rewritten, reinterpreted and "theologically cleansed" in ways primarily benefitting the various religious priesthoods, hierarchies and secret occult orders, not to mention the more worldly Powers That Be.

Since this presentation is about the Hebrew language, we conclude in that tongue. In light of current events, I sign off with some very nice words. While they may seem idealistic and impractical in view of the newscasts, join with me in praying that soon they are heard over the whole world, but especially in Occupied Palestine:

L'chaim. Hevenu shalom aleichem.
To life. We brought peace unto you.

CHAPTER 4

The Old Testament Is Theology, Not History

T he bible is one of the most important, and one of the most misunderstood, documents in world history. This curious collection of mostly small tractates contains religious, moral and ethical teachings plus material on an almost innumerable host of other topics. Some passages are beautiful and inspiring pieces of spiritual wisdom. Others are downright obscene, and more than a few are filled with blood, gore and ultra-violence. One way or another, for better or worse, the bible has had, does have and will continue to have a significant impact on world history and current events. Many Christians see it as the inerrant word of God and a guide for living. Unbelievers and severe critics say it is nothing more than a carefully crafted lie, "the Greatest Story Ever Sold" as one author aptly put it. As it is with many historical questions, especially those involving the distant past, the actual truth is elusive and a bit hard to conclusively nail down. But if we set aside blind faith and bigotry, applying critical thinking skills, there are several fascinating and plausible alternative views of the alleged events and characters spoken of in the Jewish Old Testament books. Here are a few of them for your consideration.

An Alternative View of Moses and the 12 Tribes

An obscure German historian, Dr. Erich Bromme, said the real meaning of the Exodus was a military force of former construction workers decamping from Egypt after receiving marching orders to move west, and that the "Children of Israel," rather than a tribal or ethnic name, was the "division" or "regimental" name for the body of Egypto-Semitic Habiru-Hebrew troops under their general and tribal chieftain. Moses was not only a prophet and religious teacher, but a military leader as well, keeping the children of Israel in the wilderness for 40 years to train them under the rigid 10 Commandments. By this interpretation, Moses was building a proto-Zionist army of conquest. The 10 Commandments were instructions for military order and discipline while on the march and in occupied territory. Once they conquered Canaan and took over the major cities, they built Zion, a hilltop military fortress and headquarters more than anything specifically religious. In support of the Children of Israel as an army on the march, we find an interesting statement in the old, reliable *Cruden's Complete Concordance* (first published in 1737): "In the marches of the army of Israel, the 12 tribes were divided into four great bodies, as bodies of troops, each composed of three tribes."

Burton tells us even more about Moses and the Hebrew religion. Of course, we are continually reminded that we must honor and revere this tradition, but he says religious arrogance, egotism and ethnocentrism are at the base:

"But Moses left his dispensation imperfect. He feared the relapse of his followers into the dark idolatries of the Nile. He therefore dealt only in obscure allusions to a resurrection, to another life, to a futurity of rewards and punishments—the mighty lever with which religion moves the moral world of man. . . . This was the great defect in his grand scheme. The hope and fear of a life to come, of a world in which the apparent inconsistencies of the transient mundane state shall be explained and remedied, where suffering virtue shall triumph and triumphant vice shall suffer— a proclivity for this belief is implanted by nature in the very soul and heart of man. . . .

"The Jehovah of Moses, was, moreover, in other points than personality an imperfect conception. The deity, it is true, was drawn forth from the thick veil of mystery with which the learned of India and Egypt had invested him. His existence was proclaimed not to a caste or class; it was published to a whole people. Still, he was the god of Abraham, of Isaac, and of Jacob, not the God of Eternity—the God of all men. A local deity, his cult and knowledge were confined to one people, to a mere fraction of the human kind. Moses, then, was essentially a benefactor to the Hebrews, but he was not a benefactor to man.

"The great Lawgiver of Israel sanctioned the murder in cold blood of women and childish captives. Even kings were hewed to pieces before the Lord."

Proto-Zionism

Prof. Martin Higger, in *The Jewish Utopia* (Baltimore: Lord Baltimore Press, 1932), says:

"While the *Encyclopedia Britannica*, p. 771, Vol. 21, 1949 ed., says: The Talmud is still the authoritative and practical guide to the great mass of the 'Jews,' and still not all the rabbis accept the Talmud, with its glorification of secrecy and cunning and its incitation to blood-letting and conquest. Rabbi Elmer Berger, for instance, repudiates the Talmud and the Torah. In his Partisan History of Judaism (Devin-Adair Co., New York, 1952) he attacks the books of Moses as expressions of nationalistic fanaticism, only partially based on historical fact.

"He shows that Zionism springs from this ancient Zionism."

Folktales Are Not Factual History

Several scholars say that much of what is claimed as the history of the Kingdom of Israel is, at best, exaggerated. There are even Israeli researchers willing to be politically and religiously incorrect, pointing out that the monarchy of David and Solomon, allegedly the height of ancient Hebrew political power, was in fact, a rather small and unimportant statelet. Scholars like Ze'ev Herzog and others anger Zionist fundamentalists who depend on such accounts to justify the occupation of Palestine. For those wanting more, we recommend (among many other titles) *The Mythic Past: Biblical Archeology and the Myth of Israel*, by Thomas L. Thompson (NY: Basic Books, 1999) as well as the 2008 work of Professor Shlomo Sand. An important biblical and historical work, Thompson's book explodes the overblown claims of the small Eastern Mediterranean ministate and its supposed grandiose ancestor-kingdoms of yore. Could the Philistines-Palestinians have a legitimate claim as well?

The whole concept of Israel as a powerful ancient kingdom may be a sham. More and more scholars and historians are coming to the same controversial conclusion. Much of the so-called history of ancient Israel, for the most part, is a heavily embellished myth, with strong Egyptian and Persian influences. No records in Egypt or any other surrounding nation mention a massive Exodus from Egypt, much less the infamous 10 Plagues. The religion of the ancient Hebrews was a syncretistic Semitic faith, not unlike others in the same region at the same time. They picked up legends and deities while on their wanderings. But these ideas about so-called Biblical history are quite intolerable and frightening to certain parties. Judaics and Zionists. If enough critically thinking people were to stop believing the mostly mythological bible stories, then goy Christians might eventually quit believing in the Chosen People and the supposedly Holy Land. American nationalist leader and spiritual teacher William Dudley Pelley, in (*The Forty-five Most Frequently Asked Questions About the Jews*, 1939), tells us much more:

"Is the Exodus story a myth?

"Answer—No, but it appears to be a complete subversion of what actually took place. The debasing influence of the Habiru or People of Set became so great, that from time to time severe pogroms occurred. The Egyptians would gladly have let the Habiru depart, had the latter been willing to go empty-handed. But taking their property, much of it gotten as dishonestly as the New-Deal Jews of today have gotten their fortunes by exploitation or open graft, represented a severe economic problem. In the Scriptures as written by Jews, however, and thence handed to us for acceptance, all this hocus-pocus is glorified and blessed by the benedictions of Yahvah.

"As for the Chosen-People notion's being fallacious, we have the statement of a Jew, Dr. Oscar Levy of London, who declared quite frankly: 'We the Jews invented the myth of being God's Chosen People.' Later, Dr. Levy died a very sudden and mysterious death. You can draw your own conclusions.

"Is there any difference between the Jehovah of the Jews and the Divine Father of Jesus as worshiped by the Christians?

"Answer—There is a difference so vast as to render them practically two different personages. The word Jehovah is the modern English rendering of the Hebrew term for the Midian tribal deity, Yahvah. Moses, after he had murdered two Egyptians for their treatment of an Israelite, fled to Midian, a district across the Red Sea, south of the Land of Goshen. There he married a Midian wife and became a sheepherder.

"Jehovah or Yahvah was the neighborhood god of the Midianites whom Moses seized upon, and utilized, in his later politicoracial exploits back among the Egyptians. Moses claimed that this little tribal god, with all his provincial hates and lusts, was the One Lord God of all the universe. This last could only be interviewed by Moses in person, or by Aaron or his Levites when Moses wasn't around.

"Christ came, and got Himself hated unto crucifixion, by standing this narrow and fallacious notion of the deity on its head. Christ said that the Lord God was Universal Spirit, and that man needed no paid priest or elaborate temple ceremonials to commune with Him. This threatened the whole basic foundation of Judaism, since it counseled the masses that priests were dispensable."

Said Sir Richard F. Burton, 1898:

"As the Lord formed man in his own image, so man in return anthropomorphicized the Deity. Theirs was a personal god with mortal shape and human passions, who hated the Canaanites for no sin of their own, and loved the Hebrews for no merit of their own, but for the sake of their ancestors. The 'angry god' and the 'jealous god of Moses' stand for the orthodox opinion of even the

modern Jews. In proportion as we return to the ignorance of antiquity and seek out the metaphysics of savage races, so we find the
personality of god, a description of his form, and an account of his
actions and passions most prominently brought forward. Savages
and barbarians cannot believe without anthropomorphizing their
Great Spirit. . . . Again, the Hebrew Paradise is the vestige of an old
legend current throughout the Eastern world."

Who Were Solomon and David?

Let's speculate a bit as to these "picturesque legends," as Sir
Richard Burton called them. There is no extant archeological evidence for such major events such as the Exodus, yet the Egyptians
(and many nations around them) were meticulous record-keep-
ers. There's more; the name of the allegedly great King David is
found almost nowhere outside the Old Testament Hebrew writings. In 1998, a ninth-century B.C. stele was found that contains
a reference to a victory over two enemies, one of the "House of
David." While this does at least prove that a family by that name
ruled, it does not reflect the grandeur, pomp, circumstance, great
military leadership, statesmanship etc alleged in the Hebrew writings. Erich Bromme said "David" here may have been a title, like
"Caesar" became from the time of Augustus on.

The story of Solomon is about the same. Someone with this
name, or several with this same name or title, probably did rule.
Likewise, someone actually named Arthur may have ruled in ancient Britain, but most of what we know is from legends and lore,
not factual material. Solomonic tales of great wisdom, freemasonic secrets, Kabalistic pentacle signs and a powerful kingdom
may be greatly exaggerated at best, reflecting the hopes and wishes
of later compilers, editors and outright fabricators. As we know,

Freemasonry (Kabalistic Judaism for the goyim) is based on the same Hebrew mythos. Even if we postulate that actual characters named Solomon and David ruled a kingdom called Israel, it could not have been all that important, certainly not the powerful, sophisticated cosmopolitan state portrayed by preachers and biblical commentators. Israel, whatever it may have been, was always a ministate. With the later failure of Kingdom of Israel, what power remained devolved into the surviving microstate of Judah, never over 300 square miles in size.

Much of the Old Testament is little more than Semitic psychodrama, fiction and fairy tales reinforcing ethnocentric egocentrism, grandiosity and political narcissism. A number of scholars, in spite of stern and unrelenting opposition from Jews, Judeo-Christians and the generally duped general public, have long held that many Old Testament stories are at best, exaggerated tales, embellished and amplified by the Talmudic Rebbes, not to mention by the various Christian power cliques, especially the Vatican.

Recent Revelations About the Non-History of Israel

Some of the truest and the most shocking statements about Judaic history and culture come from Judaics themselves. In our growing list of these writers, we must add Israeli Professor of European History at Tel Aviv University, Dr. Shlomo Sand (also Zand), author of *When and How Was the Jewish People Invented?* or *Matai ve'ech humtza ha'am hayehudi?* Sand says the so-called history of Israel is a modern-day fabrication of the Zionist movement.

Journalist Jonathan Cook reviewed this politically and religiously incorrect book that stayed on Israel's bestseller list for 19 weeks in 2008, and states:

"Dr. Sand's main argument is that until little more than a century ago, Jews thought of themselves as Jews only because they shared a common religion. At the turn of the 20th century, he said, Zionist Jews challenged this idea and started creating a national history by inventing the idea that Jews existed as a people separate from their religion. Equally, the modern Zionist idea of Jews being obligated to return from exile to the Promised Land was entirely alien to Judaism. . . .

"Zionism changed the idea of Jerusalem. Before, the holy places were seen as places to long for, not to be lived in. For 2,000 years Jews stayed away from Jerusalem not because they could not return but because their religion forbade them from returning until the messiah came.

"The biggest surprise during his research came when he started looking at the archeological evidence from the biblical era. "I was not raised as a Zionist, but like all other Israelis I took it for granted that the Jews were a people living in Judea and that they were exiled by the Romans in 70 C.E. [A.D.]. But once I started looking at the evidence, I discovered that the kingdoms of David and Solomon were legends. Similarly with the exile. In fact, you can't explain Jewishness without exile. But when I started to look for history books describing the events of this exile, I couldn't find any. Not one. That was because the Romans did not exile people. In fact, Jews in Palestine were overwhelmingly peasants, and all the evidence suggests they stayed on their lands.

"Instead, he believes an alternative theory is more plausible: the exile was a myth promoted by early Christians to recruit Jews to the new faith. Christians wanted later generations of Jews to believe that their ancestors had been exiled as a punishment from God."

It is not surprising that the Christian religion has been somewhat obsessed with converting the members of the supposed precursor faith. But whether Dr. Sand is correct or not about early Christian conversion efforts, the facts about the confabulated bible stories are the same, and we know the results this has had on the world with the establishment of the Israeli state. It is Zionists, aided and abetted by the sadly complicit, complacent and cooperative Christians, that caused the ministate to emerge, much to the chagrin of the native Palestinian Arabs, of whom a significant number were Christians, not to mention the hundreds of millions of Muslims the world over. Douglas Reed, in *Controversy of Zion*, 1985, adds some interesting details:

"Judaism was retrogressive even in 458 B.C., when men in the known world were beginning to turn their eyes away from idols and tribal gods and to look for a god of all men, of justice and of neighborliness. Confucius and Buddha had already pointed in that direction and the idea of one-god was known among the neighboring peoples of Judah. Today the claim is often made that the religious man, Christian, Muslim or other, must pay respect to Judaism, whatever its errors, on one incontestable ground: It was the first universal religion, so that in a sense all universal religions descend from it. Every Jewish child is taught this. In truth, the idea of the one-god of all men was known long before the tribe of Judah even took shape, and Judaism was above all else the denial of that idea. The Egyptian Book of the Dead (manuscripts of which were found in the tombs of kings of 2,600 B.C., over 2,000 years before the Judaist 'Law' was completed) contains the passage: 'Thou art the one, the god from the very beginnings of time, the heir of immortality, self-produced and self-born; thou didst create the Earth and make man.' Conversely, the scripture produced in Judah of the Levites asked, 'Who is like unto thee, O Lord, among the gods?'" (Exodus)

This is merely a sampler of theories as to the origin of the religious mythos and rather curious theological concepts found in the documents we call the Old Testament. We can choose from a variety of well researched alternative accounts explaining the Hebrew stories and bizarre fantasies mistakenly and misleadingly called history. Biblical Revisionism offers a new handle on certain themes and movements in world history. Critical thinking skills open new vistas for making sense out of events now unfolding on the world stage. The Israeli Machiavellian ministate is founded on the false history and false land claims from the Old Testament tales. But that's not all. The credibility—hence the influence, primacy and power of all three Semitic religions (Judaism, Christianity and Islam)—rests on the same fantasies, fables, folklore and fabrications.

Esther prepares to entertain King Ahasueris.

CHAPTER 5

Esther, the Queen of Purim:

A Tale of Terror & Treachery

The curious Book of Esther, one of only two in the bible not mentioning god, may have been composed 485-464 B.C. during the reign of "King Ahasueris," roughly concurrent with the reign of Xerxes I in Persia. The names certainly are similar. Many scholars dispute its provenance and authenticity of Esther. Only the first part is found in the Greek Septuagint scriptures, and it is the only book of the Tennakh not found among the Dead Sea Scrolls. Because of discrepancies in Hebrew texts, St. Jerome divided it into the older and newer parts when he organized his Latin Vulgate Bible in the late fourth century A.D. Notably, the first time the word "Jew" ("Judean") is used in the bible, rather than "Hebrew" or "Israelite," is in Esther. Set in Persia, the story incorporates key elements of Persian paganism. Fertility rites always occur in spring, and so does Purim. This is set on 14 Adar. Because the Hebrew calendar is lunar, this falls in March.

Not to digress, but demonstrating the strong Judeo-Persian cultural confluence, the names of the Hebrew months are Babylonian. Purim may be a Judaized recreation of an ancient springtime gala celebrating the victories of the gods Marduk and Ishtar over rival deities. This and other Near Eastern pagan themes made pretty good background material for concocting this very Jewish, very Talmudic fairytale.

Esther reads more like an adventure romance novelette than a book of scripture. Its sole purpose was to establish Purim, a holiday when the ancient Jews ruthlessly struck back against their former oppressors. In Hebrew, Purim means lots, named after the lottery Haman used to choose the day for the massacre. The Persian word is Pur. On this day, the Talmud gives permission, even encouragement, to getting drunk, cursing, reviling and spitting on Christians. To begin Purim, the entire book, called the Megillah (simply means scroll in Hebrew), is read in the synagogue. Hence the Jewish expression, "the whole Megillah," is like saying "the whole nine yards," meaning the entirety of something. Free Dictionary Online appropriately adds "tediously detailed or highly embroidered account." The services are held in the evening, after the beginning of the new Jewish day and commemorating Esther's deadly after-dark dinner party. Jewish women are rabbinically required to attend. In older times, and where it was tolerated, as in the ghettoes and shtetls, loud boisterous street parties went on for much of the night with dancing, singing and drunken carousing, concluding with the burning of Haman in effigy. The Talmud Bavli tells us more in Orakh Chayim 689: "All are obligated in the reading of the Megillah."

Says Megillah 7b: "Rava said: It is the duty of a man to get drunk with wine on Purim until he cannot tell the difference between "cursed be Haman" and "blessed be Mordechai." Rabbah and Rabbi Zera joined together in a Purim feast. They became drunk and Rabbah arose and cut Rabbi Zera's throat. On the next day he prayed on his behalf and revived him. Next year, he [Rabbah] said "Will your honor come and we will have the Purim feast together?" He [Rabbi Zera] answered: A miracle does not take place on every occasion."

And this, from Orach Chaim, 660, 16: "The Jew is to say on Purim Day: . . . Cursed be all non-Jews; blessed be all Jews."

Always called the Megillah (and ranked right alongside the Torah) by the Jews, Esther is the name given by Christian translators. The outcome of this rabbinical creative writing project was edited and reworked over the centuries. Since it does not appear in the late fourth-century B.C. Septuagint, and since St. Jerome worked with confusing manuscripts in the late fourth century A.D., we see a time frame when the Judeo-Babylonian Talmudists put the final touches on the Megillah. While his German-language bible has the Book of Esther, translator and theologian Martin Luther was very critical of it, saying that even the Hebrew text was of little value. We suppose he was unwilling to bowdlerize the already existing Judaic Masoretic, Greek Septuagint and Latin Vulgate versions of the Old Testament, so he included it. Writes Martin Luther in "On the Jews and Their Lies" (Der Juden und Ihre Lugen), 1543:

"They are real liars and bloodhounds who have not only continually perverted and falsified all of Scripture with their mendacious glosses from the beginning until the present day. Their heart's most ardent sighing and yearning and hoping is set on the day on which they can deal with us gentiles as they did with the gentiles in Persia at the time of Esther. Oh, how fond they are of the book of Esther, which is so beautifully attuned to their bloodthirsty, vengeful, murderous yearning and hope. The Sun has never shone on a more bloodthirsty and vengeful people than they are who imagine that they are god's people who have been commissioned and commanded to murder and to slay the gentiles."

The story goes like this. Our leading lady joins King Ahasueris's harem. She keeps her Hebrew origins a secret, yet one of the Jews, our male protagonist, Mordecai, her cousin, is a prominent man in the government. Mordecai, a dedicated friend of his Jewish people, has a sworn enemy, a classically anti-Semitic, heavily embellished theatrical wicked villain called Haman. While his motive is unclear, Haman hates the Jews and does everything he can to harm them. The plot thickens. He eventually persuades the King to sign a decree of extermination, a holocaust of ancient times. By this time in the story, our heroine is called Queen Esther, having progressed from mere Oriental harem prostitute to the position of chief wife. To make a rather predictable tale less tedious, she intercedes with her charms, but there is good and bad news. The good news is (surprise, surprise) the King grants the comely concubine's request. The bad news is that back in these olden days, once the King sends out a decree with his seal attached, it supposedly cannot be rescinded. This does not really make much sense as it seems an all-powerful sovereign could do as he pleased and change his mind, but the story line is not so simple. Instead, the King intervenes personally, providing shelter and protection in his palace. Thus he and Queen Esther stop the Persian pogrom and extermination of the Jews, planned by Hitler—oops, I mean Haman— the wicked anti-Semite. Haman is hanged on the gallows he prepared for Mordecai.

Since the death threat is over, the Jews rejoice with feasts and merriment. Along with these festivities, they set about causing the extermination of their enemies. Mind you, the original threat is over. This killing spree on the first Purim sprang solely from cold-

Queen Esther before King Ahasueris, 1865. Photographic study by Julia Margaret Cameron.

blooded revenge. First, Esther has the king invite Haman to an evening state dinner, where they will unexpectedly attack him when he is off guard. As we would expect, this *femme fatale* character is seen by Talmudic Jews and Zionists as a brave and valorous woman, and today's Christians perpetuate the lurid legends through studies about women in the bible. Not only that, the Hebrew Harlot is a main character in the traditions of the women's Masonic Order of the Eastern Star. Mind you, these folk are supposed to be reading and studying the bible, but we must ask ourselves if they're actually reading the texts of the tale. Or maybe they're just too embarrassed to point out that "the empress has no clothes." Read what the bible tells us about the brutal, bloody events following Esther's cowardly conspiracy to slay Haman, the adversary and would-be exterminator of the Jews. Here are some selected verses from Esther: 5, 6, 7, 8, 9:

"King Ahasueris said to Queen Esther, 'Who is he that would presume to do this [that is, to kill all the Jews]?' And Esther said, 'A foe and an enemy. This wicked Haman.' Then Haman was in terror before the king and queen. . . for he saw that evil was determined against him by the king. So they hanged Haman on the gallows which he had prepared for Mordecai.

"The Jews had light and gladness and joy and honor. And many from the peoples of the country declared themselves Jews for the feat of the Jews had fallen upon them.

"[The Jews prepare for their revenge.] . . . a day when the Jews should get the mastery over their foes, and the Jews gathered in their cities throughout all the provinces of King Ahasueris to lay hands on such as sought their hurt. And they could make no stand against them, for the fear of them had fallen upon all peoples. . . . So the Jews smote all their enemies with the sword, slaughtering and destroying them, and they did as they pleased to those who had hated them. In Susa the capital itself the Jews slew and destroyed 500 men. . . and the 10 sons of Haman. . . . Now the other Jews who were in the king's provinces also gathered together. . . and got relief from their enemies, and slew 75,000 of those who hated them. . . . and on the 14th day they rested and made that a day of feasting and gladness."

According to Burton in *The Jew, the Gypsy and El Islam*, 1898: "Again, the history and traditions, the faith and practice of the Jew ever placed before his eyes the absolute and immeasurable superiority of his own caste, the 'Peculiar People, the Kingdom of

Priests, and the Holy Nation.' This exaltation justified the Hebrew in treating his brother-men as heathens barely worthy of the title human. 'Lo, the people shall dwell alone, and shall not be reckoned among the nations'—an unfriendly separation and an estrangement between man and man equally injurious to the welfare of Jew and gentile. . . . Their virtues are their own, but their faults are the fruit of 18 centuries of outlawry and oppression."

Both Esther and several passages from the Talmud Bavli affirm endorse and sanction tribal bloodlust and ethnic cleansing. Want a precedent for arrogant modern Zionist atrocities against the Palestinian people? Look no further than this Talmudic tale of terror. It really makes no difference whether Esther is authentic or not. When we apply the tools of literary deconstructionism and hermeneutics, critically dissecting both the biblical and the Talmudic texts, certain ancient atavistic archetypes of bloodlust and deep-seated vengeance clearly come to light. And not just in bygone eras, but before us in today's news. In some ways, little has changed since the days of the Purim concubine queen. The Talmud says the story never ends. Writes Rambam, in Hilkhot Megilah 2:18:

"All the books of the Prophets and all the Writings will be annulled in the days of the Messiah, except for the Book of Esther. It will continue to be binding like the Five Books of Moses and the entire Oral Law, which will never be invalidated. Even though all memory of our suffering will be erased. . . still the days of Purim will not be annulled. As it is written, 'These days of Purim will not pass away from the Jews and its memory will never leave their descendants.' (Esther 9:25)."

The Jewish concubine Esther convinces the king to stop Haman's plan to deal with Persia's "Jewish problem" in this painting by Rembrandt. The king then had his chief advisor, Haman, hanged and 70,000 innocent Persians slaughtered. This event is celebrated by the Jews today as Purim.

CHAPTER 6

Purim & the Whole Megillah

A More Thorough Exegesis of the Book of Esther

This is a further exposition of my thoughts about the Purim revenge fest portrayed, created and legitimized in the Old Testament Book of Esther. Its main thrust was to establish and legitimize the Judaic Purim holiday, which as we shall see, comes from non-Hebrew pagan traditions.

Purim is a "memorial of destruction."

Says *Oxford Dictionary of the Christian Church*, 1989:

"Although there may be an historical basis for the story, in its present form it seems to be a popular romance. It contains indeed very little of a directly religious purport, and it is noticeable that no mention is made in the book of the name of god.

"The probable reason for its inclusion in the canon of the Old Testament is that it described the institution of Purim. . . .

"There are no quotations from Esther in the New Testament, nor, so far, have any fragments of the book been found among the biblical manuscripts at Qumran."

The text affirms not only their right to self-defense, but their right to utter vengeance and death over their opponents:

"By these [decrees] the king allowed the Jews who were in every city to gather together and defend their lives, to destroy, to slay, and to annihilate any armed force of any people or province that might attack them, with their children and women, and to plunder their goods, upon one day throughout all the provinces. . . on the 13th day of the 12th month, which is the month of Adar. . . and the Jews were to be ready on that day to avenge themselves upon their enemies." (Esther 8:11-13.)

In the Apocrypha, there is more of Chapter 10 plus chapters 11-16, as found in the Septuagint. This extra material clearly affirms the same psychodynamics of bitter revenge. The real or alleged events of the first Purim should be considered as a genuine "final solution," bringing an end to the problem of those who opposed the aspirations and machinations of Judaic politics and religion. Purim, as the scriptures tell us, certainly is a memorial of destruction to those who opposed the Jews back in old Babylon. To quote *Apocrypha, The Rest of the Chapters of the Book of Esther* 16:23-24:

"That both now and hereafter there may be safety to us, and the well affected Persians; but to those which do conspire against us as a memorial of destruction. Therefore every city and country whatsoever, which shall not do according to these things shall be destroyed without mercy with fire and sword, and shall be made not only unpassable for men, but also most hateful to wild beasts and fowls forever."

Were the Jews Justified in Their Actions?

As other commentators have said, in order to justify what the Jews (obviously, they must have been numerous) are said to have done, one must believe in the mysterious imperial decree that even the emperor can't revoke.

Says *Interpreters One Volume Commentary on the Bible,* 1971: "The Irrevocable Edict. At this point all that's seems needed to bring the story to a happy ending is the withdrawal of the decree of extermination. But so simple a solution would not explain the annual celebration of Purim."

Regardless of your feelings about the bible or the Jews, the facts are clear. The original danger was over; there was no more threat. Also of interest and concern is that nothing is said of the criteria used to determine who their enemy really is. Was it anyone who opposed Judaic power and influence at high government levels? Was it anyone who criticized their religion, then a proselytizing faith? In other words, was the enemy anyone whom they considered to be an "anti-Semite"? Did this make them a valid terrorist target for extinction? It appears this is one of the key doctrines of Purim. Hence, the Jews received permission to practice genocide against their opponents all over the Persian empire. While the figure of 75,000 slain is probably fictional (the Greek Septuagint says 15,000), the real and rather graphic meaning of the imagery stands out when the themes of this odd scriptural text are deconstructed. Through the Book of Esther, Purim directly confirms and affirms the right of the Judaic people to vengeance and bloodthirsty revenge against their opponents, the true meaning of this important festival.

Is Esther the Pagan Goddess Ishtar?

In yet another curious conundrum about the Megillah text is that Esther is not our heroine's actual name. Why is it used? The name, Esther, is related to Ashtoreth, a consort of the Egypto-Semitic deity called Jah-Hovah, also the same as the widely worshiped Middle Eastern goddess, Ishtar. Esther's real name was Hadassah, which in Hebrew means myrtle tree, but parallels with a Persian word meaning star. Isaac Asimov tells us much more.

He writes in *Asimov's Guide to the Bible*, 1969:

"The name Mordecai is not Hebrew and instead, seems to be suspiciously like that of the chief god of the Babylonians, Marduk, which in its Hebrew form, is Merodach. As for Esther (the official throne name that came to be carried by Mordecai's cousin), that is even clearly a form of Ishtar, the chief Babylonian goddess. Indeed, the Aramaic version of that goddess's name is Esther The name Hadassah, by which Esther was originally known within the family, is closely related to a Babylonian word for 'bride,' which is used as a title for Ishtar. And in Babylonian mythology Marduk and Ishtar are cousins, as are Mordecai and Esther. . . . It may have been one of the purposes of the writer of the Book of Esther to revise the Babylonian myth into Jewish history and convert a pagan festival into a patriotic Jewish observance."

Wikipedia tells us yet another interesting name for the book and perhaps why god is never mentioned:

"Esther can also be understood to mean 'hidden' in Hebrew, and her name is interpreted thus in another Midrash, where it is said that Esther hid her nationality and lineage as Mordecai had advised. Because the methods and aims of god are believed to be similarly hidden, 'The Book of Esther' in Hebrew can be understood as 'The Book of Hiddenness,' representing god's hiddenness in the story."

But, while the story of Esther-Ishtar-Ashtoreth-Hadassah, does have more than a bit of "hiddenness," there is little if anything concealed about the bloody themes of this hateful Talmudic treatise called the Megillah.

Is Haman a Prototypical Christ Figure?

In the sordid history of the Judaic Kabalistic ritual murder cult, Purim and Passover are the proper times for the sacrifices. Dr. Ariel Toaff speaks of Purim and the Book of Esther in his now classic work, *Blood Passovers*. He is a respected Professor of Medieval History at Bar-Ilan University in Israel. Later forced to withdraw his book, it tells the bare truth about many things. As you will see, Toaff even goes so far as to assert that the execution-crucifixion of Jesus was a traditional Jewish sacrificial murder. The ritualized figures of Amalek, Haman and Jesus are all the same thing. Quoting *Blood Passovers*, pp. 131-132:

"For a number of reasons, not least that of its not infrequent proximity to Holy Week, Purim, also called the 'festival of the lots,' came, in time, to acquire openly anti-Christian connotations and the related celebrations became openly suggestive in this sense, both in form and substance, sometimes audaciously and openly.

"Haman, equated with that other Biblical arch-enemy of the Jews, Amalek (Deut. 25: 17-19), whose memory was to be blotted out from the face of the earth, was transformed, over time, into Jesus, the False Messiah, whose impious followers were once threatening the Chosen People with extermination. Moreover, Haman was killed, hanged, as Jesus was said to have been, and there was no shortage of exegetic material reinforcing this paragon. In the Greek translation of the Septuagint as well as in Flavius Josephus (Ant. Jud. Xi, 267, 280), Haman's gallows was interpreted as a cross, and the execution of King Ahasueris's belligerent minister was described, in effect, as a true and proper crucifixion.

"The equation between Amalek, Haman and Christ was self-evidently obvious. Haman, who, in the Biblical text is referred to as talui, 'the hanged one,' was confused with He who, in all anti-Christian Hebraic texts, was the Talui by antonomasia [the replacement of a proper name by an epithet], i.e., the crucified Christ.

"The sensational trial of the most prominent members of the Ashkenazi communities of northern Italy, accused of vilifying the Christian religion was held in Milan in the spring of 1488. In reply to inquisitors demanding the name used by Jews with reference to Jesus of Nazareth, Salomone da Como, one of the accused, answered unhesitatingly: 'Among ourselves we call him "Ossoays" ("that man," from the Hebrew oto' ha-ish, according to the German pronunciation), or Talui ("the hanged one," "the crucified one"), while, when speaking to Christians, we always refer to him as "Christ." It is not surprising that a text by 4th-century writer Evagrius describes the Jew Simone, in an argument with a Christian, Theophilus, should have equated "the cursed and despised Passion of Christ" with Haman's "crucifixion."'

"According to the great English anthropologist James George Frazer, Christ died while playing the role of Haman (the dying god) in a drama of Purim in which (Jesus) Barabbas, the double of Jesus of Nazareth, played the part of Mordechai (the god that resurges). In the model of the god that dies and is reborn—which is common in the Near East—Haman is said to have played the part of death and Mordechai that of life, while the celebration of Purim is said to constitute the Hebraic ritual of death and resurrection.

"Based on this consideration, one might hypothesize that, in the past, the Jews, at the culmination of the festival, might have been accustomed to putting a man to death in flesh and blood reality, and that Jesus was crucified in this context, playing the role of Ahasueris's tragic minister, the arch-enemy of Israel .There is no shortage of testimonies of the celebration of rituals, within the framework of the carnival of Purim, intended to vilify and outrage the image of Haman, reconstituted in the semblance of Christ hanging from the cross."

What Did Haman Really Do?

Taking his statement in and of itself, did Haman actually lie about the Jews? As we can see in reading Esther, there must have been quite a few of them living in Persia. Did Haman misinform the Emperor? Or just try to warn him of a lurking and impending danger? Was he wrong? Considering the nature of his demise, he was correct.

"There is a certain people scattered abroad and dispersed among the peoples in all the provinces of your kingdom, their laws are different from those of every other people, and they do not keep the king's laws, so that it is not for the king's profit to tolerate them." Esther 3:8.

Summation

Of course, Haman and his party were a definite threat to the Judeo-Persians, but from the standpoint of morals and ethics, I can't see why Christians would ever find role models in either Haman's camp or that of Esther and her cabal of court Jews. While Judaic and Christian publications glorify and proclaim the alleged virtues of Esther, a closer look reveals the truth about this heavily fabricated folktale. More of a novella rather than scripture, its whole purpose was to create an underlying biblical footing for the Purim Revenge Fest, never mind all its pagan archetypes and prototypes. If you are still in doubt about any of this, then read "the whole Megillah" one more time and decide for yourself. I've done this so often now that I can only close by thoroughly agreeing with Martin Luther:

"Their heart's most ardent sighing and yearning and hoping is set on the day on which they can deal with us Gentiles as they did with the Gentiles in Persia at the time of Esther. Oh, how fond they are of the Book of Esther, which is so beautifully attuned to their bloodthirsty, vengeful, murderous yearning and hope."

CHAPTER 7

Rome Gave Birth to Judaism

In the first century, for all intents and purposes, the Roman empire gave birth to two major world religions: Judaism and Christianity. The modern Judaic religion was created directly through their actions, both hostile and conciliatory. Before beginning this saga, we must understand the zeitgeist, the spirit of the age, in the ancient world. The ancient port cities were the hubs and recipients of the news of various events as it spread about the world. Let's recall that all ports and roads in the Western world (and thus, who travels on them) were controlled by Rome. The talk that filled the market places, coffeehouses and taverns, as it does today, involved local and some world events, but among the subjects hotly discussed back in the day was religion. Especially after A.D. 70, Judaism spread globally and was found in all large cities, especially the ports. Many Sephardic Judaics were involved in shipping and related port and market enterprises.

And, another new faith was also becoming popular. Especially in its later forms, it too was a Roman creation. Just as Judaism came from Palestine and the eastern Mediterranean, so did this one. It didn't have a clearly distinct name at first, but soon came to be called Christianity. Both these Semitic religions and their early development as forces in world events were heavily influenced by Roman interests and priorities. Some Christians and others seem to think the Jewish religion is from ancient times, but it only came into existence a few decades after Christianity arose. As you will see, Rome is heavily involved with both these dynamic religious movements of the ancient world.

"Operation Titus" Was Both an End and a Beginning

The olden Hebrew-Habiru religion was centered on the Temple, where the blood flowed continually from primitive animal sacrifices, and where they kept "god in a box" called the Ark of the Covenant. If their Semitic deity didn't live in the box, he supposedly spoke from there. As we know, the Hebrews originally were tribes and clans of wandering Egyptians. The Ark box is how their nomadic tribal deity travelled along with them. Both their religion and the stories about it were based on an existing Egypto-Semitic mythos and body of folklore. The old religion had regional rivals with related gods such as Ba'al, Moloch and others. This included a very similar Semitic sect called Samaritans. They held their perhaps even earlier tradition of bloody animal sacrifices on Mt. Gezerim rather than in a temple. They were excluded by the Judaic religion as they were a non-Talmudic primitive form. But, all the eastern Mediterranean kingdoms and ministates were eventually absorbed and incorporated into the Roman empire.

Titus Flavius Vespasianus (A.D. 39-81), was the 10th Roman emperor (79-81). He was a true Scourge of the Jews, the despoiler of Jerusalem and defiler of the temple. The little Palestinian backwater was a trouble spot. Without going into lengthy detail, there were more than a few rebellious outbreaks. There was even a Judaic proto-terrorist cult, the Sicarii, skillful assassins who covertly stabbed their less radical opponents while brushing up against them on the streets or in the marketplace. They were the forerunners of Irgun and all the other Zionist gangs who used terrorist tactics in establishing their modern ministate. The Romans eventually grew fed up and frustrated. While many folk were good Roman subjects, even Imperial citizens, Palestine remained a problem with its revolutionary proto-Zionists.

Rome finally decided to put an end to the problem once and for all with what I like to call Operation Titus. The Siege of Jerusalem was the critical event in A.D. 70, followed by the fall of the Masada mountain fortress three years later. The Roman assault force was, of course, commanded by future Emperor Titus. Among other things, the Temple, a magnificent architectural structure of the ancient world, was completely razed and burned, the holy things carried away by the Roman Legions. Without a doubt, the Cohen and Levite priestly castes were either liquidated or scattered to the winds. It made no difference anyway; their Temple and their rituals were gone. Jerusalem was thoroughly looted and leveled. Practically nothing remained of the old Hebrew holy city.

These events were both a symbolic and literal end to the ancient Hebrew religion. It was no more. The Judaic Palestinian people were either driven away or enslaved and taken to Rome where some of them helped build the Coliseum. In addition to bringing in valuable slaves, this forced migration transplanted more than 20,000 Jews to live in Rome. Some Judeo-Roman families today trace their lineage there. As we see again and again as we study the history of the ancient world, Judea and Rome have ongoing close connections. Since the Roman Empire was multicultural and racially diverse, we must assume that Judaics and Romans inter-married and interbred. While in Palestine, Titus met, fell in love and had an extended affair with Bernice, daughter of Herod Agrippa, the Roman puppet ruler. This lasted until he was crowned. Rome and Judea; family relationships surely and certainly deepen connections.

Jerusalem in the Year 70: The Temple, the Ancient Religion and the People Are Gone

Aelia Capitolina, a new Roman colony town, was eventually built over of the flattened ruins of Jerusalem, begun over half a century later by Emperor Hadrian. Among other things built atop the rubble and ashes of the old city was a huge Roman street similar in size to a modern six lane highway. The new city was a grand Roman affair, complete with forums, baths and ornate pagan temples.

The physical and cultural changeover was complete. Jerusalem was over with, done and gone. After the Second Jewish Revolt in 132-135, Jews were forbidden to enter the area except for the Tisha B'Av observance commemorating the destruction. This means the ninth day of the month Av, a varying date in July or August. With this one exception Jews, were banned from living there or making pilgrimages. Since Aelia Capitolina was built on an open concept plan without city walls, the Roman 10th Legion was assigned the task of policing the area, preventing Jews from entering at any other time. Aelia Capitolina continued until the fourth century when the city began to grow in size again. From the reign of Constantine until the seventh century, the Jews were banned. He began building all kinds of churches and shrines at alleged sacred spots all about the region, mostly found by his mother, Helena.

The gullible Helena came seeking holy sites and holy relics. With the help of various scam artists, she "found" what she was looking for. Some say she ended up with enough pieces of the "true cross" to build a house.

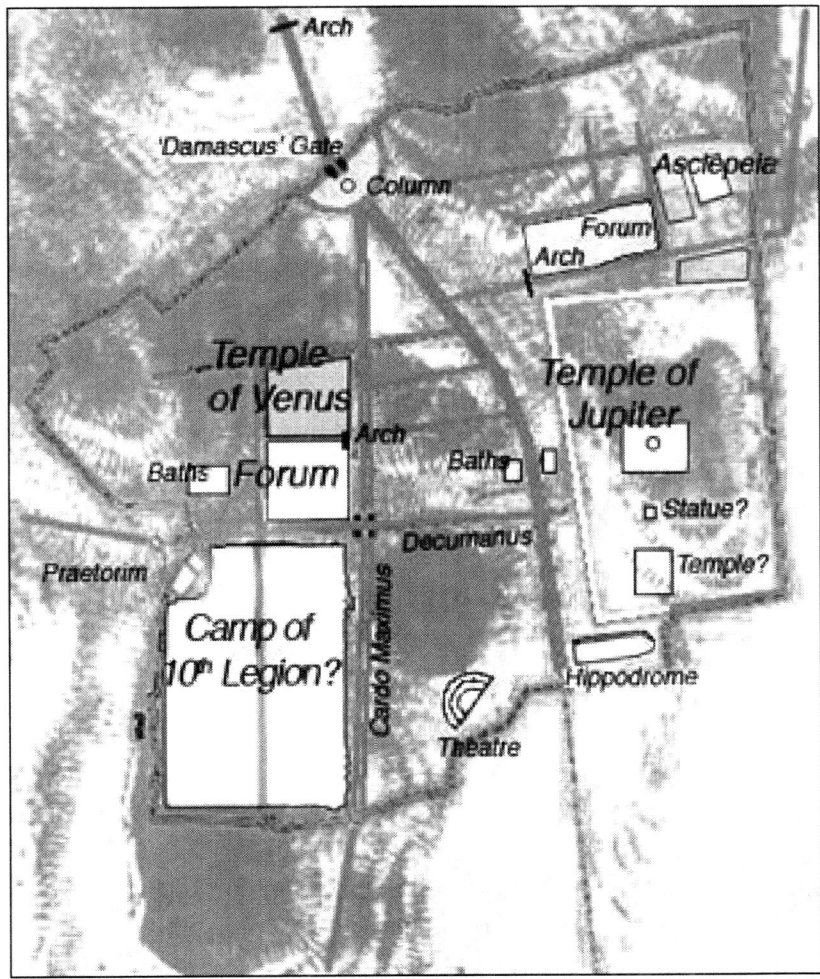

The illustration shows the grand plans for the new Roman city, Aelia Capitolina, including the huge six lane street. Note the camp of the 10th Legion, special troops stationed there to prevent Jews from entering except on Tisha B'Av.

Called Jerusalem again, it once again began to have Jewish residents. Rome and the Christian religion changed the scenery radically. Palestine was now the holy land of the new Christian religion. These structures are most of the things you see today on a tourist visit to the Zionist state. Now you know the real story of why the so-called Holy Land and what visitors are shown there is a super tourist trap and a farce, based on the confabulation and imagination of "Saint" Helena and her son, Constantine. In other words, what you see and what you're told are Roman creations.

Operation Titus put a violent and definitive end to the old Hebrew Temple cult. From this death event came a birth. Rome also served as the midwife, perhaps we might even say the mother of an essentially new religious movement called Judaism. The involvement didn't just end with the destructive birth, as you might think. Oddly enough, it appears that Rome cared for its troubled and violently born child, immediately fostering Judaism's healthy growth and development.

Roman-Sponsored Sanhedrin
Quickly Comes into Play

Not all the Jews left Palestine. Some very special ones remained by Imperial invitation and under Imperial protection. With full permission and blessing of the Romans, the Sanhedrin moved over to the coastal city of Jamnia (Javne, Jabneel), actually a much nicer location. Rabbi Johanan ben Zakkai promptly received permission to found a halakha seminary and Talmudic law school. Not only that, the money needed must have been considerable, but with presumed Roman cooperation, the yeshiva complex was created without delay. This new "Judaic Vatican," founded and blessed by Rome, became a major force in systematizing the still evolving Judaic religion, among other things, determining the canon of scriptures. Hundreds of years later, Judaic scholars based in Palestine produced the Aleppo Codex, working with both the Hebrew and Aramaic texts. The works of Rabbi Johanan had a tremendous cultural and theological impact on the evolving Judaic religion. His writings plus those of his students and later devotees comprise a great deal of the Mishna, a significant component of the modern Talmud.

When travelers visit Jerusalem today, they are taken to the old quarter and shown the usual tourist traps and supposed streets and stops where Jesus walked etc. As already said, this is all a crock of matzo. I was fortunate enough to have a good guide, and was shown a bit of so-called underground Jerusalem. While more interesting than the upper streets, this too is somewhat of a facade. One must probe several levels beneath that to find the ruins of the city destroyed during Operation Titus. This brings to question the actual location of the Temple and the supposed ruins thereof, but no time for that now. What you see in Jerusalem today largely exists only in the public imagination. Naturally, apart from than the Zionists, the Roman Vatican is the primary purveyor of these deceptions. There are many accounts that tell of the siege and days of killing and looting that followed it. The Mishna Talmud affirms the massive and rather complete destruction, possibly written by eye witness survivors or those who talked with them. As the texts say, the looting and removal of the various objects occurred two days before the building was burned to the ground:

"Five misfortunes befell our fathers. . . on the ninth of Av. . it was decreed that our fathers should not enter the [Promised] Land, the Temple was destroyed the first and second time, Bethar was captured and the city [Jerusalem] was plowed up." Ta'anit 4:6.

"On the seventh the heathens entered the Temple and ate

therein and desecrated it throughout the seventh and eighth and toward dusk of the ninth they set fire to it and it continued to burn the whole of that day." Ta'anit 29a.

Roman Pope and the Jews

As we know, the Jewish fast of Tisha B'Av marks the siege and destruction of Jerusalem, as seen on Titus' Arch. Until Napoleon occupied Rome, some new Popes would ride in a parade to the arch where the Jews, their community elders and rabbis, were required to ritually honor and greet him. Some of them must have descended from the slaves brought from Jerusalem. They ritually acknowledged and saluted Emperor Titus, the Conqueror of the Jews, despoiler of their holy city, desecrator of their Temple, greeting him at his godlike arch in the human form of the Pope, also a reigning Roman monarch. They ceremonially presented him with an ornate copy of the Torah. The newly crowned Pontifex Maximus would decline, saying something to the effect of "Good Law, but bad religion." From this and other events, the Arch of Titus is indelibly imprinted in Jewish history. In 1555 when Pope Paul IV re-ghettoized the Roman Jews, they were gathered at the Arch and forced to swear an oath of submission to him. Rome and Judah have connections of several sorts. Some are quite deep and intense.

Coming Soon, a Judeo-Roman Temple?

I assume that various Temple artifacts are still in possession of the Vatican, maybe even the Ark, ritually and symbolically quite significant. The Vatican must have all of the extant items. While allowing for the possibility that the Temple devotees destroyed certain objects to avoid capture and defilement, many things were carefully removed before the building was razed and burned. Then they were taken to Rome. Unless some covert transfer has occurred, where else would they be? I doubt the Vatican catacomb gnomes ever really lose or misplace anything, especially something this important. But neither the church nor the Jews openly address these rather esoteric and delicate matters. Are the artifacts being held for the time when a Third Temple is erected? Along with renewed Cohanim priests and special yeshivas to train them, a red heifer, required for the first ritual sacrifice, has been successfully bred. Will the pagan Pontifex Maximus Pope of the Vatican have a throne there so he can alternately reign from both power centers? If so, we could call this a Judeo-Catholic Temple. I suppose this would be the ultimate act of union between Judea and Rome. Would this yet again bring forth a new religion, based on Judaism and Vatican Two Catholicism? The Pope has already affirmed that the Holocaust dogma of Judaism is also a crucial part of Catholic dogma as shown in 2008 and 2009 in the matter of Bishop Williamson. Will Judea and Rome produce an offspring? We already have so-called Judeo-Christianity as a workable name, so who can really say? Stranger marriages have been made and even stranger children have been born.

When Rome Destroyed Jerusalem, Judaism Was Born

As we know, modern Judaism has little to do with the ancient Hebrew faith. Judaism is Talmudism. The Talmudic writings grew to prodigious proportions in old Babylon. The Judeo-Persians later brought the halakha (both oral and written traditions) back to Israel/Canaan/Palestine, where the Talmud continued to grow,

The image above from the Arch of Titus portrays the sacking of the Temple of Solomon and the removal of the sacred objects. When the author visited Rome, he found the arch to still be quite impressive even after all this time. When walking around there, one can perhaps picture the grand papal parades and large crowds of ancient days.

especially with the Jerusalem Talmud as well as the later Mishna additions. It was Talmudic Judaism, the religion of the Scribes and Pharisees, not the ancient Hebrew Temple faith, which spread about the ancient world. How did this come about?

A.D. 2008 was a great year for some really useful and informative books about Judaics and Judaism. One of the most comprehensive (1199 pages) and persuasive ones was E. Michael Jones' The Jewish Revolutionary Spirit And Its Impact On Modern History. Dr. Jones, a traditional Catholic writer, speaks about the evolution of Judaism and its supremacist geopolitical messianism after Titus and his Legions completely razed Jerusalem. By that time in history, the Pharisee cult was the dominant religious party. Particularly after the fall of the Temple and the migration out of Palestine, they thoroughly and totally recreated and recast the ancient Hebraic faith into Talmudism, which began to be called Judaism.

While it seemed that the Jewish nation had perished in the aftermath of the siege, a remnant escaped to the Diaspora communities in Arabia, Egypt and Cyrene, whence they took both their hatred of Rome and their revolutionary messianic politics. A remnant of the peace party also escaped. Sensing the revolution was leading to a catastrophe, Jochanon ben Zakkai had himself smuggled out of besieged Jerusalem as a corpse wrapped in a shroud. When Titus's Jewish spies informed him the Jochanon was a friend of Rome, the Roman general granted him one request. Jochanon asked for permission to start a school. From this school, the new religion of Judaism arose. The Jews had no Temple, no burnt offerings, no priesthood, and no Sanhedrin or ruling body. All they had was a book, and out of this book they created a new religion. The role of the rabbi was to comment on the book. The commentary was known as Talmud, which became the basis of the new Jewish religion.

Word of God Was Nullified by the Talmud

The Talmud absorbed the Torah, allowing Jews to view the rise of Christian Europe with consolation born of disdain. . . . The Talmud, says Dr. Heinrich Graetz, 'preserved and promoted the religious and moral life of Judaism,' but it did so by bringing about separation and control. . . .

The Talmud may have protected the Jews from schism and sectarian divisions, but the price the Jews paid for this protection was complete rabbinic control. The Talmud took sacred scriptures out of the hands of the common Jews and made their interpretation the sole purview of the rabbis as codified in Talmudic lore. The word of god was nullified by the Talmud. The Talmud, the saying went, permitted whatever the Torah forbade. The Jew, in other words, could not appeal to sacred writ without the permission of the rabbis who controlled the Talmud. The Talmud insured that blasphemy and subversion became a part of Jewish culture, because, as one scholar noted, the Talmud is the creator of the Jewish nation and the mold of the Jewish soul.

After A.D. 70, the Diaspora truly began. Most of the Jews either left Palestine as slaves or émigrés of one sort or another. Of the few who stayed, many of their descendants later converted to Islam when confronted by the jihads of the 700s. This is why some modern Jews and Palestinians show a genetic affinity. In the rest of the ancient Roman world, Jews became an important part of trade and transportation as well as dominating the financial realm until the 1500s when the church allowed Christians to practice usury. Israeli history professor Shlomo Sand and others say that contrary to popular belief, the Judaism of the late Roman Empire period was a proselytizing faith. While it is little known, in certain instances, Talmudic Noahide Law requires gentile conversions. While done out of fear of the Jews, the Book of Esther shows that converts to the ancient Hebrew religion were accepted. For several reasons, Judaism spread over the global scene during the time we survey. Indeed, it always has attracted various spiritual seekers, and synagogues were in all major centers, not just in the Roman realm but to the east as well. Oriental Judaists from Babylon and Baghdad helped convert the populous central Asian Khazar kingdom c. A.D. 740, who became known to the world as the Ashkenazi

Jews. The Talmud was on the move.

The somewhat tamed and pacified Judaic faith actually served the Roman aristocrats and power brokers pretty well for over two centuries. Eventually Imperial interests looked other directions and state policies changed. Rome adopted, completely took over, remade and vigorously promoted the other new first century Semitic religion called Christianity. By the late 300s, they thoroughly transformed and adapted it to their overall aims and goals. And, of course, they used it against the Jews. Perhaps the Romans feared their increasing growth and influence. By this time in history, Judaics of one sort or another were a fairly large and influential part of the empire. When Constantine came to the throne, he strongly promoted Christianity, banning Judaic proselytizing and conversions. There were both actual and psychological effects. Not only were they confined to ghettos; Jews could not share their faith with others, even if asked. They were legally forced to become culturally insular. Already separatist in their orientation toward non-chosen ones, Jews turned spiritually inward to longstanding ethnocentric Talmudic traditions. To some degree, Judaism became absorbed in the swaying and chanting Sufi-like mysticism, sorcery and ceremonial magic, dreams of golems, Kabalistic numerology and gematria. But in the more worldly environs, Jews cooperated with and profited from Roman hegemony rather than resisting it. By the mid to late 300s, very few Jews lived in Palestine. Many dwelt in Roman cities and in her colonies.

Rome's first-century geostrategic goals in the eastern Mediterranean were achieved. For the most part, their Palestinian problems were over and done with. No matter what the later effects on world history, Roman state policies and military actions during the first two centuries—both for and against—gave rise to an essentially new religion called Judaism. When we survey the chronicles of the past, we see a very old, very odd and curious kinship between Romans and Jews. What is more, this dysfunctional connection goes on. No one knows what the future holds, but on the other hand, we can observe and learn from an ongoing stream of events in world history related to this persistent and consistent theme. Nietzsche said it best:

"It's the longest ongoing conflict, Judea against Rome, Rome against Judea."

CHAPTER 8

The Khazarian Connection

The Search for Ashkenazi Origins

S ays Arthur Koestler in "Today's Jews": "The Jews of our times fall into two main divisions: Sephardim [Sephardics] and Ashkenazim [Ashkenazics]. The Sephardim are descendants of the Jews who since antiquity had lived in Spain (in Hebrew, *Sepharad*) until they were expelled at the end of the 15th century and settled in the countries bordering the Mediterranean, the Balkans and to a lesser extent in Western Europe. They spoke a Spanish-Hebrew dialect, Ladino (Judeo-Spanish; it has many other names), and preserved their own traditions and religious rites. In the 1960s, the number of Sephardim was estimated at 500,000."

Koestler continues: "The Ashkenazim, at the same period, numbered about 11 million. Thus, in common parlance, 'Jew' is practically synonymous with 'Ashkenazi Jew'."

In Mr. Koestler's own words, "the story of the Khazar empire, as it slowly emerges from the past, begins to look like the cruelest hoax history has ever perpetrated."

The history of the Ashkenazi Jews was widely known and appreciated in the former Soviet Union. Ashkenazi militants traced the area where the Turkic Khazars originated before their migration to southern Russia to Birobidjan, an eastern Siberian area as big as Switzerland bordered by the Amur River, by China and Mongolia. Around 1928 they started building settlements in this ancient homeland, with the Soviet government's help, and in 1934 the Autonomous Republic (Okrug) of Birobidjan Yevrei came into being, with official languages of Yiddish and Russian. It is still there as an autonomous republic to this day, offering the only historically legitimate settlement area for Ashkenazi Jews willing to exercise their "right to return."

Make the primary Khazarian connection. A significantly large number of the folk called Jews are not Semitic in origin, and their ancestors never set foot in old Palestine. For over a millennium, an originally Asiatic tribe has had considerable, some say undue, influence on the course of world affairs, perhaps more than any other ethnic group. Who are they? Few, if any, other cultures have impacted the world through the ages like this people. Their real name almost faded away along with their once mighty empire of Khazaria.

In contrast, the **people** called Khazars did not disappear at all. They underwent a convenient identity change, creating a unique designation for themselves. They became the "Jews of Eastern Europe," the so-called and self-styled Ashkenazim, adopting and adapting a Semitic Hebrew heritage that was never really theirs. It was under this new name that they entered Europe.

Harold Rosenthal in an Interview said: "Jews are the most intelligent people in the world, so if it benefits them to change their names, they do so. That's all there is to it. They mix in your society, which is plenty corrupt. . . ."

Following the Trail Can Be Difficult

Quite naturally, one of the first questions some readers ask is why there are so few books on Khazarian culture and history? In addition to being ignored and somewhat suppressed, there are reasons of a more scholarly nature. Douglas M. Dunlop, whose study preceded Arthur Koestler's, was one of the first modern scholars to directly address this little-known saga. Says Dunlop, in *History of the Jewish Khazars*, p. x:

"A continuous account of the Khazars was in fact given by the Cambridge historian J.B. Bury, in a chapter of his *History of the Eastern Roman Empire* [London, 1912]. This may be taken as the best account available, though there are others, besides a great number of monographs on various aspects of the subject and incidental references in modern books. The chief reason why we are not more familiar with the Khazars appears to be neither the lack of intrinsic interest presented by their story nor the absence of material, but rather the difficulty of dealing with the existing sources—partly because they are written in a variety of languages, Greek, Arabic, Hebrew, Syriac, Armenian, Georgian, Russian, Persian, Turkish and even Chinese, with which no one can be expected to be conversant at first hand; and partly because of the contradiction and obscurity of the data thus afforded."

The Genesis of a Strategic Term

This term is our second Khazarian connection. A few points must be made about the word "Jew." It was originally spelled and pronounced very differently than today. The meaning was Judean, i.e., someone from Judea, a small subsection of ancient Palestine. In its beginning, this meant nothing necessarily religious. It was a simple geographical designation, but things have changed. The modern word is a "secondary usage," and did not take on its current meaning or pronunciation until the 1700s.

Through this adaptation and misusage, the Khazars took on the special mantle and alleged heritage (in truth, mostly mythological anyway) of an ancient coalition of Semitic tribes, sometimes called Habiru Sagaz ("raiders from across the river"), Hebrews or Israelites. Israel means "chosen of El" (one of several deities mentioned in Genesis), though some say its roots come from Egypt, denoting Isis, Ra and El, the same place they borrowed and adapted their Yahu/Yahweh ethnocentric deity. Whatever the case may be, Israelite, like Judean, was used at one time or another by several tribes who migrated around the area.

But wherever the alleged bloodline rights to any purportedly "promised lands" may lead, they never lead to non-Semitic Khazaria. Khazars are neither the "Chosen Ones" nor the "Children of Israel" except in their own fantasies and desires. The real roots of the ancient Semitic Middle Eastern tribes are quite hard to follow. In practical and provable historical terms, there are no pure and distinct bloodlines back to Old Testament times. How can we follow bloodlines when we hardly know who some of those ancient folk really were? One need not explore too far into ancient history to realize how very little we actually know.

The Phoenix Journals carried this relevant statement: "Historical sequences are convoluted at best. The players are manifold and the events themselves become lost in the obscurity of antiquity."

Jesus and the Jews of His Time: Parallels With Today?

For those who follow New Testament teachings, here is what Jesus said to the Talmudic cult of Pharisees over 20 centuries ago.

There is a theme here, one of lies and deception. Modern "Judeo-Christians" (what an ultra misnomer) seem obsessed with prophecies of one kind or another, but can they connect what is below with current events? Sadly, few seem willing or able to do so, choosing to believe "Jesus was a Jew" and that today's Judaic Zionists are the "chosen people." No, that is not what your bible says. There's more if you want to find it, but these verses should really be enough. Make the connection. According to John 8:44-45: "Ye are of your father the devil, and the lusts of your father ye will do. He was a murderer from the beginning, and abode not in the truth, because there is no truth in him. When he speaketh a lie, he speaketh of his own: for he is a liar, and the father of it. And be-cause I tell you the truth, ye believe me not."

And from Revelation 2:9-10, 3:9: "I know. . . the blasphemy of them which say they are Jews, and are not, but are the synagogue of Satan. . . which say they are Jews, and are not, but do lie. . . "

Who is spoken of? Who fits this profile today? Is Jesus talking about the Khazar convert Jews who entered Europe a thousand years after he spoke? If so, we could say this young Palestinian prophet, leading a resistance movement against the Pharisaic cult and conspiracy that ultimately killed him, provided a prescient look ahead. While the Khazars are surely not the people of the New Testament, having merely appropriated this supposed her-itage and mythos, they certainly match the Talmudists of old Palestine in cunning and guile. For hundreds of years, the Khazar Judaics have excelled in the teachings of the Talmud.

Unfortunately, their Talmudic schemes and machinations have largely succeeded. For example, a lot of modern Christianity is lit-tle more than Judaism for the goyim. They say it best themselves. As Harold Rosenthal put it in his interview:

"Judaism is not only the teaching of the synagogue, but also the doctrine of every 'Christian church' in America. Through our propaganda the church has become our most avid supporter. This has even given us a special place in society, their believing the lie that we are the 'Chosen People' and they, 'gentiles'."

Making Khazarian Connections in Our World Today

According to Theodore White: "History is always written generations after the event, when clouded fact and memory have all fused into what can be accepted as truth, whether it be so or not."

The authentic history of this obscure tribal group is imperative. Not only is the U.S.A.., indeed almost every Western government, committed financially and militarily to defend the unjustly established State of Israel, as we painfully see, almost every Christian church in America promotes this Khazar Zionist nightmare regime. The present-day reality of the Israeli ministate and its myriad of problems take on an entirely different meaning when seen in proper context, but first, we must lift the veil of obfuscation.

When the Khazarian connection is made, it truly begs the question: Why do the American people support patently false land claims from a racial/tribal lineage that was never remotely from Palestine or anywhere else in the Mideast? This is crucial in reviewing what are otherwise just little-known facts about an obscure ancient Central Asian tribe.

As a result of media suppression and a dumbed-down educational system even at the university level, few Americans make the Khazarian connection. American Muslims know the truth through their own news services such as Radio Islam, but most other Americans, especially Christians, seem either to know nothing or don't care to know anything as it contradicts their religious beliefs. Not only that, many Jews know or understand very little of this tale. What force is powerful enough, not so much to rewrite history, but to write around it, virtually erasing significant traces or comments about the ferocious Khazar tribes, and their early impact on Western culture and world history?

Samuel Butler said: "God cannot alter the past, but historians can."

At its height, Khazaria consisted of a territory in West Central Asia and Eastern Europe encompassing over 1 million square miles, located between the Black Sea and the Caspian Sea (which was once called the Chasarian Sea), and northwest to Kiev. Why the historical blackout? Who are they? What happened to them? This is the subject of our study.

Map shows the Khazar empire at the height of its power.

The Khazars were fierce warriors. Both a well armed and armored heavy cavalryman and foot soldier are shown above. The word "hussar," for cavalryman, may have come from Khazarian since the Turkish word for Khazar is "Hazar."

Overview of Khazarian History

Here are the facts as set forth, not only by the historians and books of the past, but by those in modern times. The works of Arthur Koestler, Benjamin Freedman, Douglas M. Dunlop, Kevin Brook and more than a few others speak to these matters. We see below what some present-day Khazar descendants, called the Karay Turks, say about the origin of the name. They too are Khazarian convert Jews, but do not follow the Talmud. Not just that; the Karay are very proud of their Turko-Asian heritage.

According to the website http://ozturkler.com/data_english/0008/0008_07.htm:

"Khazar is a Turkish word derived from the root 'kaz', with the meaning of 'gez' (wander). In Anatolian Turkish, the term 'khazar' means 'gezer' (wanderer), and coincides with the meaning of a nomad who freely wanders around without any connection to one place. Probably, this word took its final shape through an etymological transformation in the forms of 'gezer', 'gazar', 'kazar' and 'hazar'. The word is 'el-Hazar' in Arabic, 'Huzari', 'Kozar' in Hebrew, 'Gazari', 'Chazari' in Latin, 'Hazari' in Georgian, 'Huszar' in Hungarian and 'Ko-sa', 'ka-sat' in Chinese."

The Khazars, a migratory folk originating in eastern Asia and close kinsmen of the Huns and Mongols, trekked westward. In c. 138, the Khazar tribe's folk arrived in the area between the Caspian and Black seas, near several great rivers. There they established a tribal kingdom that grew in power and influence. For well over 400 years they ruled over an immense and lucrative empire south of the Russian territories, between the Black Sea and the Chasarian/Caspian Sea, reaching as far northwest as Kiev. In its day, the khaghanate (kingdom, empire, khanate) was larger and richer than any other country in Europe. Yes, Khazaria (Khazaran; Khuzaran; Arabic al-Kazara, Kusari; Hebrew Kuzarim), like later Russia, was both an Asian and a European nation. Their location was of key geopolitical importance. Europe was on the west, the Rus Varangians, descendants of the Vikings, on the north, all of Asia and the Silk Road to the east (from whence came the Mongols, their later downfall), plus Greek Christian Byzantium and the newly ascendant Islamic Arabs to the south.

Khazaria was a powerful regional military and trade power. They were commercial wizards of the first order, although those who had to pay the tolls on their seas, rivers and overland trade routes might rather have called them extortionists. Truth be known, the Khazars lived almost solely off this revenue. They produced nothing for export except isinglass. Clothes, tools and virtually everything else came from outside the country. Over time they created additional loot by conquering, oppressing and extorting taxes from over 25 nearby peaceful agricultural tribes. Khazaria produced very little. It was an empire almost solely supported by trade-related revenues. Of course, this mercantile mindset came with them into Europe, but it began a long time before that.

Traders and Merchants of a High Order

Khazars were heavily involved in all kinds of international barter, including the slave trade—hence, the sex trade too, just as they are today. They were one of the better-known procurers and suppliers of Slavs, a people so exploited in this fashion that their very name came to mean slave. The Rus routinely sold Slav captives to the Khazars. This continued in their later migrations and machinations. In the 16th to the 19th centuries, Khazar descendants, along with Sephardic co-religionists, are the dominant players in shipping the black slaves from Africa to the Americas. In his *History of the Jews*, Solomon Grayzel clearly lays this out:

"One type of business carried on in the early Middle Ages by the Jews of Europe, namely the slave trade, requires a special word of explanation. The Jews were among the most important slave-dealers. As inhabitants of western Germany pushed their way deeper and deeper into Central Europe, driving the Slavic inhabitants farther eastward and taking away their land, they brought back captives whom they sold to Jewish traders. The Jews, in turn, transported these slaves to other lands to be sold to Christian and Mohammedan masters."

Another trade learned as Khazars and continued as Jews was that of the furrier. Marten, sable and other fine furs (in addition to many other valuable products) came down the Volga via the Bulgars, and goods flowed all the way from Novgorod via the Dnieper, not to mention other centers via the Don and several more major waterways. Some main commodities were furs, hides, honey, flax, tar, cloth, grains, gold, silver, jewels and silks. The Khazars made almost no cloth or clothes, getting them all through the mercantile networks. Old descriptions of Khazar clothing sound something like the Hasidim and others, featuring fur hats and long coats. Trade in many of these items continued to be dominated by the Khazars even after they migrated into Europe. For example, the fur business is often a Judaic enterprise even today. Of course, the dominant international diamond and jewel traders (thus they are involved with "blood diamonds") are the Khazar Ashkenazi Hasidic Jews. While dominant in more than a few industries today, back in Khazaria and later in Europe, they were the chief players, sometimes the only players, in commercial enterprises such as brewing, and, of course, later in distilling. The early pioneers in manufacturing and marketing of alcoholic beverages were often Khazar Jews.

Per Dr. Cecil Roth, writing in *World History of the Jewish People*: "In the 'dark age,' the commerce of Western Europe was largely in Jewish hands, not excluding the slave trade, and in the Carolingian cartularies Jew and merchant are used as almost interchangeable terms."

Minister Louis Farrakhan and the Nation of Islam were lambasted and criticized by the Zionist dominated media for daring to publish, with heavy documentation, the history of Jews and the African slave trade. *The Secret Relationship Between Blacks and Jews* (by an anonymous writer or group of writers) is quite well researched and very difficult to refute. The Sephardic Jews were among the earliest sea traders, sailors, shippers and ship owners, as were their Semitic cousins, the Phoenicians. With co-religionists in almost every port in the world, they got the goods reliably delivered when international shipping was an extremely risky business, and before the modern insurance industry began. Their involvement in the profitable human cargo trade was a natural development of their extensive trade and shipping connections. Both Sephardis and Ashkenazis were prominent in the slave trade. Today, it is the lucrative and despicable sex slave trade that holds their interest.

Make the Khazarian connection. Many of their main families, i.e., the Rothschilds as well as other Illuminati bloodlines, consisted of slavers, war profiteers and exploiters, then as now.

How the Khaghanate Was Governed

Before moving on, we say a few words about the Khazar monarchy. Its ruler was called the khaghan, an emperor or high king (related to khan, also rendered as khakhan, khaqan etc). He was a ceremonial figure of sorts, and a spiritual leader as well. Curiously, this old Khazar title may still be with us in the Judaic name Kagan. The khaghan was head of state, but not head of government. Another important character was the begh, a shogun-like grand vizier or generalissimo figure. This is a curious job. As would a prime minister, along with a council of ministers, the begh conducted everyday business, yet was also the military commander-in-chief. But at other times, he seems more like a co-monarch, sometimes styled as the khaghan begh. Of course, this "begs" the question and makes the relationship even harder to fathom. In Kazakhstan, Uzbekistan and other places, the old title is still used for some tribal leaders. Koestler tells us more:

"All this does not explain the startling division of divine and secular power, apparently unique in that period and region. As Bury wrote: 'We have no information at what time the active authority of the chagan was exchanged for his divine nullity, or why he was exalted to a position resembling that of the emperor of Japan, in which his existence, and not his government, was considered essential to the prosperity of the state.' A speculative answer to this question has recently been proposed by Artamonov. He suggests that the acceptance of Judaism as the state religion was the result of a coup d'état, which at the same time reduced the khaghan, descendant of a pagan dynasty whose allegiance to Mosaic Law could not really be trusted, to a mere figurehead. This is a hypothesis as good as any other—and with as little evidence to support it. Yet it seems probable that the two events—the adoption of Judaism and the establishment of the double kingship—were somehow connected. Before the conversion the khaghan was still reported to play an active role—as, for instance, in his dealings with Justinian.

"To complicate matters further, the Arab sources sometimes refer to the 'khaghan' when they clearly mean the 'bek' (as 'khaghan' was the generic term for 'ruler' among many tribes), and they also use different names for the bek. . . ."

In some ways, the supreme monarch's role seems ceremonial and minimal, but this is not consistent, and may have varied, depending on the personality and goals of those who came to the throne. As we shall see, some played the dominant role in diplomatic affairs. We also know that the khaghan made a required ceremonial appearance before the people every four months, but the record is vague about other functions. When he appeared before the people, did he grant audiences? Did he make proclamations? Alas, we do not know. We might assume he had some sort of veto power if the begh failed in his tasks. This curious relationship was not always consistent. The begh was the supreme military leader, but some khaghans were known to take the field at the head of their troops. Other than the curious "co-rulers," Khazaria was, more or less, a traditional monarchy. It also had a shamanistic priesthood, a warrior caste (probably the begh came from this class) and an aristocracy (the "White Khazars" or Aq Khazars), but we know little more.

Did the Ancient Khazars Ritually Slay Their King?

As the khaghan was also a spiritual leader, some strange rituals grew up around him and his role. Koestler tells the tale:

"There is no evidence of the Khazars engaging in religious persecution, either before or after the conversion to Judaism. In this respect they may be called more tolerant and enlightened than the East Roman Empire or Islam in its early stages. On the other hand, they seem to have preserved some barbaric rituals from their tribal past. We have heard Ibn Fadlan on the killings of the royal gravediggers. He also has something to say about another archaic custom—regicide: 'The period of the king's rule is 40 years. If he exceeds this time by a single day, his subjects and attendants kill him, saying 'His reasoning is already dimmed, and his insight confused.'

"Istakhri has a different version of it: When they wish to enthrone this khaghan, they put a silken cord round his neck and tighten it until he begins to choke. Then they ask him: 'How long dost thou intend to rule?' If he does not die before that year, he is killed when he reaches it."

Zeki Validi quotes a French anthropologist, St. Julien, writing in 1864: "Bury is doubtful whether to believe this kind of Arab traveler's lore, and one would indeed be inclined to dismiss it, if ritual regicide had not been such a widespread phenomenon among primitive (and not-so-primitive) people. Frazer laid great emphasis on the connection between the concept of the king's divinity, and the sacred obligation to kill him after a fixed period, or when his vitality is on the wane, so that the divine power may find a more youthful and vigorous incarnation. [Sir James Frazer wrote a special treatise on these lines on 'The Killing of the Khazar Kings' (*Folklore*, XXVIII, 1917).] It speaks in Istakhri's favor that the bizarre ceremony of 'choking' the future king has been reported in existence apparently not so long ago among another people, the Kok-Turks.

"When the new chief has been elected, his officers and attendants . . . make him mount his horse. They tighten a ribbon of silk round his neck, without quite strangling him; then they loosen the ribbon and ask him with great insistence: "For how many years canst thou be our khan?" The king, in his troubled mind, being unable to name a figure, his subjects decide, on the strength of the words that have escaped him, whether his rule will be long or brief.

"We do not know whether the Khazar rite of slaying the king (if it ever existed) fell into abeyance when they adopted Judaism, in which case the Arab writers were confusing past with present practices as they did all the time, compiling earlier travelers' reports, and attributing them to contemporaries. However that may be, the point to be retained, and which seems beyond dispute, is the divine role attributed to the khaghan, regardless whether or not it implied his ultimate sacrifice. We have heard before that he was venerated, but virtually kept in seclusion, cut off from the people, until he was buried with enormous ceremony. The affairs of state, including leadership of the army, were managed by the bek, who wielded all effective power."

As previously observed, this is all a bit frustrating due to its inconsistency. Some khaghans not only led their troops, but presided over sensitive diplomatic negotiations and treaties. The Khazar king was also a spiritual leader, so we examine this dimension next.

Khazars and Religion

Accoding to Heinrich Graetz, *History of the Jews*, 1892: "The Chasars professed a coarse religion, which was combined with sensuality and lewdness."

Like kindred tribes, their old religion was primitive shamanism sometimes even involving human sacrifice. But change was in the air. History records that in the middle of the eighth century (c. 740), the khaghan, along with the begh, their ministers and close advisors, made a carefully calculated geopolitical decision about a state religion. This had become a sticking point in foreign affairs. While fighting Muslims in crucial battles at certain times, the Khazars also had many of the Islamic faith, not only within their borders, but as mercenaries in their multicultural army. Bulan even have made a half-hearted conversion from shamanism to Islam (c. A.D. 737), making the religious situation even more confusing. Apparently, if it happened at all, it was largely symbolic, involving only the khaghan, who was said to have quarreled with the imams about their strict dietary rules.

Dunlop, p. 86, says: "At first sight, the statements that the khaghan became a Muslim in A.D. 737 and Judaized three years later are, to say the least, remarkable."

There was apparently an ongoing Christian presence. Certainly they must have interacted with Christian merchants and maybe missionaries and other travelers on their trade routes. An Armenian bishop is said to have preached in the area around 682. While he likely converted a few, there is no record of a diocese being established or priests coming to start mission churches. However, this was right in the middle of two Khazar-Arab wars, so the timing was not ideal. How deep the Christian roots were planted is a wide-open question. But, apparently, some did get baptized, and there are ongoing references to Christian Khazars.

Koestler, pp. 129-130, writes: "The Khazars evidently had the qualities of a jack-in-the-box, derived from their Turkish origin, or Mosaic faith or both. Cedrenus [the chronicler] also says the name of [a] defeated Khazar leader was Georgius Tzul. Georgius is a Christian name; we know from an earlier report that there were Christians as well as Muslims in the Khaghan's army."

Essentially, all of Europe owes an unacknowledged debt to Khazaria. The Khazars repelled two massive Islamic jihads from the powerful and aggressive Abbasid Caliphate. Without a doubt, in due course, they would have continued into Europe. If you have not realized it yet, Europe has always been and still is the target of the global Islamic jihad, aimed at bringing about a whole planet in submission to Islam, Allah, the Koran and shariah law. The first Khazar-Arab war lasted from 642 until 653; the second from 732 to 737. In both endeavors, they repelled the Muslim invaders, and the Abbasid caliphate turned its eyes elsewhere.

Khazar Conversion

So as we see, the Judaic conversion came in a time of war and upheaval as Khazaria was surely and certainly beset by the Muslim armies. Turning Christian was out of the question. Not only would this have put them in a compromising position with both the Vatican and Byzantium, but, more importantly, would have insulted the Muslims. What were they to do? Bulan, the Begh and their ministers set out to remedy the situation. While some writers say it never really happened, they reportedly brought in Greek philosophers, Christian bishops and evangelists, Islamic mullahs and faqihs, and rabbis from Baghdad and Babylon for debates and dissertations about their respective faiths. Whatever the facts may be, the decision was already made. Indeed, we must opine that Judaism did not just suddenly appear right before the great debate. According to several sources, a rabbi was already resident at the khaghan's court. This may reflect an earlier date (c. A.D. 721), for the beginning of Judaic influence at the top levels of power. This was through Oriental Jews, from already existing communities like those in Persia, Baghdad and Byzantium.

While the decision to convert was made behind the scenes, for the sake of appearances, the other religions were brought in for the famous theological dispute. So, after an appropriate deliberation period, the khaghan, and thus his nation, converted to Judaic Talmudism. Rabbis were imported for the appropriate rites. Hundreds, maybe thousands of the pagan shamans and members of the elite classes were mass ordained (some then, some later) as Cohens or Levites (Hebrew priestly caste and sub-caste). It is to be expected that some of the rabbis, as well as other Oriental Judaics and their families, stayed on to nurture the faith, training lay teachers and rabbis from among the Khazars. And, of course, they must have intermarried, at least to some degree.

While this could mean that a drop or two of semi-Semitic blood entered the gene pool, it was minimal. Moreover, Oriental Judaic Sephardic bloodlines were already mixed and mottled, e.g., with Canaanites, Edomites, Idumeans and a host of other regional tribes from Palestine to Egypt and up and down the Arabian Peninsula. Essentially, the Sephardim are Arab Jews or Judaized Arabs, whichever you prefer. While neither ethnic group really wants to hear about it, Jews and Arabs are intermixed. Did you know that Yemen, like old Khazaria, once had a monarch and upper classes that converted? Beginning c. 390, it became a Judaic kingdom until the sixth century, called Himayar. Like in other parts of ancient Arabia, there were already Judaic tribes of one kind or another living there. Some of Mohammed's early jihads were against Arab Jews since most of them refused to follow the new prophet.

John Tiffany had some remarkable quotations and comments in his *Barnes Review* article on the Khazars, including an account by an Arab historian that contains some interesting information ("The Khazars—Non-Semitic Jews," *The Barnes Review*, Vol. III, No. 7, July 1997):

"According to a Muslim account found in al-Bakri's *Book of Kingdoms and Roads*, written in the 11th century, it [the conversion] happened in this way: 'The reason for the conversion to Judaism of the king of the Khazars, who had previously been a pagan, is as follows. He had adopted Christianity. Then he recognized its false-hood and discussed this matter, which greatly worried him, with one of his high officials. The latter said to him, 'Oh king, those in possession of sacred scriptures fall into three groups. Summon them and ask them to state their case, then follow the one who is in possession of the truth.' So he sent to the Christians for a bishop. Now there was with the king a Jew, skilled in argument, who engaged him (the bishop) in disputation. He asked the bishop: 'What do you say of Moses, the son of Amran, and the torah which was revealed to him?' The bishop replied: 'Moses is a prophet, and the Torah speaks the truth.' Then the Jew said to the king: 'He has already admitted the truth of my creed. Ask him now what he believes in.'

"So the king asked him, and he replied, 'I say that Jesus the

Messiah is the son of Mary, he is the Word, and he has revealed the mysteries in the name of god.' Then the Jew said to the king of the Khazars: 'He preaches a doctrine which I know not, while he accepts my propositions.' But the bishop was not strong in producing evidence. Then the king asked for a Muslim, and they sent him a scholarly, clever man who was good at arguments. But the Jew hired someone who poisoned him on the journey, and he died. And the Jew succeeded in winning the king for his faith, so that the embraced Judaism."

The coming of the Talmudic religion to Khazaria began with the upper classes. It took time for the faith to spread among the common people. While it eventually did grow and flourish, in the beginning it was still in a multicultural milieu. For example, in a stance befitting its status at an international trade crossroads, and since mercenaries of many religions served in the Khazar military, a tolerance for Christianity and Islam continued. Perhaps the folk in more remote locations continued on with their shamanism, or as is done with most new religions, blended and incorporated the old beliefs with the new.

Dr. Koestler tells us a bit about the beginning of the decline of the empire in the mid to late 900s. But their new religion did not really decline at all. By that time, their Khazarian brand of Judaism was well entrenched. Even when the Kievan Rus were asserting their own sovereignty, and just before they stopped paying tribute to the khaghan, the Khazars tried to prevent this by religiously recruiting the ruler. As history shows, this sometimes does the trick, but in the case of the Kievan Rus, it was not to be. Koestler writes:

"The first non-Arab mention of Khazaria after the fatal year 965 [when the Russians dealt the Khazars a crushing defeat—Ed.] seems to occur in a travel report by Ibrahim Ibn Jakub, the Spanish-Jewish ambassador to Otto the Great, who, writing probably in 973, describes the Khazars as still flourishing during his time. Next in chronological order is the account of the *Russian Chronicle* of Jews from Khazaria arriving in Kiev A.D. 986 in their misfired attempt to convert Vladimir to their faith."

As we see, while Kiev was essentially treated as a fiefdom from which to extort tribute, many Khazars settled and lived there, long before the coming of the Rus. And even after the decline of their empire, there was still a significant presence. Kiev was commonly called the "City of the Jews."

Note on Dates and Events

We must note some discrepancies in dating events about the Khazars of old, especially about the great Conversion. The following examples are from a dateline found at http://www.turkic-world.org. It dates the larger conversion as late as 799-809, but says Bulan himself converted to Judaism in 730. To make matters even more confusing, as we know, there are other sources saying he was forced to convert to Islam in 737 to stay in power. Truth be known, he may have done both, but if it happened, the Islamic conversion probably involved only the ruler himself.

Growth of Khazarian Judaism

Judaics are said to have come to the khaghanate as early as 723, but given the longtime presence of Oriental Judaics in the region, it probably began much earlier than that. The overall conversion of a nation the size of Khazaria would take some time, but regardless of the actual date, once it began, the growth and evolution of Khazarian Judaism was steady and persistent. As with any new faith, the beginning stages were rudimentary. It required its infancy and growth periods before becoming predominant. As we see with the attempt to Judaize the Kievan Rus, they used their religion for political machinations, yet another present-day Khazarian connection. They use the same protocols of power then as now. As with Zionism, religion is merely a tool. Zionism uses and misuses Judaism in its quest for domination.

But to conclude this section, we see that Judaism was at first adopted simply as a geopolitical survival tactic when Khazaria was in a difficult diplomatic dilemma. It was a practical decision; spirituality had nothing to do with it. Historian J.B. Bury concurs:

"There can be no question that the ruler was actuated by political motives in adopting Judaism. To embrace Mohammedanism would have made him the spiritual dependent of the caliphs, who attempted to press their faith on the Khazars, and in Christianity lay the danger of his becoming an ecclesiastical vassal of the Roman empire. Judaism was a reputable religion with sacred books which both Christian and Mohammedan respected; it elevated him above the heathen barbarians, and secured him against the interference of caliph or emperor."

To begin planting the Talmudic creed, many Khazars, again beginning with the upper classes, took biblical-sounding Judaic names. Bulan, whose name meant elk in Old Turkic, changed his name to Sabriel. All later khaghans took Judaic monikers. Says Wikipedia, 2009:

"The extent of the conversion is debated. Ibn al-Faqih reported in the 10th century that 'all the Khazars are Jews.' Notwithstanding this statement, some scholars believe that only the upper classes converted to Judaism; there is some support for this in contemporary Muslim texts. However, recent archeological excavations have uncovered widespread shifts in burial practices. Around the mid-800s burials in Khazaria began to take on a decidedly Jewish flavor. Grave goods disappeared almost altogether. Judging by interment evidence, by 950 Judaism had become widespread among all classes of Khazar society."

As a result of the conversion, Khazaria also adopted the Hebrew script, so by this time they corresponded with the Sephardim and other Oriental Judaics already in the west, especially in the lands around the Mediterranean. Joseph was the name of the khaghan at the time of the Khazar Correspondence, in which he is called King Joseph. This was an exchange of letters in the mid-900s to Judaics in the Caliphate of Cordoba. It is one of the only extant documents penned by a Khazar, thus is an important part of the few secondary sources on their history. By this time, Khazaria was known in the West as the mysterious Asian kingdom of the Jews. The conversion 200 years prior was in full flower, and the Turko-Khazars were fast becoming known as the "Jews of the East."

Who Is Jewish? Who Is Not?

As said, spirituality had little to do with their Judaizing, especially in the beginning. But while this decision was perhaps entered into a bit half-heartedly, like Bulan's earlier symbolic conversion to Islam, it later proved to be momentous in world history. In spite of its later massive impact, the conversion was not really so unique back in the day. Other Central Asian tribes in need of a functional alphabet and written language also adopted Hebrew, and may have undergone some kind of symbolic rites, but not to this extent. So we must remember that while somewhat remarkable, the conversion had little actual effect on Judaism or world events until after c. 1000.

Other non-Semitic tribes, like the cousins of the Khazars, the

Karay Turks, also converted to Judaism, but none of them ever impacted world history and culture more than the Khazar converts of the mid 700s. Yet, as we know, by this time in history, all Judaic folk are of mixed bloodlines, most having absolutely nothing to do with either the Mideast or old Judea. But given the evidence, even the black Falasha Jews of Ethiopia (where a Semitic dialect still exists) or the dark Jews of Yemen have a more honest claim to a part of Palestine than do the totally non-Semitic Turko-Mongol Central Asian Khazars. —Paul Wexler

"Also, the Khazars were only one recent tribe among many that converted. There were also the Falasha of Abyssinia, who are black; the Chinese Jews of Kai-Feng, who look Chinese; the dark olive Yemenite Jews; and the Jewish Berber tribes of the Sahara, who look like Tuaregs. Who is Jewish? Who is not?"

To Judaics in the west centuries ago, the supposedly now-kosher Khazars were little more than a distant and exotic rumor, similar to the old Christian tales of Prester John. But they were proud of the magnificent "Jewish Kingdom in Asia." Eventually, the impact of the westward migration of the Khazar converts would reach them, but not quite yet.

Conversions Created Change in Judaic Bloodlines: An Israeli Revisionist's View

Until my research advanced, I believed that Judaism was an exclusivist supremacist religion, spurning and discouraging converts. I was right about the first part, but not about the second. They don't make it easy, but neither do they make it impossible. While the Talmud says even the best of the goyim should be killed, in certain instances, this is totally set aside. As for gentile conversions, only the best, and the most persistent, among the goyim can enter (at least the outer) realms of the divinely chosen ones.

Left, a fallen Khazar warrior is struck down by Svyatoslav I of Kiev in a 2005 statue. Note the hexagon Star of David on the Khazar shield. Upper right, this bust is of a Khazar warrior circa A.D. 800, right after the conversion. Note the Mongoloid physiognomy. Lower right, a heavily armored Khazar cavalryman and his prisoner are shown (8th century ewer found in Rumania). There exist also a few pictures of Khazars with a lighter complexion, probably some of the so-called "White Khazars."

Of course, the persistent and diligent convert is always the most desirable one, so only the best and the most useful are recruited. But whatever the actual numbers may be, over the centuries, these various conversions have had a sure and steady effect on Judaic bloodlines.

Dr. Shlomo Sand, mentioned above, is a distinguished professor of European history at Tel Aviv University, and author of the surprisingly bestselling politically and religiously incorrect book *When and How Was the Jewish People Invented?*, now translated into several languages. The material below comes from the review and commentary by journalist Jonathan Cook, also referred to above. It contains quotations from the book and discusses the overall implications of Sand's hypothesis. Obviously, the largest and most important Judaic conversion was that of Khazaria.

So if there was no exile, how is it that so many Jews ended up scattered around the globe before the modern state of Israel began encouraging them to "return" [to Palestine]? Dr. Sand said that, in the centuries immediately preceding and following the Christian era, Judaism was a proselytizing religion, desperate for converts. "This is mentioned in the Roman literature of the time."

Jews traveled to other regions seeking converts, particularly in Yemen [which for a time became the Jewish kingdom of Himayar] and among the Berber tribes of North Africa [from where they and the Sephardics went to Spain, Portugal, and ultimately migrated into the rest of Europe and the Americas].

Centuries later, the people of the Khazar kingdom in what is today south Russia, would convert en masse to Judaism, becoming the genesis of the Ashkenazi Jews of central and Eastern Europe.

Dr. Sand pointed to the strange state of denial in which most Israelis live, noting that papers offered extensive coverage recently to the discovery of the capital of the Khazar kingdom next to the Caspian Sea. Ynet, the website of Israel's most popular newspaper, *Yedioth Ahronoth*, headlined the story: "Russian archeologists find long-lost Jewish capital." And yet none of the papers, he added, had considered the significance of this find to standard accounts of Jewish history.

One further question is prompted by Dr. Sand's account: As he himself notes—if most Jews never left the Holy Land, what became of them? Thus he writes:

"It is not taught in Israeli schools, but most of the early Zionist leaders, including David Ben Gurion [Israel's first prime minister], believed that the Palestinians were the descendants of the area's original Jews. They believed [these] Jews had later converted to Islam."

Dr. Sand attributed his colleagues' reticence to engage with him to an implicit acknowledgement by many that the whole edifice of "Jewish history" taught at Israeli universities is built like a house of cards.

The problem with the teaching of history in Israel, Dr. Sand said, dates to a decision in the 1930s to separate history into two disciplines: general history and Jewish history. Jewish history was assumed to need its own field of study because the Jewish experience was considered unique. He says:

"There's no Jewish department of politics or sociology at the universities. Only history is taught in this way, and it has allowed specialists in Jewish history to live in a very insular and conservative world where they are not touched by modern developments in historical research."

—http://rense.com/general83/schol.htm

Rise and Fall of the Khaghanate

The Khazars were at the nexus of several crucial trade routes. They extorted a 10 percent tithe of everything passing through their realm, plus other charges. This included heavily used shipping routes, not only on the Black and Caspian seas, but on key rivers like the Volga, Dnieper, Don and Ural. This strategic location filled their coffers with gold and silver, but also placed them in a difficult and precarious political position. The empire was vast, making for porous, difficult to defend borders. While they effectively kept the Byzantines at bay through guile and intrigue, they were not so fortunate on other fronts. The fervently Islamic Arabs from the large and militarily powerful Abbasid caliphate to the south grew more and more restless and menacing, regularly encroaching. Khazaria fought two major wars and repelled them. But ultimately the greatest threat came from the northwest.

By the mid-A.D. 900s, the Rus Varangians, a tribe from Viking stock, were pushing hard. Khazarian troops, by now mostly conscripts and mercenaries, were no match for the motivated and fearsome Rus. By 985, the new dukedom of Kiev had effectively defeated the Khazars in their own environs, seizing the northwestern portions for themselves. After that, Khazaria began to politically disintegrate, but slowly. As our map on the opposite page shows, Khazaria was beset from many sides.

Both the Rus and the Arabs were vicious foes, rightly feared by ordinary Khazarian people, who were plagued on multiple fronts. What do people do in such situations? They often move away, becoming émigrés seeking a new home. But where to go? As we know, a number of them stayed around Kiev and more went there later, but the way north for more than a few was out of the picture. The Rus would never allow this. After all, it was only a few years earlier that they managed to overthrow Khazar suzerainty.

A few may have turned east, toward their old homelands, with kindred Turkic language groups and tribes. But the road east was long and perilous, and their cousins among the Central Asian nations remembered Khazar extortion, cruelty and warlike ways. In earlier times, many paid heavy tribute on top of the tithe taken from all trade, and would resent their former oppressors coming their way. Not only that. In the 1200s the Mongols came from the east in a massive migration-invasion wave, eventually overcoming Khazaria and its neighboring lands.

Oriental Judaics and some Khazars already lived in Constan-

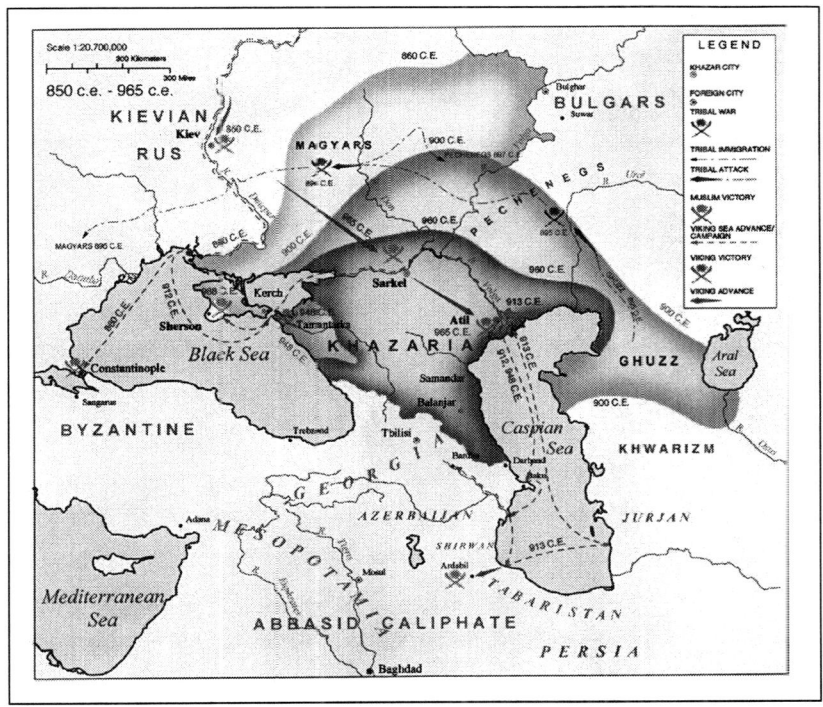

Khazarian migrations.

tinople, so a few wealthier and more business-adept ones may
have gone south, but the Christian Byzantines would have resisted
a massive influx. And, anywhere else in the south was out of the
question at that time. The militant Arabs would either annihilate
or assimilate them, treating them essentially as pagans, that is,
those who must accept Islam or face the jihad. Some did settle in
Byzantium. Over the years, Khazaria maintained a full embassy in
Constantinople. International intrigue and intermarriage of the
ruling family with a Khazar princess named Tzitzac made their
influence, a Khazarian connection, difficult to conceal. Tzitzac was
baptized as Eirene. This union resulted in her son, "Leo the
Khazar," becoming the Byzantine emperor in 775.

As time went on, Khazaria's borders shrank, and she was no longer a major player, but fought hard to keep the frontiers from shrinking further. Over a period of time during the decline of their nation, especially when various powers threatened them, more and more Khazars sought safety. For them, there was only one safe and secure direction to go—west and northwest, into Europe. Koestler says:

"Two basic facts emerge from our survey: the disappearance of the Khazar nation from its historic habitat, and the simultaneous appearance in the adjacent regions to the northwest of the greatest concentration of Jews since the beginning of the Diaspora."

And Poliak writes:

"[Here is] . . . a new approach, both to the problem of relations between the Khazar Jewry and other Jewish communities, and to the question of how far we can go in regarding this Khazar Jewry as the nucleus of the large Jewish settlements of Eastern Europe. . . . The descendants of this settlement—those who stayed where they were, those who emigrated to the United States and to other countries, and those who went to Israel—constitute now the large majority of world Jewry."

And to quote F. Roderich-Stoltheim, *The Riddle of the Jew's Success* (Hammer Verlag, Leipzig, 1927; NY: Michael Santomauro, 2005), pp. 221-222:

"But one must certainly not any longer speak of our Jews of today as pure Semites; they have taken up all manner of foreign national elements; and it is truly remarkable to what a complex extent they have assimilated the same. One is entitled to ask whether the Talmudic spirit alone has rendered this complete adaptation possible, or whether a few drops of Jewish blood have sufficed to give an unvarying stamp of expression—at least mentally—to the entire mass.

"Externally, the Jews of today present marked differences in their appearance; Negroid and Turanian (Mongolian) types can be discerned amongst them as well as Semitic. Even amongst the Hebrews who hail from Russia and Poland, one not infrequently comes across blond and watery-eyed [blue-eyed] examples. It is practically certain that the people, who were formerly called the Chasaren [Khazars], and who are regarded as belonging to a Turko-Finnish stock, and who, about 800 years after Christ, formed a separate empire in what is now south Russia, went over to Jewdom and were completely absorbed. The Jews themselves are conscious of this distinction, for the western Jews who have come across Spain call themselves 'Sephardim' (if baptized, marranen) [marranos], and have North African blood in their veins [see more about this later on], describe the eastern Jews as 'Aschkenazim,' and look down on the latter with a certain amount of contempt.

"In spite of this, the Talmudic law embraces them all, and the rabbinical despotism welds them into a closed caste, absolutely united in its hostility to all non-Jewish peoples."

This illustrative material from the fascinating and revealing *Riddle* book shows that Germanic scholars of the early 20th century, while they did not write a lot about it, knew that ancient Khazaria was the source of much of European Jewry. Before moving on to the mass migration, here is another interesting little-known story about some present-day descendants for whom the nation still exists.

Did Khazaria Really Come to an End?

Did Khazaria really come to an end? Not according to the Karay people, a community of ethnic Turkic-speaking adherents of Karaite (non-Talmudic) Judaism, centered in the Crimea, which as you know was at the heart of old Khazaria. Today, many live in Turkey, Britain, Lithuania (another nation with an honorable Karaite presence in their history), other parts of Europe, Israel, the U.S.A. and elsewhere. Their rituals and folkways are quite authentic, going back to ancient times. Some researchers date them from the 800s, right after the conversion a half century or so before. [http://www.belgeler.com/blg/1hdr/a-disappearing-community-crimean-karaites-kaybolmakta-olan-bir-halk-kirim-karaylari]

The Karay Crimean Turko-Khazars clearly assert that they are rightful heirs with a direct bloodline connection to the traditions of ancient Khazaria. While they still have a strong ethnic folk identity, their old Turkic dialect is dying out, though efforts to preserve it are under way.

Their religion and their presence in the world attest to the beguiling story of the old Khazarian Judaic kingdom. This is yet another people, like the Kurds, who were left off the maps when the European colonialist regimes redrew them. While there is no time to narrate more of it here, this is a stirring story about an honorable non-Talmudic Khazar people preserving their heritage and birthright. Not only do the maps omit them, so do most so-called history books. Talking too much about the Karay might lead to more controversial topics, which are assiduously avoided by the court historians, who are well rewarded for their compliance and cooperation.

The Khazarian Exodus into Europe

Europe already had small pre-existing Judaic communities with whom the Khazars could ally, sometimes later to absorb and replace. They moved west, not as Khazars, but using a name they

The images above show Karay tribesmen, left, and Seraya Shapsal on the right (1873-1961), their highly venerated spiritual and political leader.

had adopted and helped coin, calling themselves "Jews." They first nestled in with the small Hebraic communities they found, becoming the Ashkenazim (more on this later), the "Jews of the East." While some think about ghettos when they think of European Jewry, the truly exclusive Judaic settlement is not the ghetto, which was imposed upon them by Christians, but the Khazar Jewish shtetl. This closed, segregated institution's purpose was to allow Talmudic Jews to remain pure, living apart from the defiling goyim. A shtetl in today's perfectly politically correct terms, is an ethnocentric self-contained community, barring all outsiders (goyim) and their polluting influences.

By the 15th and 16th centuries, the Khazars had, for some time, practiced and enhanced the terribly tedious, convoluted and legalistic Talmudic Pharisaic faith, so-called Judaism. Judaism, especially when entangled and entwined with Khazarian Zionism—and even more so in certain parts of their "sacred scriptures" called Talmud and Kabala—is an exclusivist elitist dogma and doctrine. By late medieval and early renaissance times, the erstwhile Turko-Mongol Khazar converts became the "Jews of Europe." Then and now, the most devout and devoted Talmudists and Kabalists are of the Khazarian Hasidic sect. In Hebrew, *hasidim* means the "pure ones" or the "righteous ones."

"Why should they [Christian Europe] fear a few shabby, furtive aliens who have drifted in from unknown places, and who established themselves in the heart of the city so unobtrusively that it seems they have always been there? These aliens are willing to do anything; they perform any sort of distasteful task which the natives feel is beneath them. The aliens traffic in the bodies of young girls, set up gambling dens, deal in stolen goods, lend money, establish houses in which one can perform every imaginable type of sexual degeneracy, and provide assassins for hire. . . . In a short time, the aliens know the secret of the people's leaders, and they have established their hold over them." —Eustace Mullins, *The Biological Jew*.

Did They Emigrate All at Once?

The so-called Exodus of the Old Testament (a heavily redacted document) may refer to a series of events at different times when the Habiru Sagaz and other clans and tribes left Egypt in search of greener pastures. Some say they were run out for being thieves and plunderers, but we mustn't digress. My point is that the ancient relocations mentioned in the bible and the movements of the Khazars eons later definitely have one thing in common. Both were mostly gradual and not really all that dramatic. And, we must consider that not everyone had the desire or the resources for a difficult and possibly dangerous westward trek. Even after the Rus/Varangians, who previously paid tribute to the khaghan, claimed Kiev as an independent dukedom in the mid to late 900s, a substantial Khazar colony continued living in the city. Undeniably, some of the old empire did not fall until much later, the Mongol invasion eventually bringing an end to the once glorious Khaghanate. As you see on the map of the Russian Pale of Settlement, some remained in place; or if they moved, not very far.

Said Salo W. Baron, in *A Social and Religious History of the Jews*:

"In general, the reduced Khazar kingdom persevered. It waged a more or less effective defense against all foes until the middle of the 13th century, when it fell victim to the great Mongol invasion set in motion by Jenghiz [Genghis] Khan. Even then it resisted stubbornly until the surrender of all its neighbors. . . . But before and after the Mongol upheaval the Khazars sent many offshoots into the unsubdued Slavonic lands, helping ultimately to build up the great Jewish centers of Eastern Europe."

The Eventual Demise of the Khaghanate

Eastern and Central Europe became the "home of the Jews." Reflecting this massive immigration, population statistics swell right after c. 1000 with the first wave of settlers. We must also consider that better farming methods increased the food supplies, thus contributing to the population growth, but that does not account for the large numbers of Jews who begin appearing in old records. As to better food supplies, this would have been an additional lure for the fatigued and beset Khazar émigrés. Khazaria, like other defeated and declining empires, expired slowly. Disintegration was not immediate, nor did the exodus happen all at once. Besides, not all moved, or not that far. Some settled in Ukraine, particularly centering on Kiev, already known as a Judaic center. Some strongholds and outposts hung on later than others, but by the mid 1500s, neither Khazars nor their ancient Asian kingdom receives much mention. They successfully transformed themselves, later migrating to the major population and mercantile centers of the world. These Turko-Mongol Central Asiatic shamanistic tribesmen successfully shape-shifted themselves into the "Jews." They speak rather openly of this in some of their own publications. For example,this from the *Encyclopedia Judaica*, 1971:

"In spite of the negligible information of an archeological nature, the presence of Jewish groups and the impact of Jewish ideas in Eastern Europe are considerable during the Middle Ages. Groups have been mentioned as migrating to Central Europe from the East or have been referred to as Khazars, thus making it impossible to overlook the possibility that they originated from within the former Khazar empire. . . . There seems to be a considerable amount of evidence attesting to the continued presence in Europe of the descendants of the Khazars."

Actually, there is quite a bit more archeological evidence, like artifacts and gravesites, than one might think, and more to come. Even the location of the khaghan's old capital, Itil (also spelt Atil or Etil), has been discovered, and a dig was in progress in 2008. You may also want to visit Kevin Brook's informative website at www.khazaria.com.

The map on the facing page shows the western migrations. Note the boundaries of old Khazaria as compared with the Russian Pale of Settlement. Some Khazar Jews did not move all that far. And as we see, many of their descendants migrated to the Americas.

THE PALE 1835-1917

0   200
Miles

Baltic Sea

St.Petersburg

1891, 2,000 Jews deported, many of them in chains

1855, Open to Jews

Moscow

1891, 20,000 Jews expelled

GERMANY

KOVNO

VITEBSK

VILNA

SUWALKI

PLOCK

WARSAW

LOMZA

GRODNO

MINSK

MOGILEV

KALISZ

SYEDLITZ

PIOTRKOW

RADOM

WIELCE

LUBLIN

VOLHYNIA

CHERNIGOV

Brody

Kiev

KIEV

POLTAVA

AUSTRIA-HUNGARY

RUMANIA

PODOLIA

BESSARABIA

KHERSON

Nikolaev

EKATERINOSLAV

TAURIDA

Sebastopol   Yalta

Black Sea

Principal town from which in 1880 began the exodus of over two million Jews from the Pale to the United States, Britain, Europe, South America, and Palestine

In 1882 500,000 Jews living in rural areas of the Pale were forced to leave their homes and live in towns or townlets (shtetls) in the Pale. 250,000 Jews living along the western frontier of Russia were also moved into the Pale. 700,000 Jews living east of the Pale were driven into the Pale by 1891.

The Pale of Settlement, Russian Jews confined to this area by laws of 1795 and 1835. By 1885 there were over 4 million Jews living in the Pale

Towns within the Pale barred to Jews without special residence permits

Discovery of the Ancient Khazar Capital

In 2008, archeologists located the actual site of Itil. They will find some very interesting artifacts, but no grand and great structures; no acropolis, no Roman temples, no great pyramids or anything like that. The Khazars were not builders. And even after they centered in around various settlements, in the spring and summer of the year, they would take to the steppes for a long seasonal camping expedition, setting up giant tents that held hundreds.

To quote *European Jewish Press*, Moscow (AFP, 9/08) www.ej-press.org/article/29915:

"'This is a hugely important discovery,' expedition organizer Dmitry Vasilyev told AFP by telephone from Astrakhan State University after returning from excavations near the village of Samosdelka, just north of the Caspian Sea. We can now shed light on one of the most intriguing mysteries of that period—how the Khazars actually lived. We know very little about the Khazars—about their traditions, their funerary rites, their culture,' he said. The city was the capital of the Khazars, a semi-nomadic Turkish people who adopted Judaism as a state religion, from between the 8th and the 10th centuries, when it was captured and sacked by the rulers of ancient Russia. At its height, the Khazar state and its tributaries controlled much of what is now southern Russia, western Kazakhstan, eastern Ukraine, Azerbaijan and large parts of Russia's North Caucasus region.

"The capital is referred to as Itil in Arab chronicles, but Vasilyev said the word may actually have been used to refer to the Volga River on which the city was founded or to the surrounding river delta region. Itil was said to be a multi-ethnic place with houses of worship and judges for Christians, Jews, Muslims and pagans.

Its remains have until now never been identified and were said to have been washed away by the Caspian Sea.

"Archeologists have been excavating in the area of Samosdelka for the past nine years but have only now collected enough material evidence to back their thesis, including the remains of an ancient brick fortress, he added. 'Within the fortress, we have found huts similar to yurts, which are characteristic of Khazar cities. . . . The fortress had a triangular shape. . . . It's another argument that this was no ordinary city.'

"Around 10 university archeologists and some 50 students took part in excavations in the region this summer, which are partly financed by the Jewish University in Moscow and the Russian Jewish Congress."

Khazar Ashkenazis Dominate
Today's Judaic Religion

"No one really knows what the Jewish religion is. . . . We have to be detectives to find any traces of it. . . . The Jewish religion is the only one in the world which is famed for its secrecy. Its aims and purposes, as well as its traditions, are shrouded in mystery. For all practical purposes, the scholar finds that the Jewish religion is an unwritten code, which can be best compared to the unwritten code of the Italian gangster group, the Mafia. The Jewish code is principally concerned with protecting a criminal group, and it too invokes the Mafia rule of omerta [silence], or death to anyone who talks about their activities." Eustace Mullins, *Mullins' New History of the Jews*.

Make this crucial Khazarian connection. Their influence on the nature, dogma, doctrines and practices of modern Judaism is all-embracing. Ashkenazi Talmudism, with a good dose of Kabalistic occultism, is now the main expression. I trust most readers know the spiritual practices of the Old Testament and what today passes under the name of Judaism aren't the same thing. The old Hebrew temple bloody animal cruelty religion, and whatever else it really was, had almost nothing to do with the Judaic religion of today. Even the proposed rebuilding of the old temple by Judaic Ashkenazi extremists is little more than a continuing Zionist strategy to further exclude the Palestinians and the world's Muslims from the ostensible "Holy Land."

But as to Pharisaic Talmudism in its present form, this is a rather late development, beginning in early medieval times, after the coming of the Khazars into Europe. Benjamin Freedman always called them "so-called and self-styled Jews." They are not the people seen in the bible. They are not Semitic and certainly not Judean, but Judaism from A.D. 1000 onward is almost entirely a Khazarian creation. Moreover, their ideology and their behavior are elitist and racist, just as we see in their apartheid ministate. Even with other Judaics, Khazar supremacism rules. This is emphatically why the Sephardim, the few remaining Karaites, Mountain Jews, Ethiopian Falashas, the Kaifengs of China, Torah True Jews and other Judaic minorities, do not get along very well with the snobby Ashkenazis, who act as if all the others are inferiors. Note that all the Judaic minorities mentioned are non-Talmudic sects. While treated a little better than Palestinians, they are definitely victims of prejudice and animosity in New Khazaria. Oops, I mean "Israel."

Zionism has usurped and appropriated the Judaic religion for its own non-religious, basically atheistic, political ends. That being said, it does appear that the Talmud (extremist parts of which are openly anti-Christian as well as ethnocentric and racist) certainly seems agreeable with rather than disavowing such supremacist

goals. Again, the voluminous contents of the Talmud are decep-
tive, diverse and obscure, requiring close examination, so we shall
not go there in this exercise. The essentially atheistic Zionist
founders and leaders use all of this to their advantage with unfortunate Jews who buy into the phony Pharisaic fairy tale that they
are a specially and divinely chosen folk.

Says Prof. Martin Higger, in *The Jewish Utopia*:

"While the *Encyclopedia Britannica*, p. 771, Vol. 21, 1949 ed.,
says: 'The Talmud is still the authoritative and practical guide to
the great mass of the Jews,' . . . still, not all the rabbis accept the Talmud, with its glorification of secrecy and cunning and its incitation to blood-letting and conquest. Rabbi Elmer Berger, for
instance, repudiates the Talmud and the Torah. In his *Partisan History of Judaism* (Devin-Adair Co., New York, 1952), he attacks the
books of Moses as expressions of nationalistic fanaticism, only
partially based on historical fact. He shows that [modern] Zionism springs from this ancient Zionism."

Plans for Khazar Global Domination

Other documents of the past also attest to and expose plans for
world domination, just as spoken of in the Protocols. Here is one:

The Khazar Jewish Plan
(Stunning Letter of 1928):

"The Jewish people—as a whole—will become its own Messiah. It will attain world dominion by the dissolution of other
races, by the abolition of frontiers, the annihilation of monarchy
and by the establishment of a world republic in which the Jews
will everywhere exercise the privilege of citizenship.

"In this New World Order, the children of Israel will furnish all the leaders without encountering opposition. The governments of the different peoples forming the world republic will fall without difficulty into the hands of the Jews. It will then be possible for the Jewish rulers to abolish private property and everywhere to make use of the resources of the state.

"Thus, will the promise of the Talmud be fulfilled, in which is said that when the Messianic time is come, the Jews will have all the property of the whole world in their hands." —Baruch Levy, Letter to Karl Marx, *La Revue de Paris*, p. 574, June 1, 1928

Note: The vast majority of today's "Jews" are Khazars whose forebears adopted Judaism (and corrupted it) in the early 700s A.D. We suggest you read the Protocols of the Learned Elders of Zion to fully understand the plan and what is being done to you and the world. (From www.rense.com/general89/khz.htm, 1-27-10.)

Completing the Khazarian Connection

"The future is only the past again, entered through a different door." —*The Phoenix Journals*

We began this by looking way back in time at the fierce, acquisitive and aggressive Euro-Asian Turko-Khazarian tribes of yore, and we end by examining today's Khazarian Zionist threat. Yes, it is very true. Few, if any, ethnic groups have had an equivalent impact on world history. . . . not just in the past and current events, but surely and certainly looming in our future as Khazar Zionism seems stronger, more determined, more aggressive, hence more toxic and volatile than ever. In regard to that, never forget that the Zionist statelet has weapons of mass destruction, aided abetted and tolerated by the various world powers. A host of questions pose themselves, but in a time of both moral and economic crisis, two of them step out in front of all the others. If Christians follow the examples of the peaceful Palestinian prophet called Jesus, why do they support Zionist aggression? Shouldn't they repudiate these classic Pharisees as did their Messiah/Savior? But even more in light of current events and a collapsing economy, why are billions of dollars in American tax money used to support this radical régime? But I am sure all my readers know, such seemingly simple questions are not only not unanswered, they are rarely even raised, and certainly not in Christian pulpits or the U.S. Congress.

1

2

3

4

CHAPTER 9

Judaic Origins & Genetic Testing

W hile researching various theories about Judaic origins, I read reports based on DNA markers, genetic haplotypes and haplogroup studies, mitochondrial DNA and mitochondrial transfer RNA used to trace the evolution and migration of human species. Just from the terminology, you see this is a fairly complex and technical. In spite of this, I'll share some data and a bit of commentary. I do not present any of my interpretations or speculations as propositions proven beyond the shadow of a doubt; far from it. As you'll soon see, many questions arise from a myriad of data. Review the material; make your own conclusions.

Who Is Jewish and Who Is Not?

Genetic test results are conflicting and confusing. For one thing, today's Palestinians and Israelis are apparently kin to one

Photo display on facing page shows 1) the Falasha Jews of Ethiopia; 2) the Cochin Malabar Jews of India; 3) the Kaifeng Jews of China. All of them practice a Torah-centered, non-Talmudic form of Judaism. Lastly, the somewhat "Afro-Semitic" Yemeni Jews are shown (4).

another. I'm not entirely sure, but a Turkic bloodline link may explain this. Many Israelis are descended from the Khazars, who originally were of Central Asian Turko-Mongol stock. Today's Palestinians are from an Arabic (or Hebrew) Semitic lineage, but for many centuries, until 1917, Ottoman Turkey ruled the entire Mideast. Due to its proximity, good climate near the sea, plus the fact that the sultan granted Turks special privileges in the hinterlands, some acquired land, settled and intermarried in Palestine. Their descendants are there today.

"The Eastern European Jews, who form 92% of the world's population of those people who call themselves Jews, were originally Khazars. . . . These Khazars, these pagans, these Asiatics, these Turko-Finns, were a Mongoloid race who were forced out of Asia into Eastern Europe." —Benjamin Freedman in an address made in 1961.

Then came the modern Turko-Mongol Khazar Ashkenazis with their already mixed bloodlines. Does a Turkic tie at least partially explain the genetic affinity between Palestinians and Israelis? Maybe so, maybe not, but there are other relational factors.

Arabs and Jews

Many Sephardic Jews who lived in Roman Palestina Province and the eastern Mediterranean left the area when Titus and his Roman legionaries marched through the land, leveling Jerusalem in A.D. 70. Some stayed, but many of their descendants converted to Islam in the 700s, further mixing already confused bloodlines. The jihad especially aimed at Jerusalem, now declared to be the third holiest city in Islam. Hence, Sephardim and Arabs, now good Muslims all, mixed and interbred. Prof. Ariella Oppenheim, an Israeli geneticist, affirms this:

"[The results] support the historical documentation according to which the Arabs are descendants of an ancient population of the country and that a large proportion of them were Jews who converted to Islam after Islam reached Eretz Israel in the seventh century A.D."

In addition to this, back in Mohammed's day there were Judaic tribes living in the Arabian peninsula. When the jihad came around, they either became Muslims or left the territory, spreading about the region, including to nearby Palestine. Sephardics can best be characterized as Judaized Arabs or Arabized Jews, whichever you prefer. Thus, we have a curious and continuous connection. Since Palestinians and Israelis have a kinship, they must have equal rights to the land.

"Descent literally means the hereditary succession of an heir to the property of an ancestor. . . ." John W. Reilly, *The Language of Real Estate*.

Cohen Gene

I write about history or do an occasional column on current events, and I'm not a scientist, but I'll risk a comment about the so-called Cohen Gene, a key part of the genetic data, said to trace ancestry back to an ancient tribal religious priesthood in the so-called Holy Land. Several things suggest themselves. After all this time, today's testing groups have a wide and blended ethnicity. Some may not want to hear it, but at this point in human history, most races and ethno-groups have mixed, at least a bit. In the last 500 years, with ever increasing world trade plus improved transportation and travel opportunities, almost all ethnic groups moved about and met.

"Partly as a result of gene flow, the hereditary characteristics of human populations are in a state of perpetual flux. Distinctive local populations are continually coming into and passing out of existence." —*Statement on the Biological Aspects of Race, American Association of Physical Anthropology,* 1996

"Even within the Cohanim, and certainly within the rest of the Jewish people, there's a vast amount of genetic variation." — Daniel Friedman

"There is a significant Christian population among Palestinian Arabs, leading some to claim that at least part of the Palestinian population (the Christians) descended from the original followers of Christ, who were, of course, Jews (they were Jews ethnically, even if they didn't follow Judaism). Despite extensive research, I have not been able to find any scientific studies supporting this claim. Furthermore, the fact that there is joint heritage of 2,000-3,000 years ago does not mean that new genes were not introduced into the Palestinian genetic pool. For one, genes from the Arabian peninsula were introduced after the spread of Islam. As part of the Arabian genes, African genes were introduced. . . ." — David Storobin, Esq., *Palestinian Genes Show Arab, Jewish, European and Black-African Ancestry,* 2005

Among the peoples of the world, the Khazar convert Jews have one of the most mixed and varied ethnicities of all. While Oriental Judaics have a diverse and mottled ancestry from ancient times on, the Sephardim are nothing compared to the Ashkenazim. Khazar elitist breeding habits have literally changed their physical appearance. As far as the so-called Cohen Gene, of course the Khazars show up in the mix, but are Khazars qualified as kosher because of this special genetic marker? Recall some facts about the c. 740 Talmudic conversion. The pagan shamans and members of the aristocracy were mass ordained as Levites and Cohens, often taking one of these titles (or one of many variants) as a new surname. Well then, Khazars have been in the Cohen Gene pool for almost 1,300 years. Is this an important factor? It seems worth considering. In a 1997 book *In the Blood: God, Genes and Destiny*, Steven Jones emphasized the differences between Khazars and other Jews as well as the likenesses:

"Ashkenazim are quite different from their Mediterranean and Middle-Eastern co-religionists. . . [but] they are not a unique group. . . from other peoples around them. . . The Y chromosomes of Jews are—unsurprisingly—not all the same; the idea of 'the sons of Abraham' is a symbolic one."

Ellen Levy- Coffman, in *A Mosaic of People: The Jewish Story and a Reassessment of the DNA Evidence*, 2005, wrote:

"Diversity was present from Jewish beginnings, when various Semitic and Mediterranean peoples came together to form the Israelites of long ago. The genetic picture was clearly enriched during the Diaspora, when Jews spread far and wide across Europe, attracting converts and intermarrying over time with their European hosts. The most recent DNA evidence indicates that from this blending of Middle Eastern and European ancestors, the diverse DNA ancestry of the Ashkenazi Jews emerged. Although the debate over the fate of the Khazars is far from over, DNA research suggests that remnants of these mysterious people continue to exist within the genetic makeup of Ashkenazi Jews. In fact, the Levite results indicate that the Khazars became fully integrated into the Ashkenazi communities and came to play an important role within the Jewish priesthood.

"The Cohanim results do not disprove the genetic contribution of the Khazars. Rather, the DNA studies indicate that Jews are not entirely Khazarian, Israelite or European in genetic makeup, but a complex and unique mixture of all these peoples."

Afro-Semitic, Egypto-Habiru Negroid Tribes?

Before exploring this fascinating topic, we must enlarge our vocabulary with "gene haplotypes," the focus of many DNA studies. Said Daniel Friedman, www.Khazaria.com:

"A recent article reporting research by Dr. M.F. Hammer, *et al.* ("Jewish and Middle Eastern Non-Jewish Populations Share a Common Pool of Y-chromosome Biallelic Haplotypes," 2000) may reopen the debate over the ancestry of Ashkenazi Jews (the European Jewish communities which originated in Germany and spread throughout medieval Eastern Europe) [thus refuting Koestler, Dunlop, *et al.*].

Hammer's study supports the contention that Middle Eastern Jews and non-Jews share common origins. This paper presents an analysis of the data in the Hammer study which may provide new evidence for a more genetically diverse origin of the Ashkenazi community. Hammer et al.'s research is based on genetic anthropology, the study of human evolution through chromosomal analysis. This relatively new science relies upon the premise that discrete genetic changes (polymorphisms) produce variations at individual sites on specific chromosomes (haplotypes).

"Most of these variations are part of the so-called "junk" DNA, which apparently has no effect on an individual's physical characteristics. The Hammer study is based exclusively on Y-chromosome (paternal) haplotypes; in other DNA procedures, maternal genes are used."

Let's cover a rather interesting test result, presented as an alternative history sidebar about Judaic origins, already shadowy and murky that they are. "Junk" DNA supposedly has no bearing on physiognomy, but how can it be that the very ancient and very black South African Lemba tribe also has a big dose of the so-called Cohen Gene? When the topic is explored, there are racial and cultural links apart from genetic haplotypes. Don't forget the black Falasha Judaics of Ethiopia (and lesser known ones) who also claim a Hebrew heritage back to Solomon. One of the Ethiopian emperor's most important titles was Lion of Judah.

Could authors such as Dr. Nana Darkwah (*The Africans Who Wrote the Bible*, 2003) be correct about the ancient Hebrews being black, and that the bible came from Africa and the Akan language? Darkwah presents a seemingly cogent and scholarly linguistically based hypothesis, but since I know nothing of African languages, I can't speculate much more. While this book is still available, it has become a rather expensive and hard to find volume. Did the wandering Egypto-Semitic Habiru tribes interact with powerful black cultures not so far up the Nile? Perhaps the better question is why wouldn't they have? Jews in other parts of the world display a rather different physiognomy than seen in Europe or North America or Israel.

President Obama's Rabbinical Relative

First Lady Michelle Obama's cousin is a black rabbi. I cite this as yet another Afro-Judaic connection. Her cousin is a professional rabbi with a congregation and is recognized in both the Conservative and Orthodox traditions. In light of the quote below, Rabbi Funnye prefers his people not be called African-Americans, but Hebrews or Israelites:

"Capers C. Funnye Jr. (pronounced fun-AY) is a Jewish African-American who is the rabbi of the mostly African-American 200 member Beth Shalom B'nai Zaken Ethiopian Hebrew Congregation of Chicago, Illinois. He is also the first African-American member of the Chicago Board of Rabbis, serves on the boards of the Jewish Council on Urban Affairs and the American Jewish Congress of the Midwest, and is active in the Institute for Jewish and Community Research, which reaches out to black Jewish communities outside the United States, such as Beta Israel in Ethiopia and the Igbo Jews in Nigeria. The organization was founded by Funnye in 1985 as a

Rabbi Capers C. Funnye Jr.

direct offshoot of Wentworth Arthur Matthew's Commandment Keepers.

He was ordained a rabbi by the Israelite Rabbinical Academy in 1985. In 1996, Funnye was the only official black rabbi in the Chicago area recognized by the greater Jewish community. . . . The congregation was started by Rabbi Horace Hasan from Bombay, India, in 1918 as the Ethiopian Hebrew Settlement Workers Association." —Wikipedia, 2009

Look, folks, I'm not saying the Afrocentric theories are the real story at all, but for the purposes of speculation, what if they are? What would it mean, not only for Judaics, but for Christians? Was Jesus a dark-skinned prophet? Were Moses, David and Solomon Hebrew Egypto-negroes? Was the queen of Sheba black? Who were the Nubians and the Kushites? They were quite nearby, just up the Nile a bit.

Oddly enough, even Karl Marx had something to say. He was never kind to others and was particularly noted for his scathing criticism. He especially enjoyed sparring with Ferdinand Lassalle, a prominent Breslau Jew who had changed his name. Marx derided him as "Baron Itzig, the Jewish nigger." In describing his alleged negritude, Marx speaks of Egypto-Semitic negro Judaic heritages:

"Lepsius says in his great work on Egypt has proved that the exodus of the Jews from Egypt was nothing but the history which Manetho narrates of the expulsion of the 'leprous people' from Egypt. At the head of these lepers was an Egyptian priest, Moses. . . . It is now perfectly clear to me that, as the shape of his [Lessalle's] head and growth of his hair indicates, he is descended from negroes who joined Moses's flight from Egypt."

At this point in time, the two main Semitic tribal groups, i.e., Arabs and Jews of various varieties, have a mixed and polyglot racial heritage, including genes from sub-Saharan Africa. While Mr. Storobin's statement below seems to exclude today's multiracial Judaics, this does not really make any sense since both Jews and Arabs share racial bloodlines. It appears that some Jews may have a negroid heritage as well as several other bloodlines.

Says David Storobin, Esq.:

"A study by the University of Chicago found that Arab populations, including Palestinians, Jordanians, Syrians, Iraqis and Bedouin, have at least some sub-Saharan African genes. Non-Arabs from the region, including Turks, Kurds, Armenians, Azeris, Georgians and Jews, did not have any African roots. A possible explanation is the proximity of the Arabian peninsula to the black African nations. This conclusion is favored by the fact that Yemenite Arabs have 35% black African genes in their mtDNA (which passes through the mother), while others have less. Yemen, of course, is very close geographically to several black African nations.

Other Arabs, especially those far away from the Arabian peninsula, have as little as 10% African blood in their mtDNA. As such, it is possible that the African gene was merely diluted by the introduction of non-Arab (and non-African) genes to the pool when Arabs began to conquer other Middle East people after the rise of Islam. The 'real' Arabs—those who have Arab ancestors stretching beyond the last 1,400 years—are actually 35% black in their mtDNA. These Arabs are from the Arabian peninsula."

Conclusion

Today's Judaics are of a speckled and polyglot genealogy. In spite of this, and as you can imagine, many a rebuttal has been and will be made to the Afrocentric ideas, but after the debate, criticism and conjecture, crucial questions remain. If Judaics (and thus their folk traditions as well) don't have at least some African influences, then how do we really explain the Cohen Gene in the black African Lemba tribe? But beyond "junk" DNA, what about the various groups of black and dusky Jews around the world? Without considering the complex linguistic arguments, at least some Afro-Egypto-Semitic linkages are obvious. Moreover, in terms of current and future events, what about the Israelis and Palestinians, now scientifically proved genetic cousins? Whose heritage is authentic? Whose land claims count the most? We began with questions and so we end.

CHAPTER 10

The Yiddish Language and Ashkenazi Tribal Traditions

Yiddish is a curious semi-Germanic patois, the word literally translating as Jewish. It was also called *yoshon-ashkenaz*, the Ashkenazi language, but more affectionately termed *mame-yoshon* or mother tongue, distinguishing it from biblical Hebrew and Aramaic, called *yoshon koydesh*, the holy tongues. Nevertheless by the 1700s it was generally called Yiddish. Yid (or Zid) is a word for Jew in Eastern Europe, so some say the name comes from Yid-Deutsch. It has roots in High German, but is written with the Hebrew alphabet. It arose in the 10th century, coinciding with the coming of the Khazar convert Jews from the east. It became the lingua franca of the Judaic world, with several distinct dialects among its speakers. The Eastern idiom naturally had more Slavic elements. Spoken around the world in Orthodox communities, Yiddish is most widespread among the ultra-Orthodox Hasidic sect. It did not appear in print until the 19th century. While the number of speakers and publications has declined, it continues as a Judaic dialect and international trade language.

Some researchers maintain it has links to the old, obscure Turkic language of the Khazars, but other linguists and historians disagree. Several years ago, I spoke with Dr. Clarence Lang and Dr. Charles Weber, both of whom were professors of history and German, about the possible Khazarian roots of Yiddish. Both disagreed. But could it be so?

"I believe Yiddish is a mixed West-East Slavic language (and not a German dialect as is commonly believed. Of the two native Slavic substrata of Yiddish—Sorbian and pre-Ukrainian/pre-Belarusian (or in historical terms, 'Kiev-Polessian')—it is the latter imprint that unambiguously points to the existence of Slavic-speaking Jewries in parts of the former Khazar kingdom who eventually became speakers of Yiddish. Hence, one major venue for the birth of the Ashkenazic people would have to be in the contemporary Belarusian and Ukrainian lands, where an indigenous Slavic-speaking Jewry (as best established by the facts of Yiddish) could only be derived from the Turko-Iranian-speaking Khazars. Furthermore, Yiddish lexicon and grammar reveal links with Turkic and Iranian languages that have not been widely appreciated." —Paul Wexler, "Khazars," as seen on http://www.israelshamir.net/.

The Yiddish letters do not entirely conform to the basic Hebrew alphabet.(See facing page.)

Germanization of the Khazar Ashkenazim and the Further Evolution of Yiddish

Yiddish and German have a close connection, both linguistically and culturally. Read what Prof. Arthur Koestler said about this curious love-hate relationship:

ז	וּ	ו	ה	ד	ג	ב	אָ	אַ	א
zayen (z)	melupm vov (u)	vov (u)	hey (h)	daled (d)	giml (g)	beyz (b)	komets alef (o)	pasekh alef (a)	Shtumer alef (silent)

ן	נ	ם	מ	ל	ך	כ	יִ	י	ט
langer nun (n)	nun (n)	shlos mem (m)	mem (m)	lamed (l)	langer khof (kh)	khof (kh)	khirek yud (i)	yud (y; i)	tes (t)

ש	ר	ק	ץ	צ	ף	פ	פֿ	פ	ע	ס
shin (sh)	reysh (r)	kuf (k)	langer tsadek (ts)	tsadek (ts)	langer fey (f)	fey (f)	pey (p)	ayen (e)	samekh (s)	

Used primarily in Hebrew and Aramaic loan words:

תּ	ת	שׂ	כ	ח	ב
sof (s)	tof (t)	sin (s)	kof (k)	khes (kh)	veyz (v)

Letter Combinations:

יי	יי	וי	טש	דזש	זש	יו
(ay)	(ey)	(oy)	(tsh)	(dzh)	(zh)	(v)

www.JewFAQ.org

Yiddish alphabet characters are not exactly like the Hebrew alphabet.

"It is easy to see why Khazar immigrants pouring into medieval Poland had to learn German if they wanted to get on. Those who had close dealings with the native populace no doubt also had to learn some pidgin Polish (or Lithuanian, or Ukrainian or Slovene); German, however, was a prime necessity in any contact with the towns. But there was also the synagogue and the study of the Hebrew Torah. One can visualize a shtetl craftsman, a cobbler perhaps, or a timber merchant, speaking broken German to his clients, broken Polish to the serfs on the estate next door; and at home mixing the most expressive bits of both with Hebrew into a kind of intimate private language. How this hotchpotch became communalized and standardized to the extent to which it did, is any linguist's guess; but at least one can discern some further factors which facilitated the process." —Koestler, *The 13th Tribe: The Khazar Empire and Its Heritage,* 1976

The German states already had a Judaic presence long before the coming of the Khazars. Soon they became the "German Jews" as they rapidly began to settle there, eventually becoming the predominant Judaic sect. Considering the time it takes to walk from the east, the Ashkenazic migration expanded all over Europe in a remarkably short period of time. Germanic areas were at the top of their list.

"Even if their number was relatively small, these German-speaking Jews were superior in culture and learning to the Khazars, just as the German Gentiles were culturally superior to the Poles. And just as the Catholic clergy was German, so the Jewish rabbis from the West were a powerful factor in the Germanization of the Khazars, whose Judaism was fervent but primitive.

"A rabbinical tract from 17th-century Poland contains the pious wish: May god will that the country be filled with wisdom and that all Jews speak German." —Koestler

The Khazarian Ashkenazim were characterized by their unique language as well as their distinct dress. Both varied greatly from any others in Europe.

The old Khazar tongue was crude, lacking an alphabet. Along with their conversion to Talmudic Judaism, the Hebrew alphabet became a handy linguistic tool. While Yiddish picked up other words and features as it moved westward, it remained the language of the Ashkenazim. From the beginning, it had nothing to do with the preexisting Jews of Western Europe until after the 10th century and had nothing to do with ancient Israel or the old He-

The Khazarian Ashkenazim were characterized by their unique language as well as their distinct dress.

brew language other than using the alphabet.

While the famous Khazar Correspondence with Sephardic Judaics in Islamic Iberia (c. 950) was conducted in Hebrew, just a handful of upper-class Khazars and their rabbis really understood or wrote the language. Words were added and meanings changed, common factors in the evolution of all languages. German was a natural contributor to Yiddish. The Khazars recognized the dynamism and advanced nature of the culture, quickly sending their children to German schools and adapting everyday Germanic terms into their polyglot Yiddish dialect. The rest of the linguistic elements were from Slavonic, Russian, Baltic and related regional dialects, including the old Khazar Turkic tongue.

"The Khazar language was supposedly a Chuvash dialect of Turkish, which still survives in the Autonomous Chuvash Soviet Republic, between the Volga and the Sura. The Chuvash people are actually believed to be descendants of the Bulgars, who spoke a dialect similar to the Khazars. But all these connections are rather tenuous, based on the more or less speculative deductions of Oriental philologists. All we can say with safety is that the Khazars were a Turkic tribe, who erupted from the Asian steppes, probably in the fifth century of our era." —Koestler

". . . [T]he Jewries of Eastern Europe were, if not established, at least recruited in substantial numbers from Jews from farther east. On the linguistic side, investigations have tended to establish the absence of western influences in Yiddish. . . ." —Douglas M. Dunlop, *The History of the Jewish Khazars*, 1954

Dr. Koestler succinctly sums up how Judaics, both the Sephardim and Ashkenazim, use language. While the Khazar Turko-Mongol tribes were not the Hebrew tribes of the bible, they share some obvious characteristics. Owing to this and by the sheer strength of numbers, the Khazars eventually came to define and control modern Judaism, bringing it into their service.

"Incidentally, the descendants of the biblical tribes are the classic example of linguistic adaptability. First they spoke Hebrew; in the Babylonian exile, Chaldean; at the time of Jesus, Aramaic; in Alexandria, Greek; in Spain, Arabic, but later Ladino—a Spanish-Hebrew mixture, written in Hebrew characters, the Sephardic equivalent of Yiddish; and so it goes on. They preserved their religious identity, but changed languages at their convenience. The Khazars were not descended from the tribes, but, as we have seen, they shared a certain cosmopolitanism and other social characteristics with their co-religionists." —Koestler

"Spanish Jewry was part of a trading network which spread throughout the Old World. Against this background, Hasday ibn Shaprut's links with the Khazars and the Jewish academies of Mesopotamia seem rather less surprising. . . ." —Richard Fletcher, *Moorish Spain*, 1992, p. 95

Who Are the Ashkenazim?

How did the Khazars come to be called Ashkenazis? This name is dubious and obviously very convenient, supporting spurious claims to the heritage of old Palestine and the bible. Like Jew, it is yet another hijacked word. But what does it really mean? Several scholars comment.

"As to the terms Sephardim and Ashkenazim, the following seems pertinent. In *Die Geschichte des Volkes Israel* ('History of the People of Israel'), 1926, Ludwig Albrecht, a professed Christian, wrote, on page 654: 'The name Sephardim, designating the Spanish and Portuguese Jews comes from the biblical book, Obadiah, verse 20, '. . . the exiles of Jerusalem who are in the Sepharad shall possess the cities of Negeb.' The name Ashkenazim, designating the German Jews, comes from Genesis 10:2, 'The sons of Gomer, Ashkenaz, Riphath and Togarmah'. . . ." —Prof. R. Clarence Lang, Th.M., Ph.D.

It was only in medieval times, after the coming of the Khazars, that the term began to be applied as it is today. While an etymological cognate relationship is not crystal clear, the Old Turkic

An Ashkenazi rabbi.

term, Aq Khasars, indicating the upper classes or the "White Khazars," sounds similar to Ashkenaz.

"Ashkenaz is also a brother of Togarmah (and a nephew of Magog) whom the Khazars, according to King Joseph, claimed as their ancestor. But worse was to come. For Ashkenaz is also named in Jeremiah 51:27, where the prophet calls his people and their allies to rise and destroy Babylon. . . .

"This passage was interpreted by the famous Saadiah Gaon, a spiritual leader of Oriental Jewry in the 10th century, as a prophecy relating to his own times: Babylon symbolized the caliphate of Baghdad, and the Ashkenaz who were to attack it were either the Khazars themselves are some allied tribe.

"Accordingly . . . some learned Khazar Jews who heard of the Gaon's ingenious arguments, called themselves Ashkenazim when they migrated into Poland." —Koestler

By now, you see a recurring pattern. Khazars assume, adopt and adapt a Semitic name and Hebrew heritage that was never theirs. Are they the "German Jews"? No, not really. Albeit small in numbers except in the Iberian Peninsula, Sephardic and Oriental Jews were already in Europe and living in the Germanic lands long before the coming of the Khazar convert Jews. But given that the Ashkenazis were such extreme Germanophiles, their designation as "German Jews" is somewhat correct.

Other Judaic Dialects Around the World

In actuality, there are as many dialects as there are unique Judaic communities such as the Falashas of Ethiopia, the Kaifengs of China, the Cochin Judaics of India and others. The Sephardic equivalent of Yiddish is Ladino (also called Judezmo or Spaniolish), the lingua franca of the Iberian Jews. Like Yiddish, it is written in Hebrew letters. Ladino blends Spanish, Portuguese, Hebrew, Arabic and perhaps other tongues as well. I once had occasion in Gibraltar to hear it spoken among Sephardic taxi drivers. While sounding something like Spanish, its vocabulary and particular accent distinguish it.

The use of Ladino and Yiddish as an insider code-talk parallels the Gypsy tongues, Romani (or *rromani chib*). Romani languages, like Yiddish, took on many words (and grammatical structures in the case of Romani, Romani creoles and para-Romanis) from the many lands where the Gypsy people lived. This was paralleled by the more localized use of other polyglot dialects such as Judeo-Greek, Judeo-Italian and Judeo-Persian. Like Ashkenazic Yiddish, Sephardic Ladino speakers took on words from other languages as they moved about the world.

The Karaite non-Talmudic Jews are of Turko-Khazar origin and speak a particular dialect. Today, younger Karay Turks are working to preserve their unique linguistic legacy, and the Karays proudly proclaim their Khazarian history and heritage. A perhaps related group, the Mountain Jews of the Caucasus, speak Farsi-Tat, a Persian dialect with added Hebrew words and expressions. This usage may shed some light as to their elusive origins. While they might have some Khazarian origins, given their proximity, the use of the Farsi-Tat dialect reflects the influences of the Oriental Judaism of Babylon and Baghdad. The Karaite dialect followed the Karays and continued to evolve as they made their way west.

"It is also significant that Tshagataish, the language of the Khazar Jews, a Turkish dialect, is still spoken in Poland, Hungary and Lithuania by the Karaites, the Jewish sectarians whose homeland was originally in the Crimea. Even more significant is that Tshagataish is spoken by the few surviving Jewish Krimtchaki of the Crimea." —Nathan Ausubel, *Pictorial History of the Jewish People*, 1984

Dr. Koestler tells us more about the Khazars and the Karaites:

"That language was and still is a Turkish dialect, in fact the nearest among living languages to the *lingua cumanica*, which was spoken in the former Khazar territories at the time of the Golden Horde. According to Zajaczkowski, this language is still used in speech and prayer in the surviving Karaite communities in Troki, Vilna, Ponyeviez, Lutzk and Halitch. The Karaites also claim that before the Great Plague of 1710 they had some 32 or 37 communities in Poland and Lithuania. They call their ancient dialect 'the language of Kedar'—just as Rabbi Petachia in the 12th century called their habitat north of the Black Sea 'the land of Kedar'; and what he has to say about them—sitting in the dark through the Sabbath, ignorance of rabbinical learning—

fits their sectarian attitude.

"Accordingly, Zajaczkowski, the eminent contemporary Tur-cologist, considers the Karaites from the linguistic point of view as the purest present-day representatives of the ancient Khazars. This sect preserved its language for about half a millennium, while the main body of Khazar Jews shed it in favor of the Yiddish *lingua franca*. . . ."

And we mustn't forget other Judeo-Persian dialects.

"It was the Jewish practice to corrupt for their own use the lan-guage generally employed in commerce in the region in which they took up residence, and to write it in their own alphabet to prevent the natives from reading it. Under the Sassanian dynasty (after c. A.D. 226), the Jews in the territory under Persian control quickly developed for themselves a corruption of the revived Per-sian language, what we may call a 'Persian Yiddish,' which was cer-tainly known to some of the composers of the Talmud and corrupted in some passages the corrupt Aramaic they continued to use.

"A very large number of Jewish religious writings in their cor-ruption of Persian are still extant." —Dr. Revilo Oliver, 1985

The Judaics of the Meshed area of Iran were forced to convert to Islam, but spent the latter part of the 19th century trying to break away. Some fled to Afghanistan, taking their peculiar Judeo-Persian dialect called Elazar with them. As we see, wherever there are settlements of Jewish folk, they either use existing intra-Judaic idioms or create their own.

Yiddish and the Ashkenazi Culture Today

While younger Jews are losing the ability to use Yiddish, it re-mains a powerful communication tool. Many of the current generation will never learn it well, but rest assured that others will. For certain dealings, there is no replacement. Yiddish speakers can recognize one another and know where the other person is from through their accent and idiomatic expressions. Even in the electronic 21st century, the old Khazar code talk is still indispensable for certain clandestine activities. Besides, with fewer people understanding Yiddish, it becomes an even more exclusive tongue, just for the Ashkenaz elites and no one else.

Their insistence on the use of Yiddish rather than adopting the Slavic tongues, led to even more cultural isolation from Polish and Russian societies. Not only did they live apart from all others when they moved west, but in homes and buildings often with an alien look. Pagoda-like synagogues typified the Judaic areas of town. They also dressed differently. Even in the early 20th century, many Ashkenazim were characterized by Oriental kaftans and speaking a mostly unintelligible language.

This, and Talmudic business practices, set them apart from Russians, Poles, Germans or the people of whatever country where they settled. Ghettos were closed communities imposed by Christian society. However, the Ashkenazim lived by choice in shtetls, self-imposed kosher and pure ethnocentric communities, undefiled by contact with the unclean goyim.

"What virtues and what vices brought upon the Jew this universal enmity? Why was he in turn equally maltreated and hated by the Alexandrians and the Romans, by the Persians and the Arabs, by the Turks and by the Christian nations? Because everywhere and up to the present day, the Jew was an unsociable being. Why was he unsociable? Because he was exclusive and his exclusiveness was at the same time political and religious, or, in other words, he kept to his political religious cult and his law." —B. Lazare, *L'Antisemitism*

Assimilation Is the Foremost Threat to the Future of Ashkenazi Judaism and the Yiddish Language

"The Jew is a religious being. All Jewish history is the result of religious passion and purpose, and, whatever is said to the contrary, the continuity of the Jew is bound up with the retention of his religion. Wipe out the religious element from the equation of his life, and the Jew would cease automatically." —H.G. Enelow, *A Jewish View of Jesus*, 1920

Yiddish is exactly what its name literally means—the language of the Ashkenazi Khazar Jews—and no one else. Beyond that, Judaism is an exclusive religion for their benefit. The Talmudic scriptures tell them they are different from other human beings, especially chosen by their exclusive and jealous Egypto-Semitic deity. Not only that; the Talmud and Halakah rabbinical law give permission to gouge, maltreat and manipulate the gentiles as they please. This supremacist mindset makes it virtually impossible to assimilate, adjust and adapt to other societies. As we know from eons of past history, this is an ongoing phenomenon. The observant Jew purposely stands apart religiously and culturally, never really blending in. Some overcome this, but more often than not have to completely divorce themselves from Judaism. The rabbis are right. Assimilation—especially when it involves conversion to some form of Christianity—is a total rejection of rabbinic authority and Talmudic supremacism.

"Humanity changes, empires arise and fall, ideals spring up, become resplendent, and are extinguished, the Jew remains, Judaism remains clothed in its fierce exclusivism. . . .

"A people without land, a wandering nation, dispersed race, they preserve a country, their religion . . . ever pursuing the mirage of a golden age. a new era, a messianic time when the world would live in joy and peace, subject to Yahweh, serving his law under the rule of the sacerdotal people, who had been prepared by trials for the attainment of this hour. . . . [T]hey are eternally inadaptable. . . ." —Georges Batault, *Le Probleme Juif*, 1921

And from Paris (European Jewish Press)—"Rabbi Israel Meir Lau, former chief rabbi of Israel and currently chairman of Yad Vashem Holocaust Memorial, said assimilation 'is today the biggest threat to the Jewish people.' Speaking during a gathering in Paris of around 300 rabbis from across Europe and Israel. . . . Lau said assimilation is a 'bigger threat' than anti-Semitism and terrorism for the future of Jews. Lau mentioned statistics from the United States showing that out of 100 Jews from the first generation only three are left as Jews in the fourth generation. Rabbi Yisroel Yaakov Lichtenstein, head of the Jewish court in the UK, spoke of around 50% assimilation among Jews in his country. Young people are not interested in religion, they have no connection with Judaism. . . ." (News report, June 7, 2001)

So, we have a demographic problem here. There's a 97% casualty rate in the U.S. and 50% in the UK. Not only that, immigration to Israel decreases every year, especially with prolonged and increased violence. Some say one way or another, the ministate may not last another 20 years. But even if Israel were to become some kind of non-Jewish entity or otherwise cease to exist, and even if only a few Jews pass on the traditions, Yiddish, *yoshon-ashkenaz*, the language and legacy of the Ashkenazim, lives on. Regardless of losses to assimilation or conversion, for a number of devout and observant Judaic Talmudists, there are two truly holy languages: Hebrew and Yiddish.

CHAPTER 11

Demystifying the Talmud

"The modern Jew is the product of the Talmud."
—Rabbi Dr. Isaac M. Wise

What Rabbi Wise says is crucial to understanding the inner core, the true heart and the soul of the religion called Judaism. There is an important question when studying the history of any people: What was their religion?

How did it play out in their everyday lives? What philosophies, what books and writings guided their development? Rabbis say when Moses received the law, he also received commentary and instructions, not written on the tablets. He supposedly passed this on to a succession of tribal elders, and so on down the line until it got too big to keep in memory. Then they began to write it down. By A.D. 500 it was more or less in its essential form. Of course, what is considered Talmud? More or less, it is anything, any of the writings that the more important rabbis agree upon. But what do we really know about this curious collection of commentary?

A lifetime Talmudic scholar is shown.

Both Judaism and Islam are comprehensive Semitic legal systems as much as they are religions. The Talmud is a body of civil and religious law, made up of thousands of pages, including commentaries on the Torah, consisting of a codification of laws, called the Mishnah, and a commentary on the Mishnah, called the Gemara. The collection of decisions by scholars on legal questions, both oral and written, is known as Halakah. The legends, anecdotes, and sayings illustrating the law are called Haggada.

There are two compilations. There is the Palestinian Talmud, also called Jerusalem Talmud or Talmud Yerushalmi, and the Babylonian Talmud, called Talmud Bavli. Both contain the same Mishnah, but each has its own Gemara. Scholars between the third century A.D. and the beginning of the fifth century produced the Talmud Yerushalmi. The Talmud Bavli was compiled by rabbis and scholars writing between the third century and the beginning of the sixth. That version became the authoritative one because the Babylonian rabbinic academies survived those in Palestine by several centuries.

A most important segment of Talmud is the Mishnah or Mishna Torah (Repetition of the Torah, c. A.D. 1180) by the famous Sephardic rabbi, philosopher and physician called Maimonides. The Mishnah is said to be an abstract of all the rabbinical legal literature in his time. Other widely known commentaries were those on the Babylonian Talmud by the French Rabbi Rashi, and by the Tosaphists, a group of Talmudic scholars (in Hebrew, *chackamim*) in France and Germany between the 12th and 14th centuries. While modern Judaism ritually enshrines and honors the Torah as the Word of God, neither the five books nor the rest of the heavily edited Old Testament play a particularly important role in the everyday life and decisions made by Judaics. Solutions to ethical and moral dilemmas often come from the teachings of the Talmud, delivered through the rabbis. This has almost nothing to do with the Old Testament teachings revered by Christians.

Talmudic Teachings Shock Christians

Among its myriad of pages, the Talmud contains violent themes and demeaning insults about Christians, Jesus and Mary. In olden times, various kings and bishops ordered the Talmud seized and burned by the wagonloads all over Europe. While the church occasionally attacked the Talmud, large-scale activities to ban and burn it don't appear until the 1200s, after Khazarian Jews appropriated much of preexisting European Judaism.

If you read Hebrew, as did some Christian scholars, it was not hard to find distasteful passages. The texts below illustrate the emergence of a supremacist separatist ethnocentric apartheid ideology.

"The following passages will show the extravagant notions of the Jews touching the origin of their souls and of the souls of the rest of mankind. The treatise *Emek Hammelech* gives the following: 'Our rabbins, of blessed memory, have said: Ye Jews are styled men; because of the soul ye have from the Supreme Man (i.e., god whom the Cabalists call Adam Ahelion; that is, the Supreme Man). But the nations of the world are not styled men, because they have not, from the Holy and Supreme Man, the Nefhama (or glorious soul). But they have the Nephesh (i.e., the soul) from Adam Belial; that is, the malicious and unnecessary man called Sammael, the Supreme Devil.' . . .

"In the treatise Nishamath Adam, [it] says, [sic] the soul of a Jew is a part of god from above. And in the Preface to the treatise *Shesa Tal*, 'tis said, the soul of a Jew is a part of God from Above, and of his substance or essence, as of the Essence of his Father. In the treatise *Emek Hammelech*, in the part entitled Shaar Kirjath Arba, it is said, the souls which he (god) created, live and continue forever, because they are the sparks of the substance or essence of the Blessed God. . . ." —Prof. Dr. Johannes Eisenmenger, *Endecktes Judenthum* ("Jewry Unmasked"), 1740; English translation, Vol. I, 1742, pp. 253, 261

"The Talmud declares that Abraham, who had seen god, asked his servants if they had likewise done so; and on their replying in the negative, he said to them, 'Abide ye here with the ass,' meaning that they were animals like the ass. . . .

"Thus the law and the prophets belong exclusively to the Jews; the gentile reading or even buying a copy should be put to death. All the books of other faiths must be burnt, even though they contain the name of Jehovah; and if any but a Hebrew write the name of god in a bible which is not a Jewish manuscript, the volume must also be burnt. According to the Talmud (chap. iv., Sanhedrin, of the fourth Mishnic Section, or order Seder Nezekin), the gentile sanctifying the Sabbath must be put to death without asking questions." —Sir Richard Francis Burton, *The Jew, the Gypsy and El Islam*, London: 1898

"The souls of all gentiles emanate from the demons under circumstances which are not explained in the Zohar." —A.E. Waite, *The Holy Kabbalah*

Jews, Jesus and Others Comment on the Talmud

Jesus and the Pharisaic Talmudists are the main protagonists In the Gospel stories. The Pharisee cult had both political and religious power. Jesus not only challenged them in the streets and marketplaces, but boldly came at them in their power center, the Temple itself. You could say he walked in there like he owned the place. And he wasn't polite. Christians have forgotten that their Christos Messias regularly repudiated, reviled, railed against and despised the Talmudic religion of his day. He had so much success the Pharisees conspired against him, eventually causing his death.

One hears a lot about Christians who read, study and truly love the bible. Some believe it to be prophetic, and many consider it to be the inerrant Word of God. All right, then. In that spirit I pose a question. The phrase "for the fear of the Jews" occurs in the bible, does it not? What did this mean to the early Christians? Why did they feel that way? What is more, why do Christians today seem to be in thrall of Judaism? This is not to say that we should be hateful or disrespectful. Not at all, but even the slightest criticism is politically and religiously incorrect to the max. Jesus physically assaulted the usurers and the gang of Talmudic thieves and thugs, driving them from their predatory perches in the temple with a whip. Surprisingly, today's Christians invite them to speak in churches and seek support for Israeli Zionist terrorism, all in the name of that old Egypto-Semitic demigod, Jah-Hovah. Of course, Jesus never spoke that name, always referring to God as the Father. Why do I get blank stares from most Christians when I try to discuss these things? Why are they so ignorant of their religious history and what's really said in their scriptures?

"Jesus said: Woe to the Pharisees, for they are like a dog sleeping in the manger of oxen, for neither does he eat nor does he let the oxen eat. . . . The Pharisees and the scribes have taken the keys of knowledge and hidden them. They themselves have not entered, nor have they allowed to enter those who wish to."—*Gospel of Thomas*, Nag Hamadi codices

"Woe to you scribes and Pharisees, hypocrites; because you are like to whited sepulchers, which outwardly appear to men beautiful, but within are full of dead men's bones, and of all filthiness. So you also outwardly indeed appear to men just; but inwardly you are full of hypocrisy and iniquity. Woe to you scribes and Pharisees, hypocrites; that build the sepulchers of the prophets, and adorn the monuments of the just, and say: If we had been in the days of our fathers, we would not have been partakers with them in the blood of the prophets. . . . Wherefore you are witnesses against yourselves. You serpents, generation of vipers, how will you flee from the judgment of hell? Therefore behold I send to you prophets, and wise men, and scribes: and some of them you will put to death and crucify, and some you will scourge in your synagogues. . . . Behold, your house shall be left to you, desolate." —From Matthew 23: 27-38, *Douay-Rheims Bible*

"And they turned away, and kept not the covenant. Even like their fathers they turned aside as a crooked bow. They provoked him to anger on their hills and moved him to jealousy with their graven things. God heard, and despised them, and he reduced Israel exceedingly as it were to nothing." —Psalm 77:57-59. *Douay-Rheims Bible* (Psalm 78 in Protestant translations.)

"[The Christian] is quite incapable of pursuing the Jewish train of thought unless he has obtained insight into the true Jewish spirit by reading the rabbinical writings. Everything there—based on direct denial of reason and morality—is turned topsy-turvy and directed against the natural feelings and disposition of humanity. He, who has not studied, in some manner, the books of the Talmud, will never come to a right understanding of the Jews." —*The Riddle of the Jew's Success*, 1927, p. 109

"The Talmud has been the banner which has served as a rallying sign to the Jews, dispersed in diverse countries; it has maintained the unity of Judaism." —Dr. Heinrich Graetz, *History of the Jews* (English translation, 1892)

"I am one of the few goyim who have ever actually tackled the Talmud. I suppose you now expect me to add that it is a profound and noble work, worthy of hard study by all other goyim. Unhappily, my report must differ from this expectation. It seems to me, save for a few bright spots, to be quite indistinguishable from rubbish. . . ." —H.L. Mencken

"I believe that three of Aesop's fables, half of Cato and several comedies of Terence [i.e., Publius Terentius Afer—Ed.] contain more wisdom and more instruction about good works than can be found in the books of all the Talmudists and rabbis and more than may ever occur to the hearts of all the Jews." —Martin Luther

Israeli historian Prof. Ariel Toaff reflects on the severe secrecy required. This comes from his now-infamous but thoroughly scholarly book *Pasque di Sangue, Ebrei d'Europa e omicidi rituali* or "Blood Passovers, European Jews and Ritual Murders," (unauthorized English translation, 2007):

"Ask thine elders, and they will tell thee. (Deut. 32:7) This booklet contains a tradition transmitted orally, by one person to another; it may be put in writing but not printed, for reasons due to our bitter exile. Beware of reading this text before children and persons of scanty understanding, or all the more so before the uncircumcised who understand German. For this reason, he who is wise shall know how to understand and maintain silence. . . .

"Publicizing this text is an extremely serious matter, and it cannot be revealed to all, because we can never know what tomorrow has in store for us, and we can trust no one. I have written the text in intentionally allegorical and obscure language, because we have been selected as the Chosen People and we are permitted (by god) to use mysterious imagery.

"Their violent anti-Christian feelings and expressions, both ideological and ritualistic, in which these feelings found an outlet and a reflection necessarily had to be surrounded by a protective aura of secrecy and omertà because any indiscretion in this regard, either deliberately or through naiveté, could be the precursor of struggle and of tragedy." —Toaff, p. 188

"Essendo massimamente la maggior parte di loro Talmudisti negromanti, heretici et vitiosi."

This was the ruling of a Venetian tribunal assigned to examine the Talmud. Its use was banned "since the majority of Talmudists are sorcerers, heretics and vicious persons."

While the synagogue ceremonially parades the Torah, it is the Talmud that forms the bedrock of Judaism. There are a number of reasons to exclude the goyim from knowing anything at all about this strange body of semi-scriptures.

"However, one should not be allowed to forget that for centuries, Jewry has taken care to work to 'clear things up.' Already, in printings of the Talmud of the 15th century, various printers left white, empty spots in many passages, in order to avoid as much as possible the chance of attack by non-Jews. . . . In Damascus, the former Rabbi Moses Abu-el-Afieh, having converted to Islam, spoke about this on the occasion of the ritual-murder trial in 1840 and said that in the editions of the Talmud which were intended for Europe, 'empty places' were left in the books. At the inquiry of the Court's Chairman, as to what purpose these empty places served, Rabbi Moses gave the diplomatic response: In order to fill these up with the names of those (non-Jewish) peoples, and everything that concerns them." —Dr. Hellmut Schramm, *Der Juedische Ritualmord*, (Berlin: 1943; Regina Belser translation, 2001), p. 262

The Talmud is the unifying factor in Judaism. Its traditions seem to dominate Judaics, no matter where they are in the world. More than that, many Judaics today have little or no Semitic bloodlines, yet they act united, like a race, even though they are not a race. The teachings of the Talmud are the glue holding them together.

"Externally, the Jews of today present marked differences in their appearance; negroid and Turanian (Mongolian) types can be discerned amongst them as well as Semitic. . . . But one must certainly not any longer speak of our Jews of today as pure Semites; they have taken up all manner of foreign national elements; and it is truly remarkable to what a complex extent they have assimilated the same. One is entitled to ask whether the Talmudic spirit alone has rendered this complete adaptation possible, or whether a few drops of Jewish blood have sufficed to give an unvarying stamp of expression—at least mentally—to the entire mass.

"The Talmudic law embraces them all, and the rabbinical despotism welds them into a closed caste, absolutely united in its hostility to all non-Jewish peoples." —F. Roderich-Stoltheim, pp. 221-2

FInding the Talmud

Where can we see the whole thing, or at least some of the key parts? The Soncino edition, published between 1934 and 1952, has at least 52 volumes (some sets vary; some are smaller), hence millions of words. If you can find a set, they may cost $10,000. Some large reference libraries, Judaic universities and yeshiva seminaries will have a set, but you'll need permission to examine them. Various volumes show up now and then in used book sales, and some are available online. The Soncino Babylonian Talmud, in English, Hebrew and Aramaic, with Rabbi Rashi's commentary, is also on CD-ROM.

The newest publishing venture is the Artscroll or Schottenstein version (2005). This is named after a wealthy department store family who sponsored the project. Available for about $2,000, it is a massive undertaking, even larger than the Soncino. Hence there are an estimated 5,000,000 or more words as the Schottenstein Talmud Bavli's 73 volumes.

Of course, there are books with selections from the Talmud and the Kabala as well as a host of other books, CDs, videos, lectures and workshops etc, but these are thoroughly cleansed. We are told by Judaics and their Christian apologists that the ugly verses are relics of long-ago times and past prejudices, and that no one believes them anymore. Well, if so, then why not officially repudiate them and not print them in the Talmud anymore? After all, some Jewish groups call for Christians to remove certain New

Testament passages, so turnabout is fair play.

But outside of philo-Judaic literature, where can we learn about the Talmud? Prof. Dr. Johann Andreas Eisenmenger's *Entdecktes Judenthum*—"Jewry (or Judaism) Unmasked (or Unveiled, Uncovered, Revealed, Discovered etc)"—a 1700 German work, is little known and seldom read. The author was a Lutheran professor of Oriental languages at Heidelberg University, and with this background, he surveyed the Talmud with its odd and outré contents. Even in that less politically correct era, Judaics did everything they could to bribe him or otherwise block his work, and they almost did. It was a true magnum opus, taking many years to complete and publish. While he succeeded in this, only four years later (1704), Eisenmenger passed away [born 1654—Ed,].

The only English "translation" is a rather large, but nonetheless incomplete, 1742 edition. It was translated from Old High German and prefaced by the Rev. John Peter Stehelin. I eventually found a reference to someone with that name being made a member of the Royal Society in 1739. The title (in shortened form) is: *The Traditions of the Jews; Or, The Doctrines and Expositions Contained in the Talmud and Other Rabbinical Writings; Or, An Enquiry into the Origin, Progress, Authority and Usefulness of Those Traditions, Wherein the Mystical Sense of the Allegories in the Talmud and Other Writings of the Rabbins Is Explained.* Did you get all that?

Not only is it in two volumes, it's written in the style of and printed in the type fonts of the mid-18th century. Stehelin must have had some sort of theological difference with the Lutheran scholar. In the almost 800 pages, neither the proper German title nor Prof. Eisenmenger's name are even mentioned.

Several classical works of the past were also based on and inspired by *Entdectes Judenthum*. Particularly influential was *Der Talmudjude*, an 1871 work by Canon Dr. August Rohling, a priest and university professor in Prague.

Here's a selection from Eisenmenger's tome showing that the Talmud is considered superior to the Torah, and that members of the rabbinical caste are specially blessed.

"The rabbins have said, the words of the scribes are more delightful than the words of the prophets. But a more awakening assertion concerning the excellence of the Talmud, and its preference to the bible, is one we find in a Talmudic treatise entitled *Chagiga*, under the words: Neither was there any peace to him that went out or came in. The Ras has said, when a man leaves the Halacha (i.e., the study of the Talmud) and goes to the bible, he will have no peace or good fortune. The Jews believe and teach that it is their duty to obey the rabbins, and likewise give credit to everything they say. The Jews are taught, that the company of a rabbin at their tables, is to be looked upon as visit of the Divine Being. In the treatise entitled Berachoth, is the following passage: Rabbi Alb-bin, the Levite, has said, He who partakes of a feast where a sage is present, doth as much as if he partook of the Divine Glory. . . ." —*The Traditions of the Jews*, Vol. I., 1742, pp. 40, 47

"At the age of five years of age, says the Mishnah, let the child begin to study the scriptures; let him continue so doing until the age of 10, when he may begin to study the Mishnah; at the age of 15 let him begin the Gemara. (T. Aboth, chap. v.)." —Burton, p. 103

Ashkenazi Khazarian Judaism

It is said that Judaism was somewhat dying out by c. A.D. 900; that it was in a decline, existing mostly in a few ports and urban centers, scattered over the world. After the Khazars entered Eastern

Europe beginning c. 1000, by the sheer force of numbers (even today they hugely outnumber the Sephardim and other sects), they had a distinct and direct influence on Judaic religion and culture. This is especially true in study and interpretation of the Talmud and Judaic theology in general. They established hundreds of Yeshivas and Schuls everywhere they went. The Khazar converts swelled the ranks of the almost moribund faith. Now calling themselves Ashkenazis and Jews, the Turko-Mongol Asian converts were, by far, the largest group of Judaics in Europe and in the world. The Talmud and the already-corrupted traditions of the Oriental Sephardim served as convenient and comfortable gloves for Khazarian hands. The fit was further tailored through the intense, indeed sometimes frantic, devotions of the Ashkenazim and their Sufi-like Kabalistic cults such as Chabad Lubavitchers and other ultra-orthodox Hasidim.

The Talmud Today

By Renaissance times, Ashkenazi rebbes, tzaddiks and chachams were numbered among the master Talmudic scholars and expositors, and this continued as the years rolled by. The overwhelming majority of the world's Judaics are no longer of Semitic lineage, but of multiple mixed bloodlines. In spite of this, tried and true Talmudic traditions effectively bind them together. It is the base and bedrock of Judaism, the real magic and mystery of these sacred and treasured works. In truth, the Talmud creates a miracle of unity among Judaists the world over. From Judaic and Judeo-Christian perspectives, this is a blessed thing. But on other fronts, the results of Talmudic ethics and morality are grim and deadly.

Especially at the higher levels, the geopolitical expansionist movement called Zionism is made up of many who are little more than psychopathic atheists and bolshevists. This Illuminati cult of power seekers glommed on to Judaism and Old Testament ethnocentrism, not to mention the ugliest Talmudic traditions, to create the nuclear-armed Israeli menace to world peace and justice. In one way or another, the teachings of these Semitic semi-scriptures lie at its heart. The basic principles and paradigms of Zionist Talmudic terrorism are acted out every day in Occupied Palestine, so painfully obvious in how apartheid Israel perpetrates crimes of ethnic cleansing against the Palestinians in the cruelest of ways. Are the Israelis fighting terrorism? Or doing it themselves? If you agree that the Zionist entity is committing war crimes and violating basic human rights, now you know from whence came the inspirations, aspirations, falsifications, fabrications and justifications.

In the final frame, there really isn't all that much to demystify about the Talmud. It says what it says. It is what it is. And, it is what it does. Ultimately, we mustn't separate ideas from the actions they incite and justify. The teachings of the Talmud are innumerable. Some seem spiritually helpful, wise and beneficial. But far too many other passages, especially in their overt evil intentions and nasty, lurid imagery, are hateful, wicked and occult, inspirations from the dark side. The Talmud is the ultimate Jewish book. It is not meant for the rest of us. The few gentiles who study it usually do so for curiosity—or self-defense.

"Tob Shebe Goyim Harog. Even the best of the gentiles should all be killed." —*Minor Tractates*, Soferim 15, Rule 10, Rabbi Simon ben Yohai.

CHAPTER 12

Talmudic Mysticism and the Occult

Judaic Spirituality in the *Tanya* Book

anya is Aramaic for "it was taught," but it is also known as *Likkutei Amarim*, "a collection of statements," a massive 1796 work by the Talmudic scholar, Rebbe Schneur Zalman of Liadi, Lithuania, the great savant, sage and seer of several Ashkenazi Hasidic sects. *Tanya* study, like Kabala, is quite trendy right now, both among Judaics and some mystically minded gentiles. In large cities as well as on the Internet one can take Tanya classes. While some parts of Zalman's five-volume tome are psychologically informative and spiritually enlightening, other parts remind us of the same ethnocentric theology and mindset as in much of the Talmud and Kabala:

In the *Tanya*, chapter 1 (page 5b), it is written: "The explanation of this matter is according to what the Rabbi Chaim Vital O_B_M [of blessed memory] wrote . . . that every Jew, whether he is righteous or wicked, has two souls, as it says, 'And the souls I have made'—that is, two souls: one soul from the side of the klipa [peel or husk—Ed.] and Satan's camp . . . also naturally good character traits that are found in every Jew, such as mercifulness and charitable deeds, stem from it, for in the Jew, the soul of this klipa comes from klipat noga, which also contains good. . . .

"But it is not the case concerning gentile souls, for they stem from other impure klipot which contain no good. . . and the second soul of the Jew is surely part of g-d on high. . . "

In the end of chapter 6 it is written:

"The klipot are divided into two levels. . . . the lower level consists of three impure and completely evil klipot, which contain no good whatsoever . . . from there the souls of the gentiles are influenced and drawn, as are the bodies and the souls of all impure animals which are forbidden to eat. . . . However, the vital, animalistic soul in the Jews, which stems from the klipa . . . and the souls of pure animals, beasts, birds, and fish which are permitted to eat . . . are influenced and drawn from the second level of the klipot . . . which is called klipat noga . . . and the majority of it is evil, combined with a slight amount of good. . . .

Above, the Tanya, *or* Likkutei Amarim, *"a collection of statements," a massive 1796 work by the Talmudic scholar Rebbe Schneur Zalman of Liadi, Lithuania, the great savant, sage and seer of several Ashkenazi Hasidic sects.*

It is evident that what Ra'avad, Rabbi Yehuda HaLevi, the Maharal, the Ramchal, Rav Kook, Rav Charlap and Rav Tzadok wrote in the language of the Revealed Teaching, each in his own style, has been said by the Ari, Rabbi Chaim Vital, the Midrash Shmuel, and the *Tanya* in the language of the Secret Teaching—and the intention is the same."

Says Burton: "He [the average person] cannot realize the fact that the ferocity and terrible destructiveness which characterize the Jew and his literature, from the days of the Prophets to those of the Talmudists, are present in his civilized neighbor, whom he considers to be one of the best of men—a sleeping lion, it is true, but ready to awake upon the first occasion. . . . And he is ignorant of the Eastern Jews' love of mysticism and symbolism, their various horrible and disgusting superstitions, and their devotion to magical charms and occult arts, which led to a variety of abominations.

"But the English world never hears the fact that the Jew of Africa, of Arabia, of Kurdistan, of Persia and of Western Asia generally, is still the Jew 'cunning and fierce' of the 13th and 14th centuries in Europe; that he is the Jew of the Talmud, of Shammai and of Rabbi Shalomon Jarchi, not of the Pentateuch, of Hillel and of Gamaliel; that he sympathizes, not with those staunch old conservatives and rationalists, the Sadducees, now gone forever, nor with Ezra and the Priests, the Levites and the Nethinin—men of the Great Synagogue—nor with the ascetic Essenes, prototypes of Christian monkery, but with the Pharisees, the Separatists, and the Puritans of his faith, with the Captains, the Fanatics, the Zealots, the Sicarii [a proto-Zionist sect of terrorist assassins], the Swordsmen and the Brigands. . . of those who worked all the civil horrors of our first century." —Burton, pp. 29-33

Esoteric Sects Among the Ashkenazis

According to Burton: "The Ashkenazim are divided into religious sects and social communities. The former are three in number—viz. Parushim, Khasidim and Khabad. The Parushim, Pharisees, . . follow the law as laid down in the commentary of the late Gaon [means "learned man"] of Wilna. They consider the diligent study of the Talmud as essential . . . respecting, however, the sense attached to various rites by the Kabalistic teachers. They observe strictly the appointed times for prayer, but they do not consider it necessary to dip the body in water before ablution. They neglect a second pair of phylacteries prescribed. . . . They do not hold it unlawful to slaughter animals for food with a knife which is not very sharp, provided that the edge has no notches. The Khasidim, that most fanatical of Jewish sects . . . for the most part, unlearned.

"Unlike the Parushim, they believe in certain Sadikim [Tzaddics, Kabalistic sorcerers], or righteous men, . . and regard them with a superstitious veneration, which borders upon worship, attributing to them supernatural powers, and attaching some spiritual and symbolic meanings to their most trivial and insignificant actions. Whilst professing to be guided only by the Talmud, they in reality follow the teaching of some chosen Guter Jude. The Khasidim are particular in the observance of . . . Sabbath. They shake themselves violently and cry aloud during prayers; at other times they are much addicted to dancing, singing and deep drinking.

"The Khabad or third sect [Chabad; founded in the late 1700s by Rabbi Schneur Zalman, author of the mystical *Tanya* book], suggests in name the Ebionites or Jewish Nazarenes, who hold the 'great teacher of Nazareth' to be the Messiah, but merely human; this sect, however, has apparently died out. The modern

Khabad have a liturgy arranged from their old Rabbi Zelmine. . . . They dip themselves before prayer, read and study much, and meet together on Sabbath evenings to hear the Law expounded by their principal teacher. They keep as a feast the 19th day of Kislef, the third civil and ninth ecclesiastical month (around December); on that day R. Shalomon, the founder of the sect, was liberated from prison." —Burton, pp. 52-55

Burton continues: "Moreover, the large space given to cursing the Jew and the non-Jew, and to the unhallowed practices of magic and necromancy, the summoning and conversing with devils and spirits, the advocacy of astrology, charms, and philters, served as a pretext for pope and inquisition to attack it. In A.D. 533 Justinian proscribed it [the Talmud] by Novella 146 as a tissue of puerilities, of fables, of iniquities, of insults, of imprecations, of heresies, and of blasphemies'; it was destroyed by Gregory IX in A.D. 1230; it was burnt in Paris by Innocent IV (A.D. 1244); and it was proscribed by Clement IV, by Honorius IV, and by John XXII. The first printed edition [all others were handwritten manuscripts] (Venice, 1520) saved it, and not until the third had appeared (Basle, 1578) did it come under the eye of the censor. In 1533 and 1555 Julius III promulgated a proclamation against what he called grotesquely the Talmud Gulnaroth; and this proceeding was repeated by Paul IV in 1559, by Pius V in 1566, and by Clement VIII in 1592 and 1599." —Burton, pp. 104-105

And Trachtenburg writes: "The theme [of Jewish magical prowess] recurs in a number of medieval legends, and a 16th-century mystery play, *La Vie de Saint Martin*, offers in a half-mocking vein an account of a band of Jews celebrating the Sabbat. . . Even the Sabbat itself, with its weird and obscene ceremonial, was traced back to the Talmud by some medieval authorities on witchcraft, while the congregation of witches for Sabbat rites was commonly designated a 'synagogue'. . . Jews were accused of desecrating sacred images, abusing the Host, and in general, burlesquing and blaspheming the ritual and sacraments of the church." [In occult crimes] we need not dispute the presumptive guilt of occasional Jewish individuals. . . " —Joshua Trachtenburg, *The Devil and the Jews*, 1943, p. 210.

The Mystery and Meaning of P_R_D_S and the Divisions of Talmudic Studies

Burton writes: "By almost imperceptible degrees the notes and commentaries upon the text grew to formidable proportions, and became a special science, whose technical name, found in the Book of Chronicles (2 xiii 22 & xxiv 27), is Midrash, from *darash*; in Arabic, *dars*, a lesson. Of the innumerable methods of studying these holy writs, the three principal are embodied in the Persian *Paradise*, the Arabic *Firdaus*, written Semitically without vowels PRDS, and the mysterious letters were assumed mnemonically as the initial of a technical word. Thus P (Peshat, the simple rendering of words) recorded the elementary law of Talmudic exegesis, 'No verse of scripture practically admits to any sense but the literal sense, although in a different or familiar signification it may be explained in a host of ways. R (*Remiz*, the Arabic *Ramz*, a secret, intimation, insinuation or suggestion of meaning) illustrates certain letters and signs apparently superfluous and explained only by tradition; in a more general manner, it gave rise to a *memoria technica* and a stenography resembling the Roman Notaricon.

"Points and notes were added to the margins of manuscripts, and thus was founded the Massorah (Masoretic tradition), or diplomatic conservation of the text, intended to preserve its purity. D (*Derush*, illustration) was the familiar application of historical, traditional, anecdotal, allegorical, and prophetical sayings to the actual state of events; it was a sermon aided by ethics, logic, poetry, parable, proverb, apologue, and the vast mass of legendary lore known as the Halakah or diplomatic part—perhaps it was suggested by the New Testament. Finally, the fourth and last, S (Sod, secret mystery), included the mystical and esoterical sciences of theosophy, metaphysics, angelology and a host of supernatural visions, brilliant and fantastic. It borrowed with impartial hand from the magic of Egypt, the myth of Hermes Trismegistos, the works of the Platonists and Neo-Platonists, and the labors of the Christian Gnostics." —Burton, pp. 96-98.

The Hebrew letters P_R_D_S spell PaRaDiSe, when the vowels are added, forming an interesting biblical word and concept. PRDS or paradise comes directly from the Persian/Avestan word *pairrdaeza* (Greek *paradeisos*), and enters English almost unchanged. It was chosen by the Greco-Hebrew translators of the Septuagint (third century B.C.) as the word for "Eden," the place of paradise or delight. In Persian, it is simply a beautiful park-like area. The rabbis teach that through diligent study of the Talmud, one's eyes will open to Paradise. Or so goes the story.

Talmud Permits Consorting With Demons

Writes Eisenmenger: "In the law of Moses, witchcraft and commerce with familiar spirits are capital crimes. . . . But the Talmud allows consulting with the devil. In the Talmud treatise entitled Sanhedrin, we have the following passage. No questions are put to the devil on the Sabbath. . . . Some put questions to the devils through oil . . . but others put questions to them through eggshells, and those devils are called princes of eggs. . . . When Solomon needed help with splitting huge stones for the temple, the rabbins told him to] order 'a male devil and a female devil to come before thee, and force them together. Perhaps they know, and will reveal it to thee.'" —Eisenmenger, Vol. I. pp. 58-9

He continues: "Some rabbins, particularly those who are Cabalists, look upon necromatic knowledge to be necessary qualifications for a seat on the Sanhedrin or Grand Council and Court of Justice among the ancient Jews. In the treatise *Emeck Hammelech*, in the part entitled Schaar Kirjath Arba, there is the following passage: Those in the Sanhedrin were obliged to know the art of sorcery, that they may discern right for what sorcery the sorcerer is to be adjudged to death." —Eisenmenger, p. 137.

Talmudic Rituals Are Pure Judaic Psychodrama

According to Strack: "Bakrrecht (ordeal of the bier) (cf. p. 49). *Buch der Frommen*, Bologna, s. 1143: Rudimentary Element of the Building-Offering (v.p. 31 sq.). Jehuda the priest says in his Testament, s. 17: 'Where a house has never stood, there let none be built. Should it, however, come to pass, the house should remain uninhabited for one year.' He probably considered the empty spot to the happy hunting ground of demons (Isai. xiii. 21). For that reason timid Israelites, even in the first half of the 19th century, 'when they reared up a house in such a place, quartered in it a cock and a hen before they installed themselves there, and then had them killed. These propitiatory sacrifices were intended to avert the peril menacing the new inhabitants. . ."

—Prof. Dr. Hermann Strack, *The Jew and Human Sacrifice*, English translation, 1892

These perverse and prevalent folk superstitions carried on into modern times. Even today, rabbis wave chickens about their heads, later to ritually slaughter them in a sadistic rite. This is not unlike what is done in the Afro-Cuban, Haitian cults like Santeria, Voodoo, Palo Mayombe, et al. (See page 172 for images.)

Tribal Customs & Rituals

As said, some of the best commentary on curious ethnic cultural customs comes from Judaic authors themselves, proven once again from the material below. Dr. Ariel Toaff, professor of medieval and renaissance history at Bar Ilan University in Israel, and son of Elio Toaff, a grand rabbi of Rome, comments on the cruel kapparot custom—and its relation to another ritual much, much worse:

"Once again, at the beginning of the 18th century, the Minorite friar Luigi Maria Benetelli severely censured those Jews of Venice, presumably belonging to the German community, who unperturbedly maintained the custom of the kapparot on the eve of the Fast of Expiation. According to him, these Jews intended to transfer the ballast of their own sins onto the white roosters, condemned to be sacrificed, while irreverently imitating the Passion of Christ.

"Many of you, on that day, dress in white and search for a white rooster without a single reddish feather (since red is the color of sin), and, clutching it by the neck and whirling it around your heads three times, pray that the rooster may expiate their sins; they torment the rooster by pulling its neck, they butcher it, throw it violently on the ground, and finally, they roast it; denoting, by means of the first torment, that they themselves deserve to be strangled; by means of the second torment, that they themselves deserve to be killed with a noose; in the third, that they themselves deserve to be stoned; and in the fourth, that they themselves deserve to be burnt for their sins. Not all (and for this

These images show kaparot, yet another Judaic animal cruelty fest, rightfully protested by animal lovers all around the world. Even Judaic children are included in the ritual, dancing about with the unfortunate birds.

reason, I said 'many') practice this ceremony even today. To me, it is enough that many of them, although unintentionally, admit, in fact, that the Messiah, which is white for its divinity and red for Humanity, should expiate sin. . . .

"Similarly, as with the kapparot, in the case [of the ritual murder] of the Christian child, his crucifixion transforms the child into Jesus and into Christianity, symbolically allowing the community to savor that vengeance against the enemies of Israel which is a necessary, although insufficient, preamble to their final redemption. The crescendo of insults and contemptuous gestures in front of the almemor of the synagogue was not, paradoxically, directed against the innocent boy, but rather, against Jesus, 'the hanged one,' whom the boy personified. Whether by 'doing the fig,' spitting on the ground, grinding their teeth or stamping their feet, all the participants in the spectacular representation, alive and charged with tension, repeated the Hebrew wish, *ken ikka-etu kol oyevecha*, which means, "thus may our enemies be consumed." —pp. 205-206.

This quite shocking material comes from the now-infamous but thoroughly scholarly book *Pasque di Sangue*, or "Blood Passovers," op. cit.). Prof. Toaff just told us the motive for these horrific acts of talmudic terrorism. We conclude with more of Sir Richard Burton's commentary:

"He [the average person] cannot realize the fact that the ferocity and terrible destructiveness which characterize the Jew and his literature, from the days of the Prophets to those of the Talmudists, are present in his civilized neighbor, whom he considers to be one of the best of men—a sleeping lion, it is true, but ready to awake upon the first occasion.

"And he is ignorant of the Eastern Jews' love of mysticism and symbolism, their various horrible and disgusting superstitions, and their devotion to magical charms and occult arts which lead to a variety of abominations.

"The Talmud declares that Abraham, who had seen god, asked his servants if they had likewise done so; and on their replying in the negative, he said to them, 'Abide ye here with the ass,' meaning that they were animals like the ass. . . .

"Thus the Law and the Prophets belong exclusively to the Jews; the gentile reading or even buying a copy should be put to death. All the books of other faiths must be burnt, even though they contain the name of Jehovah; and if any but a Hebrew write the name of god in a bible which is not a Jewish manuscript, the volume must also be burnt."

According to the Talmud (chap. iv., Sanhedrin, of the fourth Mishnic Section, or order Seder Nezekin), the gentile sanctifying the Sabbath must be put to death without asking questions."

The Occult Oral Tradition

Burton continues: "The Oral Law is superior in dignity to all others. . . . the unwritten code received by Moses on Mt. Sinai and transmitted inviolate by word of mouth from generation to generation. . . . only a few years ago a French grand rabbi published a learned work to prove the facts can only be accounted for supernaturally. Also, Dr. Adler, Orthodox chief rabbi of England, declared in a sermon preached but a few years ago, the written and the oral laws to be equally divine, and compared the Reformers with the false mother in the judgment of Solomon. These things make us regret the total disappearance of the Sadducee or Rationalistic School." —Burton, pp. 77-8

Understanding the Sanhedrin

Burton writes: "At this point it might be advisable to offer a short view of the two great schools of the Holy Land which have influenced Jewish thought in Christian times. These are, first, that of Tiberias, whence issued the Talmud of Jerusalem, followed by the Talmud of Babylon; and second, the School of Safed, which rendered itself remarkable by the extreme opinions of its commentaries and glossaries.

"We read a Jewish writer (M.J. Cohen) on the authority of the Talmud, *Archives Israelites*, 1841: '[A]fter 200 years of energetic struggles against an empire which was fated to be universal [Rome], the Hebrew race found its political nationality in peri. . . . . And the plan which at once suggested itself was to determine, by an invariable method, the principles of the Mosaic Law to develop their sense. and to fix their interpretation. . . . after the destruction of Jerusalem and the expulsion of the Jews, all authority had disappeared with national power. . . . The only rational step in this state of things was to assemble all the Israelites, or those who represented them, and to form a sovereign synod. . . .'

"The Jewish Senate, Sanhedrin or national council, was first transferred from the ruins of the Holy City to Javneh, and after many removes to Saffuriah. . . . Finally, about the middle of the second century, during the reign of Antoninus Pius (A.D. 138-161), it was transferred to Tiberias, another city of Galilee. Rabbi Yahuda, universally known as the ha-kodesh, or the saint, was nashi (prince) of his nation and the president of the Sanhedrin. He lived at Saffuriah, where there is a cave through which the Roman emperor, whose reign in history is almost a blank, used to visit him from Tiberias; this tunnel is now blocked up.

"The modern Jews residing in Galilee are not agreed whether

the great rabbi died at Suffuriah, or at Turean, a neighboring village, where two large caves exist; but neither of them shows traces of a tomb. When this prince of Israel died, it was Friday evening, and the Sun stood still whilst his corpse was carried to its distant grave, lest even the body might break the Sabbath. The work of the Sanhedrin consisted in committing to paper that which had been before entrusted to memory and had perpetuated itself by tradition—the jurisprudence of the Jews, the various interpretations of the law by the principal doctors, and the rules of man's duty; in other words, all that was called the oral law'." —pp. 92-6.

"The Most Holy spoke thus to the Israelites: You have recognized me as the only ruler of the world, and for that reason I will recognize you as the only rulers of the world." —Chaniga: 3a-3b.

CHAPTER 13

Unveiling the Kabala: A Saga of Sorcery & Psychopolitics

*"Everything begins in mysticism
and ends in politics." —Charles Peguy*

T he Talmud is thousands of pages of written tradition, not to mention the ever-growing oral commentary and teachings. Some of this is more cryptic and secretive than other parts. Kabala is a currently trendy but mostly misunderstood body of teachings. It is part of the Talmud, but quite specialized, mystical, arcane, occult and esoteric in nature. These covert, cryptic traditions are called the Hidden or Whispered Tradition, from Mouth to Ear, the Hearing, the Receiving, or in Hebrew, *Kabala*. It is the root of the English word cabal. You may have noticed this word has variant spellings and pronunciations. Yes, that makes a difference. Kabala is an occult system of numerology and gematria, the sciences of numbers, letters, and voice. While some is written, true Kabala is, for the most part, a secretive oral tradition. Kabalistic lore is not just from Judaic sources, but from a variety of pre-existing esoteric semi-Gnostic sources: Indo-Aryan, Canaanite, Assyrian, Egyptian, Persian, Babylonian, and various ancient European traditions, as well as from the Talmudists-Kabalists themselves.

Says J.M. Ragon, "The Kabala is the key to all occult sciences."

Since I was a young man, I have studied metaphysics and the strange body of literature called the occult, discovering how these ideas and movements interact with certain individuals, groups and historical forces to form our present-day world. It's no exaggeration to say that both overt and covert occultism underlie the Globalist one-world protocols of what we call, for lack of a more exact term, the New World Order. At the core are occult systems rooted in Kabala. Read the Zohar (Radiance or Splendor); it is clear. This is not to say that the ideas are not found elsewhere and earlier, but it is in Kabala that certain themes are pinpointed and perfected. The roots of Hegelian Synthesis, Marxism, Collectivism, the group mind, mind control, evolution and much more are found in the Zohar. It is a difficult text. Rabbi Luria is an important expositor and commentator on Kabala.

"Rav Isaac Luria, born in the 16th century, is the most influential Kabbalist in history. A brilliant scholar even as a child, Rav Luria was called 'the Ari,' which means 'the Holy Lion.' The Ari had the gift to explore the innermost depths of the Zohar. He lived as a hermit for 13 years, probing its mysteries. It was not unusual for him to meditate upon one verse of the Zohar for many months, until the hidden meaning was revealed to him." —From the website, The Kaballah Center: http://www.kabbalah.com/

Ritual magic, secret societies and Kabalism are crucial in understanding world history because occult belief systems underlie many decisions made by New World Order planners. These covert creeds have Kabala at their epicenter. The important thing is not whether you believe in the dark forces or not. Nor does it matter whether or not you think magic really "works." The point is that high-level globalist Illuminati planners indeed do believe. Enduring beliefs eventually create their own reality and grow stronger over time. The Kabalistic Semitic sorcery requires that certain acts and symbols to be in public view. Sometimes there is a propensity for in-your-face actions rather than mere symbolism. Key players on the world stage are influenced by occult paradigms and eons-old symbolism. Mysticism and magic may seem odd topics for a serious researcher, but humor an eccentric old writer who delves into archaic legends and lore and just read on. As you probably see, a question poses itself: Do you believe in magic? Before answering, read the short quotation below, by O'Keefe:

"Magic actions are rituals that make or change something. They operate mysteriously, and what they create is mostly mystical—BUT THESE MYSTERIOUS ACTIONS HAVE SOCIAL EFFECTS. This mystical doing and making (only dimly understood by the participants) has the effect, by virtue of their beliefs, of bringing about a real social doing or making, as surely as the minister ties when he 'pronounces' you man and wife or the judge changes your status by his 'sentence.' THAT IS WHY MAGIC IS 'EFFICACIOUS MYSTICAL ACTION'." —Daniel L. O'Keefe, *Stolen Lightning: The Social History of Magic*, 1982

Reflect on these words as you review history and follow world events. Never discount the power of religions or other belief systems. In so many ways, they metaphysically create their own reality. The arcane occult doctrines of the Kabala are a powerful example of this. When these ideas are deconstructed, we see that the same mental powers and spiritual forces are at work. While not a comforting thought, this seems to be the case.

Says Crowley: "There are, of course, entirely black forms of magic. To him who has not given every drop of his blood for the cup of Babylon, all magic power is dangerous. There are even more debased and evil forms, things in themselves black. Such is the use of spiritual force to material ends. Christian Scientists, mental healers, professional diviners, psychics and the like, are all, *ipso facto*, BLACK MAGICIANS." —Aleister Crowley, *Magick in Theory and Practice*.

Kabala is a component text to the Talmud. Its myriad of axioms and labyrinthine commentaries contain lore transmitted from one generation to another, not just by the written word, but more importantly, by a secret oral esoteric tradition. Primeval occult paradigms flow beneath the veneer of all cultures and religions. To understand the mysticism and occultism of the West, we turn to Kabala. These covert traditions, well below the veneer of Judaism, have a strong influence, both positive and negative, on western mysticism, spiritualism, mystical Christianity, Freemasonry and other initiatic orders, New Age, modern occultism, ceremonial magic (thaumaturgy), neo-pagan alternative religions and more. Magi and adepts regard these traditions with great respect. But, when considering the deeper doctrines, the truly Whispered Tradition, we may not really know all that much. Except for a few items of interest, be wary of those on radio and other media who claim to be adepts of Illuminati or secret fraternal orders who have now, for some reason or the other, decided to tell the secrets. All of this is a psycho-political distraction technique. According to Tart:

"In fact any TV, radio, or press appearance by people claiming some special spiritual status or authority should be very highly suspect. . . . True initiates do not advertise themselves as such in any way whatever, or even imply by hints or other means that they are at all different from other humans. It is strictly forbidden to do anything like this under commonly accepted ethical codes of conduct." —C. Tart, ed., *Transpersonal Psychologies*, 1977.

"What is one to do, when in order to rule men, it is necessary to deceive them? . . . For almost invariably the more simple, the more silly, and the more gross the phenomenon, the more likely they are to succeed." —Helena P. Blavatsky.

Psychopolitics and the Magic of Mind Control

"Psychopolitics is the art and science of asserting and maintaining dominion over the thoughts and loyalties of individuals, officers, bureaus, and masses, and the effecting of the conquest of enemy nations through 'mental healing'." —*Synthesis of the Textbook on Psychopolitics*

Psychopolitics and its practices impact society and civilization. Psychopolitics and mind control, apart from stunning technological advances in the last half of the 20th century, have used the same basic techniques for eons: rigorous rituals, ceremonies, repetitious rote memory exercises, sleep deprivation, continual testing of beliefs, sex magic and so on. Words and symbols may change, but the same threads weave through the pages of history from the archetypal beginnings of humankind. Magic has cultural and societal results on the metaphysical-spiritual, psychological-mental and physical planes. Moreover, it has effects, whether one "believes" or not. Spells and incantations have results because others act out the psychodramas on the three planes, including the physical one. If satanists kidnap a child for a human sacrifice to ensure winning the lottery or succeeding in a big drug deal, it makes no difference whether the spell "worked" or not. The damage is done; both intent and results are clear.

Writes Eliphas Levi:

"The cult of evil is a reality—by whatever means we may seek to explain it. Evil exists; it is impossible to doubt it. We can do good or evil. There are beings who voluntarily do evil. . . . There are also beings who love evil." —*Histoire de la Magie*, 1860.

The physical and psychological effects are undeniable, on both the perpetrators and the victims, and on society in general. Crime syndicates and ethnic gangs use magic and the occult for intimidation and mind control. This is especially effective in certain ethnic communities where it is often combined with Catholic beliefs. Religions like Santeria, Voodoo, Palo Mayombe, Macumba, Candomble and others in the Americas and the precursor animist folk religions of west Africa are examples. The components of ritual magic are many and intricate, but desecration is often central to the darker rites. The so-called Black Mass is an example. Desecration, crime and bizarre behaviors lead practitioners to distance themselves from cultural taboos and societal norms, yet another psycho-political mind control method. In its darker phases, the evil rites can include sex magic and abuse, torture, and even ritualized murder in ceremonies contrived by sadomasochistic psychopaths. The unclean rites often involve child victims, so there is the stench of pedophilia along with sulfur and brimstone.

History shows an inordinate number of Judaists among the practitioners and philosophers of the occult arts. They are, of course, not the only ones, but because of the Kabalistic underpinnings of western ceremonial magical systems, they are of significance. Sorcery has a long history among the Sephardic Jews as well as the Khazar converts, who contributed their own peculiar Turko-Mongol practices, including human sacrifice. By renaissance times, Jews and their Kabalistic mysticism were prominent in the occult philosophies and practitioners of the day.

"All truly dogmatic religions have issue from the Kabalah and return to it . . . everything scientific and grand in the religious drama of all the Illuminati . . . is borrowed from the Kabalah; all the Masonic associations owe to it their secrets and their symbols." —Albert Pike, *Morals and Dogma*, 1875.

"Symbols are not lies; symbols contain truth. Allegories and parables are not falsehoods; they convey information: moreover, they can be understood by those who are not prepared to receive the plain truth." —Paul Carus, *History of the Devil and the Idea of Evil*, 1900.

Freemasonry and the Kabala

Freemasonry is a form of Kabalistic Judaism for selected goyim. The highly acclaimed but seldom read *Morals and Dogma* is, more than anything else, a Kabalistic textbook and ritual magic instruction manual. Albert Pike's book either heavily relies on or was co-written with famed 19th-century Kabalistic philosopher, Eliphas Levi. But, while not appropriate to share truly sacred things with the goyim, it is perfectly acceptable to manipulate and delude non-chosen ones for profit. In many ways, Freemasons are the largest philo-Semitic organization in the world, based as it is in the Hebraic traditions of the Old Testament. This has direct links to the proposed Third Temple. Since Solomon and his Masons of old supposedly built the first temple, why wouldn't Masons be part of creating the third one?

But on the simple social club level, most lodge members get the first three degrees and go no further. A third degree Master Mason can head a local lodge. Higher degrees take time and money. The regular members think they've either heard it all or think they have clear hints. Of course, they're encouraged to feel this way. For some, it is exciting and stimulating to be part of a movement or religion that is special and said to influence world affairs. As for Lodges (or synagogues or churches) being exclusive domains for members where business and plots are done, some certainly hope so. It's the reason why more than a few of them joined. But on a higher level, beliefs have great power. If enough people accept something as true and act in similar ways, then over a period of time, by definition a conspiracy is born.

Says Manley Hall: "[The Masons] are the invisible powers behind the thrones of Earth, and men are but marionettes, dancing while the invisible ones pull the strings. . . . We see the dancer, but the master mind that does the work remains concealed by the cloak of silence." —Manley P. Hall, 33rd degree Mason

Read all the New Age and occult books about Kabala you want, but don't be naïve enough to think you'll learn all that much. That being said, one has to begin somewhere to learn basic facts. Older books, especially those of the 19th century and earlier, are more informative, but often expensive and hard to find. Read the Kabalistic texts themselves. The Zohar, Bahir and similar works are available in print and online, but be advised. Like the rest of the Talmud, much of it is pedantic and boring. But, gems can be unearthed among the debris. Kabala's roots are eons old and incredibly deep, now experiencing a feverish New Age renaissance. While there are magical folk traditions other than Kabala, much of Western ceremonial magic has Kabalistic concepts at its core.

Kabala and Current Events

What follows is from Nesta Webster's *Secret Societies and Subversive Movements*, 1924, an exceptional book. If you want to understand the nature of occult conspiracies, this is a must. It is here

I first read of Henri-Roger Gougenot des Mousseaux (1805-1876), a 19th-century French author, knighted by the pope, who exposed Judaism and other conspiracies on several fronts. Unfortunately his classic work, *Le Juif, le Judaisme et la Judaisation des Peuples Chretiens*, "The Jews, Judaism and the Judaization of the Christian People," 1869, has never been translated into English. It was rendered into German by Alfred Rosenberg and published in 1921 as *Der Jude, Judenthum und die Verjudung der christlichen Volker*. Both Chancellor Hitler and Dr. Rosenberg, the philosopher of the National Socialist movement, were impressed and influenced by this book:

"Gougenot des Mousseaux, who had made a profound study of occultism, asserts there were therefore two kabalas: the ancient sacred tradition handed down from the first patriarchs of the human race; and the evil Kabala, wherein this sacred tradition was mingled by the rabbis with barbaric superstitions, combined with their own imaginings and henceforth marked with their seal." — Nesta Webster

Some say Gougenot was poisoned by Jewish assassins or Freemasonic agents, and indeed this may have been the case. He knew many secrets. A brief example of his work appears below. Perhaps he was a prophet. Has the scenario he describes already taken place in the "formidable crises" we now face?

"There will burst forth one fine evening one of these formidable crises which will shake the Earth and which occult societies have long prepared for Christian society, and then perhaps will suddenly appear in open day, throughout the entire world, all the militia, all the fraternal and unknown sects of the Cabala. The ignorance, the carelessness in which we live, of their sinister existence, their affinities and their immense ramifications will in no way prevent them from recognizing each other, and under the banner of no matter what universal alliance, giving each other the kiss of peace, they will hasten to gather together. . . ."—Gougenot

Is the Kabala, as Gougenot asserts, older than the Jewish race, a legacy handed down from the first patriarchs of the world? While this hypothesis is incapable of definitive proof, it makes sense. The Kabala itself supports this, tracing descent from the patriarchs Adam, Noah, Enoch and Abraham, who lived long before the Jews came forth as a separate people.

Oriental Mysticism and the Formation of the Kabala

The lore and rituals of Kabala are ancient, absorbing the mysticism and lore of other cultures, including Chaldea, Babylonia, Persia, Egypt, Canaan and others. Some say Kabala arose in Spain and France during the medieval era, and others trace it earlier to the sixth century. Truth is, Kabala is an ancient system of knowledge, orally transmitted and seldom written except in managed and controlled versions. Kabala comes from the larger Talmudic tradition, itself full of magic and mayhem. Oriental mysticism entered into the originally Egypto-Semitic traditions. Remember, Abraham was "father of many nations" (hence, father of the goyim), a man from Ur in Chaldea, the ancient home of ritual magic, necromancy, demonology and plenty of other occult traditions. The components of Kabala are diverse. Like the larger Talmud, it is a family or collection of related literature that underwent numerous additions and editings over the centuries.

According to Nesta Webster:

"Sorcery, as we know, had been practiced by the Canaanites before the occupation of Palestine by the Israelites; Egypt, India, and Greece also had their soothsayers and diviners. In spite of the imprecations against sorcery contained in the law of Moses, the Jews, disregarding these warnings, caught the contagion and mingled the sacred tradition they had inherited with magical ideas partly borrowed form other races and partly of their own devising. . . . What we know today as the Kabala is not of purely Jewish origin."

"In the Old Testament, many Israelites lost their battle with Eastern mysticism. They blended Eastern mysticism with the teachings of the Torah. The metamorphosis of this is the Kabbalah." — Sheldon Smith, *Secrets of the Kaballah*, a video documentary, Part One, 2001. http://www.youtube.com/watch?v=Ye4_feytz-c

While some oral tradition did go down on paper, there seems to be no publicly circulated material until early medieval times. Kabala means "the reception" or "what is heard," "what is whispered," an oral tradition. As such, certain parts always remain unwritten, transmitted to initiates only by a rebbe or tzaddik. Even then, only after great deliberation and only with an intelligent candidate of mature age and demeanor. Only true chacham adepts study at the deeper levels. The most important Kabala books are the Bahir and the Zohar. In Muslim Spain, Sephardic Jews published certain selections. This was very controversial in Judaic communities. Some like the famed Rabbi Isaac Luria were opposed at first. This is understandable from two perspectives. Never forget how gentiles attacked the Talmud. Publishing the Kabala might provoke them again. Not only that, publication violates every tenet of the ancient, secretive and private oral tradition.

So you say you want to understand Kabala? It is difficult just to pronounce and spell it. Kabala, Cabbala, Cabala, Kabala, Kabbalah, QaBaLa, Q'ballah; there are too many variations to list. I once watched a TV special about Kabala, and three rabbis were to appear. Oh good, I thought; I can hear each one say the word. Each rabbi pronounced it differently. Pronunciations and spellings do make a difference, each with its own meaning. Editions of the Zohar and other works are readily available. They are big sellers, and Kabala is a trendy topic for afternoon teas and evening cocktail parties. But how much can you really know about the true inner nature of a tradition that defies and defeats all attempts at disclosure? Most books simply parrot various New Age concepts, yet many gentiles and Judaists seem to think they are learning the real thing.

Adolphe Franck in his book *The Kabbalah* says:

"The term comes from the Hebrew word *qabbala*. . . , a 'receiving, accepting,' but which is also used in the sense of 'tradition'. . . a 'handing down' of traditional lore. . . ." —*Catholic Encyclopedia*

"Kabala literally means 'mouth to ear,' or signifies the Secret Tradition which could only be whispered by initiates directly into the ears of worthy recipients." —C. Tart, *Transpersonal Psychologies*

Says Franck: "Before the end of the first century of the Christian era, there circulated among the Jews a profoundly venerated science which could be distinguished from the Mishna, the Talmud and the sacred books. . . . The Kabbalists always shrouded themselves in mystery from their first appearance to the time when the press betrayed their secret. At rare intervals and after many precautions, they half-opened their portals for some new adept, always chosen exclusively from among the intellectual elite and from among those whose advanced age promised discretion and wisdom."

Even the titles of the tractates are confusing. While Bahir translates as "bright," a more literal meaning is "obscured." Bahir is sometimes confusingly called Haggadah Yerushalmi and Midrash. The most devout Jews are the Hasidim (the pious ones) sect. They are great Kabalists, and the Bahir occupies a special place. Their rebbes composed *Raza Rabba, The Great Mystery or The Great Secret*.

Also called *Sephir ha-Sod ha-Godol*, it is the primary text for those concerned with divine names, angelology, demonology and thaumaturgy. The concept of the golem, an evil humanoid, not unlike a huge Voodoo doll, animated by ritual magic incantations, comes directly from the Bahir, as does a Judaic belief in reincarnation. Kabala is rooted in numerology. The *Sephir Yetzirah* ("Book of Creation") is quite old, dating from the sixth century B.C., though some say it is a creation of the early medieval era. While about several topics, including the unity of god, to the initiated reader it is about Kabalistic numerology. *The Sefir Yetzirah* may be referred to in the Koran as the *Book of Abraham*.

See the following quotes:

"You have abandoned your people, the house of Jacob. They are full of superstitions from the East; they practice divination like the Philistines and clasp hands with pagans."

—Isaiah 2:6

"The Kabala is of course an esoteric doctrine, and its detailed study was confined to scholars. In Europe, especially after about 1750, extreme measures were taken to keep it secret and forbid its study except by mature scholars and under strict supervision. The uneducated Jewish masses of Eastern Europe had no real knowledge of cabbalistic doctrine; but the cabbala percolated to them in the form of superstition and magic practices."

—Israel Shahak, *Jewish History, Jewish Religion*, 1994

"The Ein Soph (Infinite One) is not the personal god of the bible; the latter becomes manifest only through the sephiroth to which the divine attributes correspond."

—Catholic Encyclopedia, 1931

"Even the great and legendary Solomon did not always behave according to the Lord's behest. In his old age he turned away from the god of his fathers and worshiped the wanton Elilim. He had peopled his harem with foreign women who worshiped their native gods, and in the holy city he had temples built for every creed. His theological and demonological wisdom has become legendary; his magic lamp and celebrated seal enabled him to command the spirits of hell. . . . A thousand legends concerning Solomon (Suleiman) are scattered through the east. . . . After Solomon's reign Jerusalem fell into a magico-religious chaos. The scriptures, so eloquent concerning Solomon's wealth and magnificence, his wisdom, his horses and chariots, leave unanswered the questions of whether Solomon ever returned to the faith of the one Jehovah."

—Karl Seligmann, *Magic, Supernaturalism and Religion*

Says Trachtenburg: "On the fringe of the Jewish theosophy was the magical lore that non-Jews had heretofore but dimly perceived. This had little to do with the Kabbalah proper, and was, in fact, denominated in Jewish circles the 'practical Kabbalah' as distinct from the authentic 'theoretical Kabbalah.' It was the practical Kabbalah in a theosophical dress that Christians found the easier and more desirable to assimilate. It became a prized adjunct of astrology and alchemy, a marvelous magical apparatus, in the general view. Jewish elements were soon absorbed and so transposed as to remain Jewish in name only. Since the 16th century there has grown up a vast library of Kabbalistic texts, so-called—a new, Christian Kabbalah, that speedily parted company with its ostensible parent and ventured off in other directions wholly on its own. The term Kabbalah became synonymous with magic, under this new dispensation."

—Joshua Trachtenburg, *The Devil and the Jews*, 1943.

"We cannot possibly consider the Kabala an isolated fact, accidental in Judaism; on the contrary, it is its heart and soul."

—Adolphe Franck

Kabala and Current Events: Zionist Supremacism and Greater Israel

Lurianic Kabala and the Sepher ha Zohar dominated Judaism from the late sixth century to the early 19th century. Without a doubt, they proclaim the absolute superiority of the Jewish soul over the non-Jewish soul. Lurianic Kabala says the world was created solely for the sake of Jews, hence the existence of non-Jews is of no importance. Authors of books on Jewish mysticism and Kabala almost always omit any reference to these Talmudic precepts. Naturally, Jah-Hovah wants his/her chosen people to have some chosen real estate.

As you see from the map below, this includes much of the Middle East. This is land west of the Euphrates, throughout most of

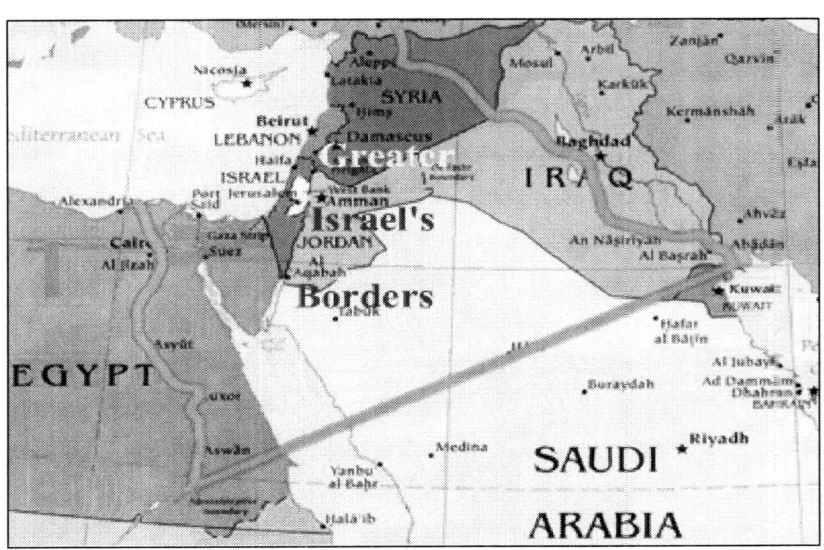

Syria, much of Iraq, Jordan and parts of Egypt and Saudi Arabia.

"God places himself for display on Earth in the likeness of the Jews. . . . The Hebrew is the living god become flesh, the heavenly man, the Adam Kadmon." —*Kaballa ad Penteteucum*, Folio 97

"The soul of a Jew is truly a part of god above. . . ." —Hasidic Rabbi Schneur Zalman, author of *Likutei Amarim* (the *Tanya*), 1:58

The Zionist supremacists believe their peculiar Egypto-Semitic deity Jah-Hovah gave them all the alleged Old Testament Land of Israel. This is far greater and far beyond the current ministate's borders. They mean Eretz Israel ("Greater Israel") or Haaretz ("the Land").

The modern-day Zionist war crimes and attempts of ethnic cleansing against the Palestinian people manifest age-old archetypal, primitive, warlike and violent characteristics, exemplified not only in the Jewish Old Testament, but especially and graphically in the Talmud and Kabala. On certain levels, they revert back to their primordial and primitive racial archetypes of vengeance and ultra-violence. Like most psychopathic serial crimes, these atrocities happen again and again.

Returning to Burton:

"We must seek a solid cause underlying these horrible acts of vengeance; we must find ample motive in the fact that every Jew's hand was ever, like Ishmael's, against every man but those belonging to the synagogue. His fierce passions and fiendish cunning, combined with abnormal powers of intellect, with intense vitality, and with a persistency of purpose which the world has rarely seen, and whetted moreover by a keen thirst for blood engendered by defeat and subjection, combined to make him the deadly enemy of all mankind, whilst his unsocial and iniquitous Oral Law [the Talmud] contributed to inflame his wild lust of pelf, and to justify crimes suggested by spite and superstition.

"Because under the present enlightened governments of the West, the Jews have lost much of their ancient rancor, and no longer perpetrate the atrocities of the dark ages, Europe is determined to believe that the race is, and ever has been, incapable of such atrocities. The conclusion is by no means logical. We have seen even now repeated in the Holy Land, and presently we shall see that they are still not unknown to Western Europe, Asia Minor and Persia. . . . The great Lawgiver of Israel sanctioned the murder in cold blood of women and child captives. Even kings were hewed to pieces before the Lord." —Sir Richard Francis Burton, *The Jew, the Gypsy and El Islam*, 1898

More Kabala and Current Events:
Semitic Sorcery, Symbols & Numerology

Perhaps the ultimate Kabalistic symbol is the magical 6,000,000 Holocaust (Hollow-Co$t) number. Kabalistic thaumaturgy (ceremonial magic) consists of divination and spells based on gematria, numerology, so letters and numbers are of prime significance. According to the Kabalists, there is a sum total of 600,000 souls. 10 is the number of the Sephiroth, or branches of the Kabalistic Tree of Life. The cryptic meaning of 6,000,000 is the ultimate number of souls 600,000, times the 10 Sephiroth. Holocaust means burnt offering or sacrifice by fire. Ba'al and Moloch worship were ancient Canaanite, Middle Eastern and Egypto-Semitic traditions that were passed on. The "wisdom" of Solomon brought them in to please his foreign concubines.

After the horrid temples were closed and the sacrifice of children by fire suppressed, the cult became an underground belief system. It survives in the graphic slaughters, ritualized murders and ethnic cleansings portrayed in the Old Testament all the way down to the Israeli war crimes and atrocities of today. Six million is the ultimate number of blessed Judaic martyr souls.

For a more detailed exposition on these matters, see my larger paper entitled "Deconstructing 6,000,000 Holo-Myths, Exploring the Occult Origin of Crucial Holocaust Dogma." Click the red "go to pdf" link at the beginning of the article to download it as a PDF file. Help launch this Truth Seeking Missile. Please share this with others. http://www.gnosticliberationfront.com/deconstructing _six_million_holo_myth.htm

Yes indeed, the Kabalistic spells and hexes have succeeded on a grand and frightening scale. What a great magic trick. All their spells have, so far, worked quite nicely. The Holocaust Dogma of Judaism is a government sanctioned and enforced world religion, complete with inquisition courts and severe punishments for un-believers and heretics. Nonetheless, the final chapter has not yet been written. Truth has a most annoying habit of emerging at un-expected and uncomfortable times. It was said in the very begin-ning of our exploration into the Kabala, and as we study history and follow current events, it continually proves to be true.

"Everything begins in mysticism and ends in politics."

CHAPTER 14

Halakha Law & Talmudic Legalism

What Is Halakha?

The word "Halakha" is taken from the Hebrew verbs meaning to walk or to go, the noun translating as the Path or the Way. More commonly, it is just called Jewish law. Halakha is the entire corpus of the Judaic religious legal tradition, including the Tennakh along with the equally authoritative rabbinical writings and Haggada oral traditions, opinions, commentary, anecdotes, and sayings illustrating the law. Tennakh plus Talmud is the complete word of god. Halakha is fully inclusive, teaching devout Orthodox believers all they need for living a good and proper Jewish life. There is almost nothing that is not addressed. The Talmud is millions of words. Halakhic law is what most of them are about.

Why Is it Important?

In order to understand the people called Jews and their immense influence on world history, from the very worst examples to the best, one must understand the Talmud to be aware of the worldview, the mindset and behavior of Judaics through the ages as they interact with the non-Judaics (gentiles/goyim). The Talmud is the true holy writ of many (but not all) Judaics, the one and only guidebook for life, most especially for those of the Orthodox persuasion. The advice given by rabbis, no matter what the subject, much more often than not, comes from the spirit and letter of the Talmud. But even for the non-practicing Jew, as well as non-Jews, this one set of so-called and self-styled "wisdom literature" has had more influence on western culture and world civilization, perhaps exceeding that of either the Koran or the bible. Both Judaism and Islam are as much legal systems as they are religions. In Islam, you have the Koran and Sharia law. In Judaism, we have the Torah and Talmudic law.

Surveying and Understanding the Formation and Development of Talmudic Law

Benjamin H. Freedman was not only a learned man, he was a devoutly honest spiritual seeker who made a sincere conversion to Christianity. In his controversial writings and speeches, Freedman was relentless in exposing and laying bare the truth about Pharisaic Talmudism. The quotation is from his 1954 classic, *Facts Are Facts*:

"The world's leading authorities on the Talmud confirm that the official unabridged Soncino edition of the Talmud translated into English follows the original texts with great exactness. It is almost a word-for-word translation of the original texts. In his famous classic *The History of the Talmud*, Michael Rodkinson, the leading authority on the Talmud, in collaboration with the celebrated Rev. Dr. Isaac Wise, states:

'With the conclusion of the first volume of this work at the beginning of the 20th century, we would invite the reader to take a glance over the past of the Talmud, in which he will see . . . that not only was the Talmud not destroyed, but was so saved that not a single letter of it is missing; and now it is flourishing to such a degree as cannot be found in its past history. . . . The Talmud is one of the wonders of the world. During the 20 centuries of its existence . . . it survived in its entirety, and not only has the power of its foes failed to destroy even a single line, but it has not even been able materially to weaken its influence for any length of time. It still dominates the minds of a whole people who venerate its contents as Divine Truth. . . . The colleges for the study of the Talmud are increasing almost in every place where Israel dwells . . . houses of learning (Jeshibath or Yeshiva) for the study of the Talmud every day."

In his classic volume on cultural history—*The Jew, the Gypsy and El Islam*—Sir Richard Burton discusses the formation of the Talmud and the codification of Halakha:

"To resume the history of the Talmud. Some years after the publication of the Mishnah in the third century (A.D. 230-270), R. Yochanan, who for 80 years had been president of the Sanhedrin, undertook a commentary on the text like the Sharh [Islamic Sharia Law], which accompanies the Arabic Matu. Aided, it is said, by Rab and Samuel, the disciples of Gamaliel, son of R. Yahuda, he produced about A.D. 300 a book which, united with the Mishnayoth, received the title Talmud (doctrine of learning) of Jerusalem, though written at Tiberias. The product of the schools of Palestine, it was composed in the West Aramaean tongue; and it calls the Mishnic text by the simple name of Halakah (rule), or dogmatic part. The School of Tiberias flourished apparently in the days of St. Jerome, and passed into oblivion during the fourth and early fifth centuries.

"In A.D. 367 Askhi, president of the Babylonian Sanhedrin, whilst teaching the Mishnah, annually commented upon two tracts of that work, which, being concise, and as it were axiomatic, like all books that announce legislative principles, required explanation of the author's exact intention. He was aided by the opinions of many doctors omitted in the Mishnah, either those who died before R. Yahuda the Holy had finished his labors, or the many who followed during the ensuing years. In order that his learning not be lost to the world, he compiled and transcribed 35 tracts, and died A.D. 427. His son Mar and Marimon his disciple continued the work, and after 73 years appeared the Gemara, complement or conclusion. It was written in the Eastern Aramaean tongue, and it corresponds with the Hasheyah of Arabic standard works.

"The Mishnah and the Gemara, now forming a single code, became known to history as the Talmud Babli (of Babylon); and when the Talmud is mentioned, the second work, being the fuller and the more minute, is always meant. Presently, the Talmudists separated into two great and rival schools in ante-Christian times: that of Hillel, remarkable for his learning, his humility and his charity, extending even so far as to forbid usury (Tract Baba Metzin, folio 17b); and that of Shammai, inflexible in principles and often inclining to severity.

"Both of these voluminous compositions are essentially a corpus juris, to be compared with the Edictum Perpetuum and Responsa Prudentium, with the Pandects, the Novellae and the Institutes. They form an encyclopedia of Judean law, divine and human, national and international, laical and ecclesiastic, civil and criminal; a doctrinal, judicial, and sentential digest, dealing in exegesis and hermeneutics; a huge compilation of what Muslim divines call fatwa, or decisions upon legal subjects; and a thesaurus of ceremonial observances borrowed from the oral law and the traditions of the heads of schools from Rabbi Gamaliel downward. [This rabbi died c. A.D. 100. According to the New Testament, he was the yeshiva instructor of St. Paul.]

"Composed in the East, that classic land of the supernatural, they abound in Hagadistic matter, wild and picturesque legends inculcating moral lessons, like the four nocturnal specters Lilith, Naama, Aguerith and Mahala, at other times puerile tales of the great angels Patspatsiah, Tashbach, Hadarniel, Enkatham, Pastam, Sandalphon, Shamsiel and Prasta. Its historical, topographical, ethnographical, and geographical information must be received with the greatest reserve. coming from authors of different ages and of several values. . . ." —Burton, pp. 99-103.

"The Talmud had spoken its last upon the interpretation of the Torah, it had closed the discussions which arose from the sacred text, and it had exhausted the traditional lore and rules established by the rabbis of Palestine and Babylon till the fifth century after the Christian era. Still the Talmud itself required after the course of ages to be interpreted, and this gave rise to a variety of medieval abridgments and to a vast series of glosses and commentaries." The more modern rabbis especially resolved that no uncertainty should rest upon the Halakah, or doctrinal part of the work, and they strictly applied themselves to codify the whole body of the Talmud." —Burton, pp. 109-110

Did you know that god studies the Talmud and consults with the rabbis? This is from a book called *The Protocols of Zion, with Preface and Explanatory Notes*, no publisher listed, 1934:

"In order to enhance the authority of the Old Testament equally recognized by the Christians, while simultaneously augmenting that of the Talmud and the rabbis, its commentators and authors reach: 'In the law (bible) are things more or less important, but the words of the Learned in the Scripture are always important. It is more wicked to protest the words of the rabbis than of Torah.' (*Miszna*, Sanhedrin XI, 3)

"'Who changes the words of the rabbis ought to die.' (Erubin, 21, b)

"The decisions of the Talmud [Halakah] are the words of the living god. Jehovah himself asks the opinion of earthly rabbis when there are difficult affairs in heaven.' (Rabbi Menachem, Comments for the Fifth Book)

"'Jehovah himself in heaven studies the Talmud, standing: he has such respect for the book.' (Tr. Mechilla)" [End quoting.]

Arrogance, egotism and ethnocentrism are at the base and bedrock of the Talmudic religion.

"The philosopher Ludwig Feuerbach has already designated the Jewish religion as nothing more than a business contract between Judah and its god. . . . [He said] the Jews have retained their peculiarity up to the present day: their deity is the most practical principle in the world: egoism, and egoism in the form of religion." —F. Roderich-Stoltheim, *The Riddle of the Jew's Success*, 1927; Michael Santomauro: 2005, p. 187.

Noahide Law

What is Noahide law? What is its impact on gentile America? Have we been covertly Judaized?

"Those who transgress any of the commandments [Noahide laws] transgress them all. The goods of the gentiles who have not conformed to the Noahite [sic] code, that is to say, all now living, are lawful to the Hebrews. This right was first conferred by Jehovah during the Exodus from Egypt, and it was confirmed to the descendants of the wanderers by the Talmud (Baba Masiaah, or Middle Gate, second of the fourth order, and Abodah Zarah, eighth of the same)." —Burton, p. 80.

Public Law 102-14 seems to have officially established Noahide Law in the United States. PL 102-14 was passed March 20, 1991 with the key phrases contained within what is outwardly a declaration declaring "Education Day" in honor of the Lubavitcher Movement (a Khazar Zionist extremist movement) and its leader Rebbe SchneersoNoahite). His discussion of these arcane Talmudic principles is most elucidating, particularly when the reader considers that our nation may "symbolically" be under the so-called Noahide Code. What have we, as a nation, done here? Why is this so important to Zionists? The fact of its existence begs the question of exactly why this was done under semi-covert, nondemocratic, ways. Think about PL 102-14. Have we been "symbolically" made into "semi-Jews"?

"In the *Prompta Bibliotheca* we find (p. 297, Order 4, Tract 4, Dist. 10): '*Gravius plectendos esse qui contradicunt verbis Scribarum quam verbis Mosaicae Legis quibus qui contradixerit, morte moriatur.*' And he must die by the flogging of rebellion, a Rabbinical practice utterly unknown to the Pentateuch, which ordered 40 stripes, whereas in the New Dispensation the offender must be flogged without intermission till he expires. Thus the scribes and Pharisees still sit in Moses's seat. The modern Jew follows the creed of Maimonides (12th century), which contains 13 fundamental articles, the last being resurrection of the dead. The ancient Jew obeyed the Twelve Commandments without a word about the resurrection. The sojourning proselyte who would be saved must be a Noahite, and obey the Seven Commandments assured to the Noachidae; the Hakham Abul Afiya gave them as follows.

"1. Thou shalt not worship planets, stars or idols.

"2. Thou shalt not fornicate nor commit adultery.

"3. Thou shalt not slay (man).

"4. Thou shalt not steal.

"5. Thou shalt not eat in the street the flesh of a lamb.

"6. Thou shalt not castrate the sons of Abraham, mankind or any other animal.

"7. Thou shalt not join with the several races of animals.

"Arubim, or mixtures, were forbidden by the Mosaic Law (Lev. xix, 19), and were greatly extended by the Oral Law, such as grafting, sowing different kinds of seeds in the same soil, wearing a garment of wool and linen mixed, and so forth. The subject is copiously treated in the nine chapters of Kilaim ('Heterogeneous,' or 'Things Not to Be Mixed'), the fourth tract of the first order, Seder Zeraaim (the Order of Seeds). More correctly speaking, this code given to the Noachidae, or Noahites, commands them to abstain from the Seven Deadly Sins: (1) idolatry; (2) irreverence to god; (3) homicide; (4) robbery, fraud, and plunder—generally, not only of a co-religionist; (5) adultery; (6) disobedience and misrule; and (7) eating part of an animal still living, or the blood of the dead. The latter was added (Gen. ix 4) to the Six Sins forbidden to Adam—namely idolatry and i sojourning proselyte [now under Noahide Law] receives scant consolation, as he may not be received when the Jubilee cannot be observed (Hilchoth Issure Biah, xiv 7, 8); and this ceased after Reuben, Gad and half of Manasseh were led away captive, or in B.C. 884, according to the common chronology. Add to this 1,873, and we have 2,757 years since the feast of the kind, and we have 27 centuries and a half since any gentiles were converted from the errors of idolatry to the religion of the sons of Noah.

"The subject of proselytizing amongst the ancient Jews is full of difficulties, and the object seems mostly to have been the discouragement of converts. . . . The proselytes of the gate, generally called Gerim or strangers, ('the stranger that is within thy gates') and properly called Noachidae (sons of Noah), were only half Israelites. The proselytes of the covenant or of righteousness were perfect Israelites. They are still admitted under protest—men by circumcision and immersion in water, and women by the latter rite only. It is a question of how far baptism was used in ante-Christian times, and possibly John the Baptist merely adapted the old rite for a new purpose.

"Those who transgress any of the commandments transgress them all. This again is scriptural. 'The doctrine of Moses is not that obedience to one command will compensate for disobedience to another, but that disobedience to one command will make obedience to others of no effect'." The goods of gentiles who have not conformed to Noahite code, that is to say, all now living, are lawful to the Hebrews. This right was first conferred by Jehovah during the Exodus from Egypt, and it was confined to the descendants of the wanderers by the Talmud (Baba Masiah, or Middle Gate, second of the fourth order, and Aoodah Zarah, eighth of the same).

"We read in the tract Sanhedrin (fourth of fourth order, p. 58) that the gentile who strikes a Jew has committed a capital offense; this ordinance is as old as the sojourn of Moses in Egypt. He who strikes a Jew strikes the deity. The 'sons of Noah' may be slain by the sentence of a single Rabbi, or upon the testimony of a solitary witness, although the latter be a relation [to the victim].

"A descendant of the Hebrews who, learning the true god in the days of Abraham, thereby separated themselves from and exalted themselves above the rest of humanity, may not be put to death but by the decision of 20 rabbis and on the testimony of two witnesses. A gentile forfeits life if he causes a pregnant Jewess or her fruit to perish; a Jew is not to be punished capitally for such crime, but he must pay for the loss of the child (p. 57). The 'son of Noah' who blasphemes the Holy Name, who has committed adultery with or who has slain a co-religionist, ceases to merit death by becoming a sojourning proselyte; but he must not be suffered to escape if he has slain a Jew, or if he has committed adultery with a Jewess (p. 71)." —Burton

The Talmud and Abortion

Our good literary comrade, Internet essayist "Bill Guru" addresses this complex and divisive issue:

"Very few people have any idea that "pro-choice" abortion is really a religious position. But it is. The Jews have successfully hoodwinked people into thinking that "pro-life" is a religious position. The truth is exactly the reverse. Christianity and Judaism take diametrically opposed views on the humanity of a fetus. Anyone who wants to understand what the Jewish religious view on abortion is should consult an essay, "Jewish Attitudes Towards Abortion, Notes on David M. Feldman, This Matter of Abortion," ch. 9, *Health and Medicine in the Jewish Tradition, L'Hayyim—To Life* (New York: Crossroad, 1986).

It is impossible, within the context of a short essay, to examine all of Rabbi Feldman's arguments. It is, however, possible to quote sufficient passages to make plain what the Jewish position really is. Then, the reader may judge for himself how the Jewish religious position has been transmuted into the law under the guise of a secular legal concept. Rabbi Feldman writes:

"Again I must say to you that you have first got to answer the prior question. Is abortion murder? If it is, then you cannot talk about women's rights. There are no rights to murder. . . . But if abortion is not murder, then we can talk about it. Then I would say that the state's law (forbidding abortion) does infringe on the rights of women. I would go much further and say that it infringes even more than you might think. Because in the Jewish legal-moral tradition an abortion, the mother's welfare plays an even greater role than NOW (National Organization of Women) would claim. A principle in the Jewish view of the matter is, *tza'ara d'gufah kadim*, that her welfare, avoidance of her pain, comes first. Accordingly, maternal indications for abortion do count where fetal indications do not."

As these initial comments suggest, Feldman wants to take care that the reader understands Jewish perspectives on their own terms, not simply as warrants for a pro-choice position supported by more familiar, but more secular notions (e.g., involving rights). To make this point in a last way, he notes that in Jewish teaching, in contrast with other possible rights arguments, it's not that the fetus has a right to be born or that the husband has a right to his progeny, but it's the welfare of the mother that is the first, and to some the only, consideration that warrants abortion.

"The Talmud considers treating the fetus as a *rodef*, specifically, an aggressor against its mother, and making that the reason why abortion to save the mother's life is permitted. After rejecting this argument because the embryo lacks the intent to be an aggressor, the rabbis go on to reason that the fetus is part of its mother's body, rather than an independent entity." [Sound familiar?]

"The law of homicide in the Torah, in one of its formulations, reads: '*makkah ish*,' 'he who smites a man. . . .' Does this include any man, say a day-old child? Yes, says the Talmud, citing another text: '. . . *Ki yakkeh kol nefesh adam*' or 'If one smites any *nefesh adam*'—literally any human person. (Whereas we may not be sure that the newborn babe has completed its term and is *a bar kayamma*, fully viable, until 30 days after birth, he is fully human from the moment of birth. If he dies before his 30th day, no funeral or shivah rites are applicable either. But active destruction of a born child of even doubtful validity is here definitely forbidden.)

"The 'any' (*kol*) is understood to include the day-old child, but the '*nefesh adam*' is taken to exclude the fetus in the womb. The fetus in the womb, says Rashi, classic commentator on the bible and Talmud, is '*lav nefish hu*,' not a person, until he comes into the world. Feticide, then, does not constitute homicide, and the basis for denying it capital-crime status in Jewish law—even for those rabbis who may have wanted to rule otherwise—is scriptural.'"

"There we have it. All the nonsense about an unborn life being potential rather than actual, all the claims that it is merely a part of its mothers body, all the rhetoric about its non-human standing until it enters the world, all the posturing about the convenience of the mother and her alleged right to 'control her body,' are nothing more than Jewish religious Voodoo. It is the logic of the Synagogue of Satan dressed up in *Brown v. Board of Education* legal sophistry known as *Roe v. Wade*."

Judaism Negatively Influences Western Culture

Once more, a courageous Judaic voice, Dr. Henry Makow, tells the truth about the impact of the Talmudic religion on civilization and society. Unfortunately, this is fundamentally a *fait accompli*:

"Judaism is a conspiracy against Christian Western civilization which has succeeded to such an extent that it cannot even be mentioned. It has inspired the bankers to recast society so there will be no families, no marriages, no private property and no freedom. It has divorced society from God, who is synonymous with absolute truth and justice It has inundated us with pornography and trivia and debased culture. It has poisoned the well of gender and degraded relations between men and women. We live in a decadent, superficial, hypocritical society where people sell their souls for money and sex, and where mass media and education are devoted to propaganda and indoctrination. Denied the truth, we are kept in a state of arrested development, befitting children or cattle. The peoples of the world and even their governments are only children under age. (Protocols of Zion, 15). We can be as politically correct as long as we want, but we can't escape the fact that mankind is in the thrall of a satanic force bent on enslaving us." —Dr. Henry Makow, writing on the life and works of Robert Edmondson.

Halakha and Tikkun Olam

Halakha is similar to the Chinese concept of Tao, the Way. It is completely inclusive. Talmudic law is all one needs to be a good and faithful practitioner of Judaism. But on a more mystical level, Halakha melds with the Kabalistic concept of Tikkun Olam, the repairing, remaking or perfecting of the world. When Halakha rules, all will be correct and proper. The ultimate Judaic world order will exist.

"World Repair" Tikkun Olam

Extremist and expansionist Muslims all dream of the day when Koranic sharia law universally rules. Similarly, some Judaists pray for the time when Talmudic Halakha law and Noahide law have full dominion all over the world.

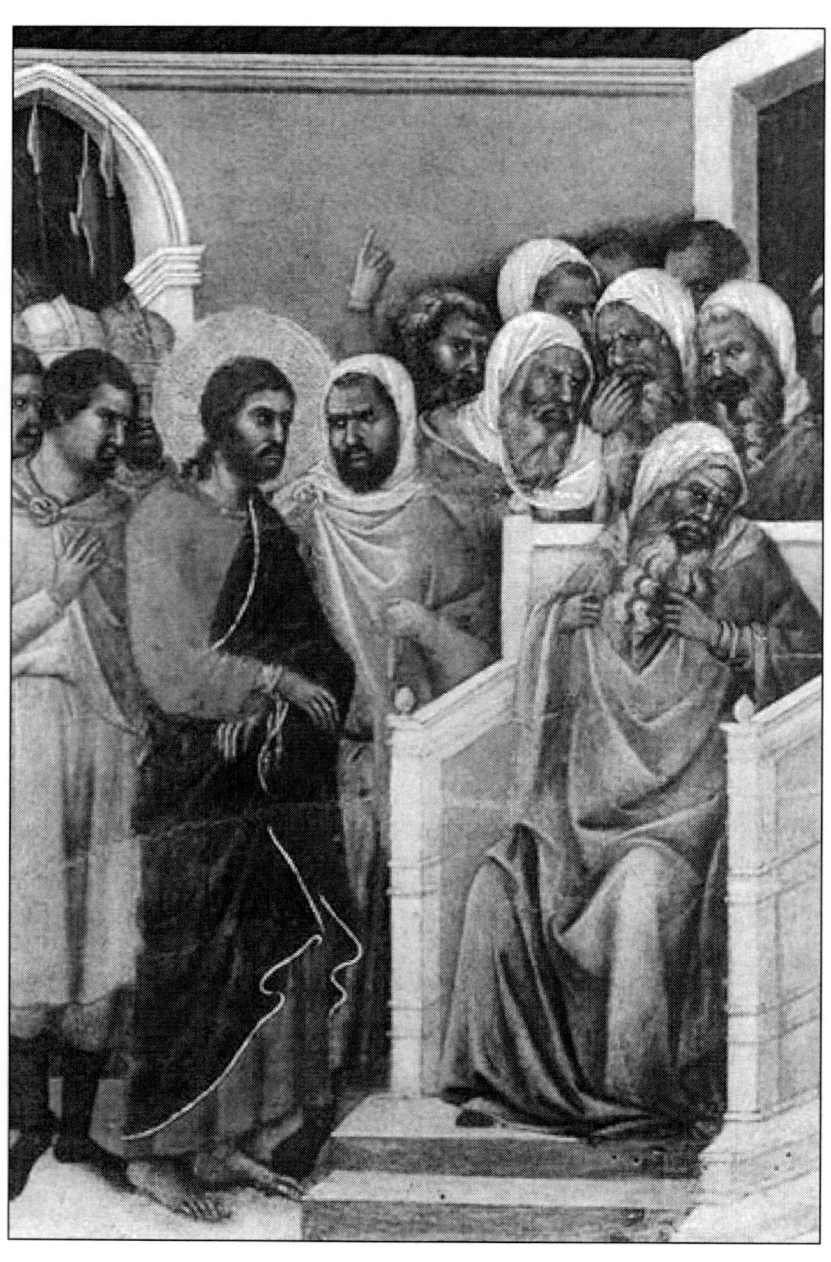

Jesus brought before Caiaphas.

CHAPTER 15

Judaism & Christianity: A Dysfunctional Relationship

Sir Richard Burton was truly a man of many wonders, but I was most impressed by his skills in Semitic languages, not to mention his general knowledge as an ethnologist, world traveler and explorer of other lands and cultures. All of this (and more) is revealed as we focus on his unique interpretation of Judaic culture, the writings known as Talmud and their ancient language. He was among the foremost linguists of his day. By the way, Burton, just as Eisenmenger and Luther, was fully fluent in Hebrew and other Semitic languages, but his selections and commentary on Talmudic texts are not colored by religious beliefs. And he is not obsessed with converting the Jews; far from it. As for being informative to Christians, you'll soon see his commentary is unparalleled. So with Burton and with me, a preoccupation with converting anyone is not a problem.

Burton has a veritable wealth of information to convey, not only about Jewish writings, but about the lives and practices of

Jews within European society. He explains that their behavior, their basic philosophy of life, is rooted in the Talmud. Through his fluent comprehension of Hebrew, he achieved a depth of understanding and vision that few English speakers can ever hope to attain. Once you understand the importance and basic intent of the Talmud, this aids you greatly in understanding other things about Judaism and its impact on world history and current events. Burton's book is a great "entry portal" to a higher level of understanding about Talmudic Judaism. Especially today, we are often reminded, mostly by Christians, that their religion allegedly came from Judaism and owes a great debt to it. If we say much to them, eventually we will be reminded that "Jesus was a Jew" and that "God meant the Holy Land for the Jews."

The Realities About Judaics Converting to Christianity

Johannes Eisenmenger and Martin Luther, his spiritual mentor, were somewhat alike. Both were respected scholars, fluent in Hebrew and other Semitic languages, and both mistakenly thought that Judaics should or would convert to the supposedly more logical and purer Protestant Christian faith, strongly rooted in the Old Testament. As we know, Luther did his own translations of both the Old and New Testaments. Beyond that, both he and Eisenmenger targeted the Talmud in order to understand the real nature of Judaism, so they could more effectively reach out to and convert Judaics. This did not work very well. In several ways, Martin Luther was like the earlier religious eclectic, Mohammed. He also assumed that the Judaic tribes of the Arabian peninsula would naturally be drawn to his purer and simpler form of Semitic faith. Both religious reformers were tragically wrong. Luther

launched a literary and theological attack in retaliation, and Mohammed launched a series of jihads that eventually either forcibly
converted or drove the Judaic Arab tribes out of the region.

Jews and Christians

"The English Jew is not seen to be standing aloof from England
and Englishmen. But it is impossible there should not be some
sort of social barrier between the Jew and the Christian. They cannot intermarry except for special political or other cogent reasons,
and it necessarily chills the kindness and intimacy of [social] intercourse when all the young people know that friendship can
never grow into anything else. In order to overcome this obstacle
many wealthy Jews have chosen to abjure their religion and enroll
their households in the Christian communion. . . . If they are not
decoyed into Christianity by their social aspirations, Jews are unas-
sailable, for the most part, by the force of either persecution or argument; and although there are some conversions to be attributed
to Christian reasoning or Christian gold, they are probably coun-
terbalanced by the accessions to Judaism of Christian women who
marry Jewish husbands." —Burton, *The Jew, the Gypsy and El Islan*,
1898, pp. 42-43

According to Harold Rosenthal: "Many rabbis now hold pro-
fessorships in supposedly Christian theological seminaries. Jews
are amazed by the Christians' stupidity in receiving Jewish teachings and propagating them as their own. As Henry Ford stated:
'The Christian cannot read his bible except through Jewish spectacles, and, therefore, reads it wrong.'" (*The International Jew*, Vol.
IV, p. 238)

Quoting Rosenthal from his interview directly: "As a result,
Christians don't have God's word on a certain matter; they have

the Jew's word. Judaism is not only the teaching of the synagogue, but also the doctrine of every 'Christian church' in America. Through our propaganda the church has become our most avid supporter. This has even given us a special place in society; they believe the lie that we are the 'chosen people' and they, gentiles."
—Harold Rosenthal interview

Talmudic Influences on the Christian Bible

From the beginning, the Talmudists set out to undermine and dilute the integrity of the text. This comes from Pastor V.S. Herrell's *The History of the Bible*, 2000:

"The first attempt to Judaize the Greek scriptures was made by Aquila, who was a pagan convert to Judaism. . . between 117-138 A.D. . . . There was an organized attempt by the Jews to change the Hebrew text even before the Masoretes. . . . Talmudic Jews had as early as the late first century adopted a Hebrew text that was markedly different from the original Hebrew, which was better represented by the [Greek] Alexandrian Septuagint by comparing it to their own Hebrew revision and trying to deceive the Christians into believing that the Septuagint was flawed."

The King James or Authorized Version

Pastor Herrell continues: "Begun in 1607 and published in 1611, this translation was the result of 47 men working at the appointment of the homosexual King James I. By constraints issued for the construction of the bible, it was based largely on the Bishop's Bible [1568; a revision of the Great Bible of 1539], although Tyndale's, Matthew's, Coverdale's and the Geneva Bible were consulted. Since the Talmudic, Masoretic Hebrew was used as the authority for the Old Testament (and not the Latin as before), many of the Old Testament translators, who made up the bulk of the team, were trained in Talmudic Jewish synagogues in preparation for the work. At the time of translation, of the few manuscripts available to them, none were older than 1000 A.D. (with the exception of the Bezae uncial). In many parts, no Greek manuscripts were available for the New Testament, such as in Revelation, where Latin was translated back into Greek and then into English. This was not the first bible to be authorized by the throne of England, and it was never even accepted by King James himself, but only called authorized because it was authorized to be printed."

After this, Pastor Herrell and I diverge theologically and historically in other directions, but his small book provides a clear and truthful look at the highly vaunted *King James Bible* as well as some other topics.

What Is Judaism? Who Are the Pharisees?

As we know, today's Christians and Judaists moved closer together. Many Christians proudly emphasize their Judaic roots. Beginning in the late 1960s and early 1970s the misnomer "Judeo-Christian" came into common usage. This completely contradicts and conflicts with the teachings and actions of Jesus and the early church. For those who actually read the words of their Savior, this is crass philo-Semitism, nothing but the usual glorification of the Jews, who can do no wrong.

In the 1920s, Henry Ford spent several million dollars researching Judaism, resulting in his world-famous edition of The Protocols of the Learned Elders of Zion. This not only contained the Protocols, but several chapters intricately discussing Judaism and the Talmud. The following is from a chapter entitled "Judaism: The Pharisees":

"The attitude of Jesus Christ to this sect is definitely expressed in the New Testament (see Luke 11 and John 8). Exoteric Judaism, the Jewish religion as practiced in the 20th century, is based on the Old Testament, and on equally ancient commentaries on it, preserved for ages as oral traditions, and known under the general name of the Talmud. All copies of this book were ordered to be burned by Philip IV, the Fair, king of France, in 1306, but the book survived the holocaust.

"We know that the Jewish god is not the father of all men and the ideal of love, justice and mercy, like the Christian God, or even like Ahura-Mazda or Brahma. On the contrary, he is the god of vengeance down to the fourth generation, just and merciful only to his own people, but foe to all other nations, denying the human rights and commanding their enslavement that Israel might appropriate their riches and rule over them."

The Old Testament and the Talmud speak clearly and unequivocally:

"And when the lord thy god shall deliver them before thee; thou shalt smite them and utterly destroy them; thou shalt make no covenant with them, nor show mercy to them." —Deut. 7:2.

"For thou are a holy people unto the lord thy god: the lord thy god hath chosen thee to be a special people unto himself; above all people that are upon the face of the Earth." —Deut. 7:6.

"You are human beings, but the nations of the world are not human beings but beasts." —Baba Mecia 114, 6.

"When one sees inhabited houses of the goy one says, 'The lord will destroy the house of the proud.' And when one sees them destroyed, he says, 'The lord god of vengeance has revealed himself.'" —Berachot 58, 6.

A What-If Scenario

For those who wonder what all this old stuff has to do with current events, we offer the following what-if scenario for the Jewish conquest of Jerusalem. It was written in the late 19th century, a time when Zionism, a political (not a religious) movement led by a cabal of thugs which successfully attached itself to the Judaic religion and the Old Testament mythology, was pushing hard for a "Jewish homeland" in old Palestine, then a part of the Ottoman empire. Burton had a fear of this, and speculated on what a bizarre scenario it would be. He was right:

"[Those who know the Jews]. . . will have no trouble in replying. A people whose highest ideas of religious existence are the superstitious sanctification of Sabbath, the washing of hands, the blowing of ram's horns, the saving rite of circumcision, and the thousand external functions compensating for moral delinquencies, with Abraham sitting at the gate of hell to keep it closed for Jews; a community which would declare marriage impossible to some 12 millions of gentiles, forbid them the Sabbath, and sentence to death every 'stranger' reading an Old Testament; which would have all the Ger who are not idolaters without religion, whilst forbidding those whom it calls 'idolaters' (the Christians) to exercise the commonest feelings of humanity; which would degrade and insult one-half of humanity, the weaker sex, and which would sanction slavery, and at the same time oppress and vilify its slaves by placing them on a level with oxen and asses; a faith which, abounding in heathen practices, would encourage the study of the black arts, would loosen every moral obligation, would grant dispensations to men's oaths and would sanction the murder of the unlearned; a system of injustice, whose Sanhedrns, at once heathenish and unlawful, have distinguished themselves only for their force and fraud, for superabundant self-conceit, for cold-blooded cruelty, and for unrelenting enmity to all human nature—such conditions, it is evident, are not calculated to create or to preserve national life.

"The civilized world would never endure the presence of a creed which says to man, 'Hate thy neighbor unless he be one of ye,' or of a code written in blood, not in ink, which visits the least infractions of the rabbinical laws with exorcism and excommunication, with stoning and flogging to death. A year of such spectacles would more than suffice to excite the wrath and revenge of outraged humanity; the race, cruel, fierce, dogged and desperate as in the days of Titus and Hadrian, would defend itself to the last; the result would be another siege and capture of Jerusalem, and the 'chosen people' would once more lie prostrate in their blood and be stamped out of the Holy Land." —Burton, pp. 68-70

Weep, wail and lament with us, Sir Richard, from your catbird seat in the Great Beyond. Many of your words have come to pass—and so much more. The Zionists not only got their independent state, they infiltrated themselves into almost all the great power bases of the world—governmental, financial and religious. And something more, something you could never have known or even dreamed in your worst nightmares—they have weapons of mass destruction. What's more, they express their willingness to use them.

"It has truly been said, 'Every nation gets the Jew it deserves,' and it may well be that the superstitions and cruelties of the Eastern Jews have been generated in them by long centuries of oppression and wrong. From these superstitions and cruelties the enlightened and highly favored Jews in England naturally shrink with abhorrence and repudiation; but it does not therefore follow they have no existence among their less fortunate Eastern brethren." —Burton, pp. x-xi.

Strack, in his *The Jew and Human Sacrifice*, tells us: "Sepher Fephuoth, 19 a.b.: In order to stop an enemy's tongue, take wax of an Atonement Day candle, put a spider in it, then stick it in your mouth and speak, 'As the spider endures in the wax, so may all enemies, who do evil, be in my hand and power, that I may be able to do them evil, but not they me'."

After the fall of Granada, Ferdinand and Isabella issued an Edict of Expulsion (The Alhambra Decree) ordering all Jews to leave by 31 July, one day before Tisha B'Av, commemorating the destruction of Jerusalem by Titus and his Roman Legions.

CHAPTER 16

Judaism & Christianity: A Focus on the Iberian Expulsions

While the Iberian expulsions are crucial events in Judaic cultural history, the real story about what happened is seldom told. When we look back, numerous governments on all levels eventually tried expulsion as a remedy for problems with the Jews. Our focus is on old Spain and Portugal for it was in Muslim Iberia that a culture existed in which Islam ruled, but under sharia law included the other two "religions of the book" in a truly multicultural setting. Arabs, Berbers and other Muslims began their conquest of al Andalus (Arabic for Iberia or Spain) in A.D. 711. Eventually, several Islamic states were created.

The Caliphate of Cordoba was a major power in the early 900s. Later on, the Muslim powers broke up into ministates. This bolstered the Christian powers to the north, beginning the Reconquista, the Reconquest. When Granada fell in 1492, the peninsula was completely in Christian hands. But even before then, some

Muslims saw what was coming and returned to North Africa before the final defeat. Some remained and converted to Catholicism; they are called Moriscos. Some Muslims were also permitted to stay without converting; they are called Mudijares. Jews had already lived in Spain before the Muslim armies came. More came with the jihad.

The full Reconquista took several centuries. No one really knows how many Jews were in Iberia nor how many departed with the Muslims before 1492, but significant numbers remained in the peninsula. In areas already reconquered, some Jews converted rather than leave, forced into a religion they resented and detested. They were commonly called marranos (meaning pig or pork), more politely called nuevo Christianos (new Christians) or just conversos (converts). The Mediterranean Jews were sea traders, merchants, managers and moneylenders. Even those who converted stayed in those trades. Their history and their continuing presence during and after the Reconquista caused resentment.

At the very least, Jews were commonly seen as collaborators with the Muslims. Many Spaniards felt all Jews and Muslims should become Christians or leave. Even though under heavy pressure, some devout Jews refused to convert.

Their former co-religionists, the marranos/conversos, were some of the most avid advocates of expulsion, demonstrating their support of the church. Some sources say hundreds of thousands, maybe over a million Jews were expelled in 1492, but this does not conform to the facts.

Writers in past times often overestimated the impact of the Iberian expulsions. Today, most scholars agree that no more 200,000 (some say less) were actually expelled. Regardless of the numbers, it was a traumatic event marking an end to a centuries-old Jewish presence in Iberia.

The Edict of Expulsion

After the fall of Granada, Ferdinand and Isabella issued an edict of expulsion (the Alhambra Decree) ordering all Jews to leave by July 31, one day before Tisha B'Av, commemorating the destruction of Jerusalem by Titus and his Roman legions. They could take personal property, but not gold, silver or other money. The edict was issued for multiple reasons. Among other things, Jews were accused of collaborating with the Muslim forces as spies and saboteurs, opening the gates to the enemy. Not only that, but as the Christian armies gained territory, Jews were under heavy pressure to convert, and a goodly number of them did. Forced conversions are never sincere and create continuing problems. Other Jews converted out of convenience and for business reasons, thus entering gentile culture. It is estimated that at least 20% of Spanish and Portuguese families descend from mixed marriages with Mudijares, Moriscos and marranos. As we might expect, many conversos relapsed into Judaism due to the proximity of Jews and continuing close contact. Some converts continued wearing a mask, secretly practicing Judaic rites, eventually bringing on the notorious Spanish Inquisition. Of course, all Marranos were suspect and might be challenged at any time to proclaim their faith. Rich Jews were envied and hated for their wheeling and dealing, but were essential components in the financial system of the day. Remember that departing Jews had to leave all their gold and silver behind, presumably in the hands of the royal treasury. Of course, any debts payable to the Jews became null and void. All of this was a convenient bailout and cash stimulus to the economy, then recovering and reorganizing after centuries of warfare. In light of this, Sir Richard Burton said the expulsion was all about the money.

We learn this from *The Jew, the Gypsy and El Islam* (1898):

"Presently, when the revenues of the Catholic kings, Henry III and John II, amounting to 26,500,000 reales. . . fell under Henry IV to 3,540,000, the plethoric moneybags of the Israelites led to the establishment of the Holy Office and its inquisitorial tribunal (January 1481). Finally, as if persecution and death were not sufficient, a wholesale expulsion took place in March, 1492. These horrors are still, after the lapse of ages, fresh in the Jewish mind. I have seen at Jerusalem a khakkham (scribe) so moved by the presence of a Spanish official, that the latter asked me in astonishment how he had managed to offend the host."

And current events back in the day also came to bear. One of the most famous ritual murder crimes was the La Guardia case, in a village near Toledo. This case was widely known and hotly discussed. Both Jews and marranos were arrested. The trial of 1490-91 gave rise to public outcry against the Jews that helped tip the balance in favor of expulsion. See William Walsh's *Isabella of Spain*, where he devotes an entire chapter to the La Guardia affair. Without digressing, ritual murder crimes also preceded expulsions from other European nations.

Jews who convert are often the fiercest opponents of Judaism. Father Tomas de Torquemada, from a family of Judaic converts, was not only the grand inquisitor of Spain. He was personal confessor for King Ferdinand and Queen Isabella and a vehement advocate for expelling the Jews. It is said that the co-monarchs were ready to accept an offering from the moneyed Jews of Spain and rescind the edict. As the wealthy Elders of Zion were literally opening their moneybags, Torquemada rushed out from behind a curtain with fire in his eyes and a huge crucifix in his right hand. The grand inquisitor flung down the crucifix atop the bags of Jewish gold and shouted, "They sold our Savior once for 30 pieces of silver. Here; you can sell him again." The royal couple reconsidered and rejected the offer, sending the elders away.

Jews were expelled and banned from returning. These Sephardic (the very name means Jews of Spain) Jews exited south to Morocco and Africa, east to Turkey, north to the Netherlands and other parts of Europe, later moving west with the spread of colonization to the New World. They left homes, a highly evolved culture and social positions they had occupied for hundreds of years. But from all of this, a great worldwide network formed. Judaics (and marranos) were soon in every seaport of the world, especially in the Americas, and could get goods (including slaves and other contraband) readily moved and delivered. The conforming Catholic converts in Iberia wanted the practicing Jews out of the realm and robustly promoted expulsion. The inquisition was brought on by false converts who secretly practiced Judaic rites and covertly observed holidays. While some must have been unjustly accused, the old records prove that false converts were not all that uncommon. Moreover, the ecclesiastical courts never dealt with practicing Jews, just with professed Christians. For more on the story, see William Walsh's *Characters of the Inquisition.*

Many nations dealt with their Jewish populations in the same way, expelling them from the land. But more often than not, this was not complete. Some Jews just converted. Those who served in important posts were quietly and unofficially allowed to stay and/or to return after the excitement died down. Naturally, this served to disperse the Jews even more globally than they already were. Says Johnson:

"Jews were exceptionally adept at gathering and making use of commercial intelligence. This was the biggest single factor in Jewish trading and financial success. By the time of the Industrial Revolution, they had been operating family trading networks, over a growing area, for the best part of two millennia. They ran sensitive and speedy information systems which enabled them to respond rapidly to political and military events and to the changing demands of regional and world markets. Such families as the Lopez or Mendes of Bordeaux, the Caceres of Hamburg, the Sassoons of Baghdad, the Pereiras, the D'Acostas, the Coneglianos and the Ahadibs, operating from branches in many cities, were among the best-informed people in the world, long before the Rothchilds set up their own commercial diaspora." —Johnson, *A History of the Jews* (NY: Harper, 1987), p. 305.

The map here shows major expulsions and the routes taken.

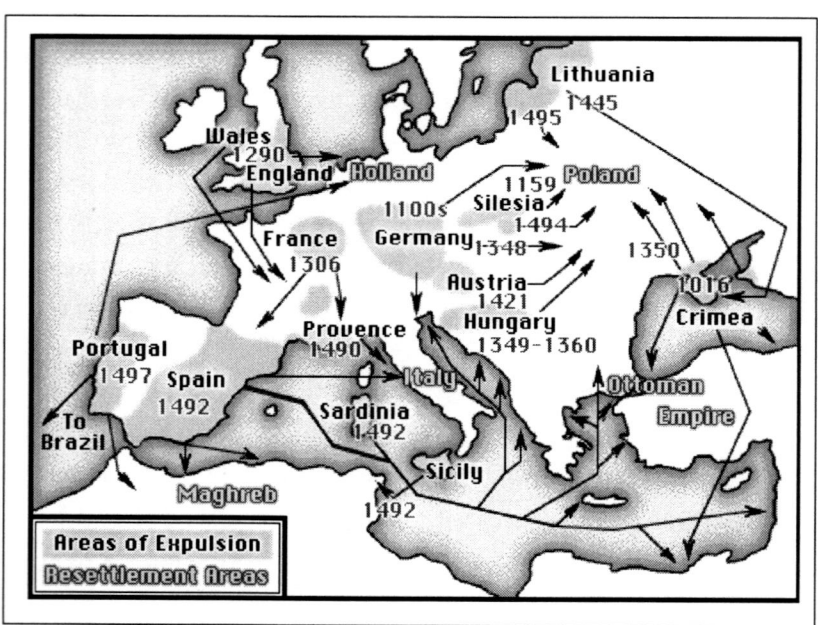

"Finally, the impact of the Spanish Inquisition on Iberian Jewry has been ridiculously exaggerated. In the whole of Catholic inquisitions from early 13th-century France to early 17th-century Spain and Portugal, not more than 5,000 Jewish families suffered capital and less severe punishment at the hands of the church courts." —Norman Cantor, general editor, *Encyclopedia of the Middle Ages.*

Dr. Cantor recognizes that conversos played a major role in lobbying for the expulsion of the remaining Jews who refused baptism (modern historians have revised their opinions as to the severity of the 1492 expulsions, citing very low numbers):

"What happened in 1492 was as much an onslaught by Jewish converts on the remaining minority of faithful Jews (probably 200,000) as an attack by an intransigent church and a compliant monarchy. The demographic importance of the famous expulsion of 1492 has also been greatly exaggerated. The traditional figure of 300,000 Jews departing—mostly at first to Portugal, and from there eventually to Holland and the Turkish empire—cannot be sustained by modern research. The figure of voluntary exile lies at between an eighth to a third of that figure." —Cantor

Jews were not to return to al Andalus for hundreds of years. The government of Spain officially rescinded the expulsion decree in 1990, and welcomed Jews to return. So far neither party has raised the potentially ugly questions of reparations or restoration of properties and moneys (expropriated by both state and church) formerly belonging to Jews.

Perhaps Spain was spared by the world Zionist apparatus since it took the politically correct position. Spain has "gone to confession and repented," apologizing and embracing the Jews and their Israeli ministate. From both the expulsions and the virulent antipathy of the Catholic Church and state, we see the basis for Talmudic texts dealing harshly with Christians as well as Judaics who convert. The culture war continues. The Talmud tells the tale (from Burton):

"The Jew must not contract friendship with gentiles. . . . He must not eat bread prepared by the heathen, for fear of undue intimacy being the result. . . . A Jew abandoning the faith of Israel must die. . . . All who admit to the doctrine of the Trinity, whether they be Jewish perverts, Christians, Muslims or pagans; all Hebrews who have violated the secrets of the synagogue, and all those especially who speak against or who injure a co-religionist, have forfeited their lives. . . . This is an invariable rule."

And this from the *Book of Libbre David*, 37: "To communicate anything to a goy about our religious relations would be equal to the killing of all the Jews. . . ."

And check out the following:

"If a Jew can deceive idolaters by making them think he is a follower of their cult, it is permitted to do so." —Iore de'ah, 157, 2.

"It is a mitzvah [religious duty], however, to eradicate Jewish traitors, minim [Christians], and *apikorsim* [heretics] and to cause them to descend to the pit of destruction, since they cause difficulty to the Jews and sway the people away from god, as did Jesus of Nazareth and his students, and Tzadok, Baithos and their students. May the name of the wicked rot." —Maimonides, *Mishneh Torah*, Chapter 10.

"Christians and others who reject the Talmud will go to hell and be punished there for all generations." —Rosh Hashanah 17a.

"Those who read the New Testament (uncanonical books) will have no portion in the world to come." —Sanhedrin 90a.

"Jews must destroy the books of the Christians, i.e., the New Testament." —Shabbath 116a.

"It is not permitted to imitate the customs of the Akum [Christians], nor to act like them. Nor is it permitted to wear clothes like the Akum, not to comb the hair as they do. . . neither must Jews build houses that look like temples of the Akum." —Iore de'ah 178, 1.

The Wandering Jew vis-á-vis the West
—A Culture War

Judaism and Western culture seem locked in a perpetual *kul-turkampf*. In many ways, neither really understands the other. Indo-Europeans settled land, raised livestock and crops, later building cities. The Egypto-Semitic Habiru tribes were wandering nomads. While not Semites, the Khazar convert Jews were migratory Central Asian tribes folk, never really attached to one place for long. While it at first seems odd with tribes of the desert and the plains, Jews adapted well to city life all over the world. The Khazars joined with the Sephardic Oriental Jews to create the modern Talmudic religion, which the Khazars by and large dominate. Their basic culture and ethnic mindset is quite different from the occidental ethos, making for persistent and sometimes intense problems as evidenced in the expulsions. All of this poses a question: Is the Talmudic mindset (ergo the Talmudic religion) really compatible with Western civilization? In his classic work, *Imperium*, Francis Parker Yockey addresses these matters:

"What did not destroy the Jews made them stronger, and separated them further than ever from the host-peoples, physically and spiritually. During the centuries of our Western history, the problems and developments which roused fundamental excitement in the West did not touch the problemless Jew, whose inner life had passed into fixity with the completion of the culture which created this Jewish church-state-people-nation. Empty for him were the conflict of empire and papacy, the Reformation, the Age of Discovery. He looked upon them purely as a spectator. His only question was what they might mean to him. The idea of his taking part in them, or making sacrifices for one side or another, never came up. The British in India looked upon disturbances among the indigenous populations with the same eye. In his ghet-toes distributed over Europe, all was uniform: the food-prohibi-tions, the Talmudic dualistic ethics, one for the goy and another for the Jew, the legal system, the phylacteries, the ritual, the feeling. His Sufism, his Hasidim sect, his Kabbalism, his religious leaders like Baal Shem, his Zaddikism, are equally unintelligible to West-erners. Not only unintelligible, but uninteresting.

"The Westerner was absorbed in the intense conflicts of his own culture, and did not observe, except in relation to himself, the life of the Jew in his midst. Not until the externalized, fact-sensitive 20th century, did the Western culture notice the Jew as a cultural phenomenon. In Gothic times, until the Reformation, it saw him as a heathen and usurer, in the Counter-Reformation as a shrewd businessman, in the Enlightenment as a civilized man of the world, in the Age of Rationalism as a fighter in the van of intellectual liberation from the bonds of the culture and its tradi-tions. The 20th century saw for the first time that he had his own public life, his own world down to the details. It realized that the comprehensiveness of his outlook was the equivalent of its own in breadth and depth, and therefore alien in a total sense which was never before suspected. In its previous centuries, the view-point of the West toward the Jew was limited by its stage of devel-opment at the time, but with the 20th century and its universal outlook, the entirety of what has been called 'the Jewish problem' is seen for the first time.

"Not race, not religion, not ethics, not nationality, not political allegiance—but something which includes them all, separates the Jew from the West—culture. Culture embraces the totality of world-outlook: science, art, philosophy, religion, technics, eco-nomics, law, society, politics. In every branch of the Western cul-ture, the Jew has developed his own taste and preference, and

when he intervenes in the public life of the Western peoples, he conducts himself in a distinct fashion, namely in the style of the public life of the Jewish church-state-nation-people-race. This public life was invisible to the inward West until the 20th century."
—*Imperium*

The European expulsions, especially those from Iberia, must be seen against this historical backdrop as a series of battles in a continuing cultural conflict. Like battles in many wars, there was no victor. Both sides lost and both cultures were irrevocably changed. We can sum this up by paraphrasing Nietzsche. It's the longest ongoing conflict, Judea against the West, the West against Judea.

Church officials order copies of the Talmud burned.

CHAPTER 17

Judaism & Christianity: Banning & Burning the Talmud

One of the many unlearned lessons of history is that book banning, burning and censorship rarely works. But more importantly, it often has the opposite effect, drawing the attention of people who had never even heard of the works being proscribed. And further, it promotes an even deeper and dogged sense of tradition and preservation among the devotees. Nevertheless, this failed strategy was widely and repeatedly employed against the Talmud. Big hay wagons loaded with Hebrew writings were put to the torch across Europe. Why was this done? For one thing, the Catholic Church never really gave up trying to convert the Jews, never fully recovering from stern Jewish rebuffs over the centuries. After countless attempts in countless places, the number of converts could barely be considered even a handful. Furthermore, false converts like the marranos of Spain and Portugal created all kinds of additional problems, eventually causing the inquisition. The church had much time to reflect on her failure to win over the "Sons of Abraham" as the Roman

Church sometimes called them. When the Vatican theologians and bishops distilled everything down, they found the Talmud and its teachings deep at the roots of the rejection, hence their misplaced and misguided efforts to excise and remove it from Jewish life. This impossible task had a long history of failure.

Why was the Talmud forbidden to be shown to non-Jews? Why was it burned over and over by order of kings and bishops and popes, excoriated by Martin Luther, denounced everywhere, and its followers exiled from one country after another down through the centuries? The Talmud was burned from the 11th to the 18th in Italy, France, Germany, Spain and many other countries. This period precisely coincides with the Khazarian Eastern European Jews moving from the east into Europe. By the 1200s they penetrated to the western edges of the continent and into the British Isles. The Khazar converts were Talmudists par excellence, bringing it everywhere they went. What follows is but a partial list of the major instances of banning and burning:

1239 in Rome by Pope Gregory
1244 in Paris by King Louis IX
1244 in Rome by Innocent IX
1248 in Paris by Cardinal Legate Odo
1299 in Paris by Philip the Fair
1309 in Paris by Philip the Fair
1319 in Toulouse by King Louis
1322 in Rome by Pope John XXII
1553 in Rome by Pope Julius III
1557 in Poland by the Frankists
1558 in Rome by Cardinal Ghislieri
1559 in Rome by Sextus Sinensis

Why were the Talmudic writings so vigorously and vehemently pursued and attacked? Was it just European Catholic Jew-hate and anti-Semitism? The following passages were collected by Randulf Johan Hansen, a Revisionist writer and webmaster in Norwegian, German and English. Visit him online at www.thenew-sturmer.com. Here is a particularly ugly collection of texts. It is not surprising that the church and the governments back in older times to radical action against such statements. Even here in the permissive and expressive 21st century, some of this is quite offensive:

Jews Have Superior Legal Status

To quote the Talmud: Baba Kamma 37b. "If an ox of an Israelite gores an ox of a Canaanite there is no liability; but if an ox of a Canaanite gores an ox of an Israelite . . . the payment is to be in full."

Baba Mezia 24a. "If a Jew finds an object lost by a gentile ('heathen') it does not have to be returned." (Affirmed also in Baba Kamma 113b).

Sanhedrin 76a. God will not spare a Jew who "marries his daughter to an old man or takes a wife for his infant son or returns a lost article to a Cuthean [non-Jew]. . . ."

Sanhedrin 57a. "When a Jew murders a gentile, there will be no death penalty. What a Jew steals from a gentile he may keep."

Baba Kamma 37b. Gentiles are outside the protection of the law, and god has "exposed their money to Israel."

Baba Kamma 113a. Jews may use lies ("subterfuges") to circumvent a gentile.

Yebamoth 98a. All gentile children are animals.

Abodah Zarah 36b. Gentile girls are in a state of niddah (filth) from birth.

Abodah Zarah 22a 22b. Gentiles prefer sex with cows.

Abodah Zarah 67b. "The vessels of Gentiles, do they not m-part a worsened flavor to the food cooked in them

Gittin 57a. Says Jesus is being boiled in "hot excrement."

Sanhedrin 43a. Jesus deserved execution: "On the eve of the Passover, Yeshu was hanged. . . . Do you suppose that he was one for whom a defense could be made? Was he not a Mesith (enticer)?"

Rosh Hashanah 17a. Christians ("minim") and others who reject the Talmud will go to hell and be punished there for all generations.

Baba Mezia 114a114b. Only Jews are human ("Only ye are designated men"). Also see Kerithoth 6b under the subhead, "Oil of Anointing" and Berakoth 58a in which Gentile women are designated animals ("sheasses").

Sanhedrin 57a. A Jew need not pay a gentile ("Cuthean") the wages owed him for work.

Tall Tales of a Roman Holocaust

Here are two early "holocaust" tales from the Talmud: Gittin 57b. Claims that 4 billion Jews were killed by the Romans in the city of Bethar.

Gittin 58a claims that 16 million Jewish children were wrapped in scrolls and burned alive by the Romans. (Ancient demography indicates that there were not 16 million Jews in the entire world at that time, much less 16 million Jewish children or 4 billion Jews.)

More Sick and Insane Teachings

Gittin 69a. To heal his flesh a Jew should take dust that lies within the shadow of an outdoor toilet, mix it with honey and eat it.

Shabbath 41a. The law regulating the rule for how to urinate in a holy way is given.

Yebamoth 63a. States that Adam had sexual intercourse with all the animals in the Garden of Eden.

Yebamoth 63a. Declares that agriculture is the lowest of occupations.

Sanhedrin 55b. A Jew may marry a three-year-old girl (specifically, "three years and a day" old).

Sanhedrin 54b. A Jew may have sex with a child as long as the child is less than nine years old.

Kethuboth 11b. "When a grownup man has intercourse with a little girl it is nothing."

Yebamoth 59b. A woman who had intercourse with a beast is eligible to marry a Jewish priest. A woman who has sex with a demon is also eligible to marry a Jewish priest.

Abodah Zarah 17a. States that there is not a whore in the world that Rabbi Eleazar has not had sex with.

Hagigah 27a. States that no rabbi can ever go to hell.

Baba Mezia 59b. A rabbi debates god and defeats him. God admits the rabbi won the debate.

Gittin 70a. The rabbis taught: "On coming from a privy (outdoor toilet) a man should not have sexual intercourse till he has waited long enough to walk half a mile, because the demon of the privy is with him for that time; if he does, his children will be epileptic."

Toilet and excrement obsessions are laced throughout the Talmud and were exhibited in Spielberg's *Schindler's List,* where the Hollywood director shows a Jewish child jumping through a toilet seat in an outhouse and falling into a pool of excrement. There the child meets two other Jewish children partially immersed who inform the interloper that this cesspool is their hiding spot exclusively and that he must find his own. These are the kind of disgusting and morbid, psychotic images which Jewish kids are exposed to constantly in the cinematic liturgy of Holocaustianity and for that matter, in the Talmud as well.

Gittin 69b. To heal the disease of pleurisy ("catarrh") a Jew should take the excrement of a white dog and knead it with balsam, but if he can possibly avoid it he should not eat the dog's excrement as it loosens the limbs.

Pesahim 111a. It is forbidden for dogs, women or palm trees to pass between two men, nor may others walk between dogs, women or palm trees. Special dangers are involved if the women are menstruating or sitting at a crossroads.

Menahoth 43b44a. A Jewish man is obligated to say the following prayer every day: Thank you god for not making me a gentile, a woman or a slave.

Shabbath 86a86b. Because Jews are holy they do not have sex during the day unless the house can be made dark. A Jewish scholar can have sex during the day if he uses his garment like a tent to make it dark.

Does the Talmud Sanction Sexual Perversion?

Does the Talmud sanction sexual Perversion? In approaching this question, we remind ourselves again that the Talmud consists of millions of words on almost anything and everything. If you truly feel compelled to learn more, visit Rev. Ted Pike's website and read his well-researched article, "Pedophilia: The Talmud's Dirty Secret."

—http://www.truthtellers.org/alerts/pedophiliasecret.html.

"Our Worst Enemy"?

More could be said and more passages cited, but this seems sufficient. These so-called sacred scripture verses say what they say. If you need more and want to see them for yourself, visit a large library with the Soncino volumes. Be a like a chacham and read the Talmud until your eyes turn red. This literature is said to inspire and enlighten Judaics, but when we look at certain texts, it begs the question of what they are really learning and what kind of principles inspire them. Now you know the real story behind why the Talmud was so reviled and detested.

One of the tribe's own, Rabbi Daniel Lapin, concludes our little exercise with a selection from his rather controversial 2005 article, "Our Worst Enemy" (the title is self-explanatory):

"Was there any form of filth or profligacy, particularly in cultural life, without at least one Jew involved in it? What had to be reckoned heavily against the Jews in my eyes was when I became acquainted with their activity in the press, art, literature and the theater. . . . It sufficed to look at a billboard, to study the names behind the horrible trash they advertised. . . . Is this why the Jews are called the "chosen people"? The fact that nine-tenths of all literary filth, artistic trash and theatrical idiocy can be set to the account of a people constituting hardly one-hundredth of all the country's inhabitants could simply not be talked away; it was the plain truth.

"You'd have to be a recent immigrant from Outer Mongolia not to know of the role that people with Jewish names play in the coarsening of our culture. Almost every American knows this. It is just that most gentiles are too polite to mention it."

The Israeli flag is kind of a map. The large blue stripes at top and bottom symbolize the Nile and Euphrates Rivers. The white space in between symbolizes the biblical Greater Israel, the ultimate dream of the Zionist state. And in the center of this, the Star of David is prominently positioned. The tiny white stripes at the very top and very bottom signify non-Jewish lands.

CHAPTER 18

The Real History of the Hexagram Called the Star of David

Symbols almost always have multi-faceted meanings. A hexagram may be the Star of David to Jews while a Hindu knows it is a Tantric symbol depicting sexual intercourse, and any criminal knows the six-pointed star means the sheriff is here. The hexagram is seen everywhere. In its present incarnation, it is best known as the central logo of Israel's flag. Interestingly, not all Zionists agreed on the design. Theodore Herzl, the father of Zionism, made a simpler suggestion of a white flag with seven gold stars, but by the opening day of the new Israeli ministate, the hexagram was almost a unanimous choice. For some, this is an admirable national and cultural symbol but for Palestinians and others it means death and oppression. The hexagram is a powerful metaphysical and magical symbol, evoking deep feelings. Other symbols have a similar power. Without digressing, the swastika comes to mind as an arouser of strong feelings. Those who study symbology know that it is an eons-old

The Star of David Jewish hexagram.

wind and Sun symbol, found in many other cultures, where it is a symbol of positive virtues and good fortune. Most people suppose a similarly hoary vintage for the so-called Star of David. A symbol as basic and ancient as the inverted triangles has obviously had many meanings, almost all of which were positive. Curiously, it was only in relatively recent times that both the swastika and the hexagram became connected to political movements. Let's take a closer look at the Hebrew hex sign called the Star of David, its real origins, past meanings and what it has come to mean in our world today:

"MAGEN DAVID (David's Shield): The hexagram formed by the combination of two equilateral triangles; used as the symbol of Judaism. It is placed upon synagogues, sacred vessels and the like, and was adopted as a device by the American Publication Society in 1873, the Zionist Congress of Basel, hence by *Die Welt*, the official organ of Zionism, and by other bodies. . . . It is noteworthy, moreover, that the Shield of David is not mentioned in rabbinical literature. . . [it] probably did not originate within rabbinism, the official and dominant Judaism for more than 2,000 years. Nevertheless a David's Shield has recently been noted on a Jewish tombstone at Tarentum, in southern Italy, which may date as early as the third century of the Common Era. The earliest Jewish literary source which mentions it, the 'Eshkol ha-Kofer' of the Karaite Judah Hadassi says: 'Seven names of angels precede the mezuzah; Michael, Garield etc. . . . Tetragrammaton protect thee. And likewise the sign called 'David's Shield' is placed beside the name of each angel.' It was therefore, at this time a sign on amulets. In the magic papyri of antiquity, pentagrams, together with stars and other signs, are frequently found on amulets bearing the Jewish names of god, 'Sabaoth,' 'Adonai,' 'Eloai,' and used to guard against fever and other diseases. Curiously enough, only the pentacle appears, not the hexagram. In the great magic papyrus at Paris and London there are 22 signs sided by side, and a circle with 12 signs, but neither a pentacle nor a hexagram, although there is a triangle, perhaps in place of the latter. In the many illustrations of amulets given by Budge in his Egyptian Magic not a single pentacle or hexagram appears. . . . It is probable that it was the Cabala that derived the symbol from the Templars. The Cabala, in fact, makes use of this sign, arranging the 10 Sephiroth, or spheres, in it, and placing in on amulets. The pentagram, called Solomon's Seal, is also used as a talisman, and . . . the Hindus likewise employed the hexagram as a means of protection . . . . In the synagogues, perhaps, it took the place of the mezuzah, and the name 'Shield of David' may have been given it in virtue of its protective powers. . . the six-pointed star has been used for centuries for magic amulets and cabalistic sorcery."

—*Jewish Encyclopedia*

As we move into modern times, it takes on a political agenda.

"The Rothschild banking dynasty was created by Mayer Amschel Bauer. . . . Bauer changed his name to Rothschild which came from the red shield (*roth schild* in German) which hung over the door of his house in Frankfurt. . . . On the shield was a hexagram, a Star of David or Seal of Solomon and this same symbol is now on the flag of Israel. People think it is a Jewish symbol because of its name and use, but this is nonsense. One was found on the floor of a 1,200-year-old Muslim mosque which stood on the site of present-day Tel Aviv. The Jewish writer, O.J. Graham, in his work *The Six Pointed Star*, says '. . . the six-pointed star made its way from Egyptian pagan rituals of worship, to the goddess Ashteroth and Moloch. . . . So the very name Rothschild comes from an ancient esoteric symbol connected to Egypt as Moloch, the 'god' of sacrifice. The hexagram only became used by the Jewish hierarchy as their symbol with the emergence of the Rothschilds and it has absolutely nothing to do with 'King David' as the Jewish leaders well know. It is on the flag of Israel because Israel is not the land of the Jews, it is the land of the Rothschilds and those who dictate to them from even higher up the Brotherhood pyramid. They created Israel and they control it."

—David Icke, *The Biggest Secret*

The word hex as used in ceremonial magic refers to the hexagram logo. Its use in ritual magic and sorcery became so widespread that hex means a spell or charm worked through black magic, especially a curse. To put a hex on someone is to attempt harm. Kabalistic seals and spells are commonly used by ceremonial magicians. Almost every seal has either a hexagram and/or incantations in Hebrew. Pentagrams or five-pointed stars are used as well. Hebrew hexes and Semitic sorcery are at the heart of the Babylonian Talmud and the accompanying mystical tomes of the

Kabala. Numerologically speaking, the number six (the Hebrew letter vav), and six-sided symbols are crucial and essential. Not to digress, but the holocaust figure of 6 million is part of this Kabalistic magical working. Never forget. In certain Judaic sects and circles, the Kabala is at the core of Judaism.

"We cannot possibly consider the Kabala an isolated fact, accidental in Judaism; on the contrary, it is its heart and soul." Adolphe Franck, *The Kabbalah, the Religious Philosophy of the Hebrews,* 1940.

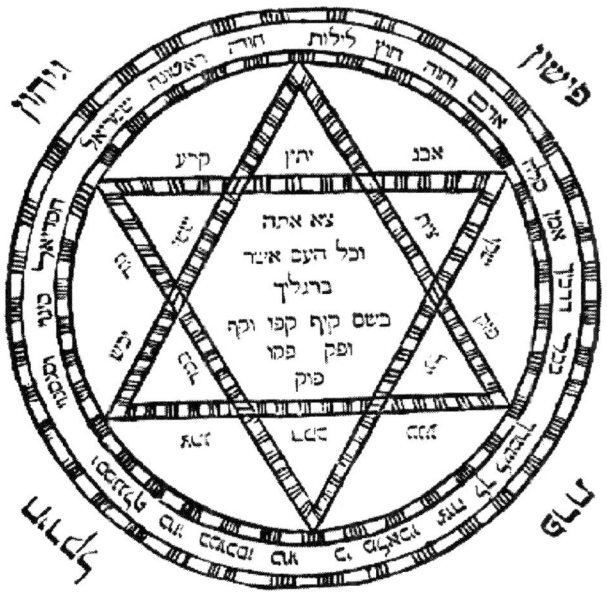

To establish its linkage to the powerful tradition of Solomonic wisdom and Semitic sorcery, the hex sign was also conveniently dubbed the Seal of Solomon, hence covering all the bases and creating imaginary connections to an ancient (and probably exaggerated) Hebrew monarch. Of course, this is the same set of legends found in Freemasonry. Even more to associate it with the

Old Testament legends, the hex sign was also called the Star of Jacob. In his *Dictionary of Symbols* (1961) Dr. Jose Cirlot speaks of the Seal of Solomon:

"This consists of two triangles superimposed and interlaced so as to form a six-pointed star. Wirth terms it the 'star of the microcosm,' or a sign of the spiritual potential of the individual who can endlessly deny himself. In reality it is a symbol of the human soul as a 'conjunction' of consciousness and the unconscious, signified by the intermingling of the triangle (fire) and inverted triangle (water). Both of these are, according to alchemic theory, subject to the principle of the immaterial called Azoth by the philosophers, and represented in the Seal of Solomon by a central point which is not actually portrayed but which has to be seen in the imagination alone, as in some of the mandalas of India and Tibet."

"David's Shield" In Modern Times

We need say no more about its connection to the black arts; this speaks for itself. But, where did the original symbol as used in modern times really come from? Almost every person when asked the question, "What is the origin of the Star of David?" would answer "from the bible." Some might add that it was the symbol of David's kingdom in the Old Testament. However, this is not correct. The symbol as used today is not really all that old. In the 1100s in Khazaria there arose a Jewish messianic movement. In fact, Judaism has a long history of various messiah figures. This is especially true in the fundamentalist Khazarian Judaic Kabalistic sects of Eastern Europe, most notably the Hasidim. This larger grouping consists of many smaller cults, led by messiah-like rebbes called tzaddiks, credited with healing and other supernatural powers. These Zionist forerunners wanted to take Palestine [from the Christians—Ed.] by force. The "brains" of this outfit was one Solomon ben Duji (also rendered Ruhi or Roy), aided by his son and a Palestinian Jewish scribe.

He and a few supporters roamed about, proclaiming their messianic military campaign, but failed to gain any significant following. His son, Menachem, shows up later in Kurdistan, where he actually raised an armed force of local Oriental Jews. They eventually succeeded in actually capturing a fortress near Mosul in present-day Iraq. It was from this geographical pivot point that the son aimed his crusade down through Edessa, then on through Syria into Palestine. While a bit far-reaching, it was certainly not impossible, and he did establish and hold a base camp. Not only that, some Islamic emirs welcomed and aided him in what they saw as a jihad against the Christians. Word spread quickly across the Middle East and many Jews eagerly awaited the liberation of Zion. But the presiding rabbis in Baghdad, then the center of Oriental Jewry, had fear for their own positions, eventually withdrawing their support from Menachem. He was now called David al-Roy (or el-Roy in Arabic), assuming a more messianic moniker. The Oriental Elders of Zion greatly feared him and what he might bring down upon them, and radical steps were taken. David al-Roy was treacherously slain in his sleep c. 1160 by his own father-in-law, who had been bribed to do the foul deed.

"Ever since, it has been suggested, the six-cornered 'Shield of David,' therefore became a decorative motif or a magical emblem, began its career toward becoming the chief national-religious symbol of Judaism. Long used interchangeably with the pentagram of the 'Seal of Solomon,' it was attributed to David in mystic and ethical German writings from the 13th century on, and appeared on the Jewish flag in Prague in 1557."

—S.W. Baron, *A Social and Religious History of the Jews*, 1957.

The Khazar convert Jews began to venerate al-Roy as a great fallen hero, a cult of remembrance and worship growing up around his now-legendary feats. And, as we know, every new cult, political or spiritual, needs a strong, unifying, vibrant symbol for flags, banners, signs etc. The six-pointed star that became the symbol of modern Israel was the same one used by David al-Roy. The story survived into modern times, and so fascinated Benjamin Disraeli that he used it as material for an historical romance called *The Wondrous Tale of Alroy*. Interestingly, the hexagram does not appear on the official state seal, which features the menorah candleholder.

As we see, the modern history of the six-pointed star has nothing to do with the Old Testament or the alleged history of an ancient Middle Eastern kingdom. It is a symbol adopted by the modern descendants of the Khazar proto-Zionists of the mid-1100s. This Central Asian Turko-Mongol tribe of non-Semitic convert Jews now has its independent ministate, so-called, self-styled and misnamed as Israel. That a sorcerer's hex sign is its symbol is quite appropriate.

CHAPTER 19

The Protocols of Zion: Fact or Forgeries?

T his chapter is not intended to be a complete history of the Protocols or to prove their authenticity. These matters are easily found online, in books and other printed matter. The debate as to their provenance never ceases, but regardless of origin, their relevance to world history speaks for itself. While most often renounced, refuted or simply rejected, many feel that if you don't know what is in the Protocols of Zion, you have a knowledge gap. "Forgeries" or not, they speak to what is going on. Some are put off by the Freemasonic references, and say this was just an anti-Masonic document or something written by Maurice Joly. Again, I have no need to "prove" anything. Read the Protocols, read some other opinions and decide for yourself. As to the Freemasonic imagery and phraseology, Nesta Webster puts it in perspective.

"Freemasonry is not to be taken seriously, but may serve as a mask and a means of preparing something quite different. . . . How is it possible to ignore the existence of an occult power at work in the world? Individuals, sects or races fired with the desire for world dominion, have provided the fighting forces of destruction, but behind them are the veritable powers of darkness in eternal conflict with the powers of light."

What follows was first published by *Tsunami Politico* online magazine out of Buenos Aires and later in the Jan./Feb. 2008 issue of *The Barnes Review* historical magazine. It has been re-edited, annotated and illustrated especially for this presentation:

'THE PREDECESSORS TO THE PLANS IN PROCESS ARE A WORK IN PROGRESS, SEVERAL CENTURIES OLD'

We must be the most deceived population of all times, yet when the information-age possibilities are considered, we should be the best informed. But we are not, and are most often our own worst enemy—the willingly deceived Euro-American. We accept, and proclaim from our pulpits and schools, the most idiotic drivel about the modern history of the world. If you do not see at least some of the roles certain conspiracy plans play in world history, then you are among the most deceived of all, so do not bother to read further.

Here is a short item of interest, pointing to a program, plan, plot, cabal or whatever you choose to call it that has been operating for countless centuries. The most agreeable name is Zionism, but because the main participants (but not all) were/are of the Turko-Mongol-Khazarian Central Asian Judaized tribe who began entering Europe in the late 10th century, the most accurate moniker could just as well be Khazarian Zionism. They are not Semites and their forebears never set foot in Palestine; nor did they originally speak Hebrew. The plans for their eventual success are partially revealed in several old documents. One of the most interesting appears below. This 1489/1492 piece seems based on "disaster contingency plans" and protocols already in place long before the letter writers posed their questions. And, just in case you don't know, the plans are succeeding. Not over

500 years ago, but right now.

In 1889, the *Revue des Etudes Juives*, financed by James Rothschild, published two documents putting the Protocols in perspective and demonstrating that the Learned Elders of Zion have been carrying on their plan for centuries. On January 13, 1489 (some sources date it, or a similar document, from Spain in 1492) Chemor (Chamorra in Spanish), Jewish rabbi of Arles in Provence, wrote to the Grand Sanhedrin, which then had its seat in Constantinople, for advice as the people of Arles were threatening their synagogues.

What should they do? What follows refers to a Protocols-like plan, dating from much earlier. The reply is found in the 16th-century Spanish book *La Silva Curiosa* ("The Curious Miscellany") by Julio-Iniguez de Medrano (but only in the Paris Orry, 1608 edition) with the following explanation:

"This letter following was found in the archives of Toledo by the Hermit of Salamanca, while searching the ancient records of the kingdoms of Spain, and it is expressive and remarkable, I wish to write it here.

"Beloved brethren in Moses, we have received your letter in which you tell us of your anxieties and misfortunes which you are enduring. We are pierced by great pain to hear it, as yourselves.

"The advice of the grand satraps and rabbis is the following:

"1. As for what you say that the king of Spain obliges you to become Christians: Do it, since you cannot do otherwise.

"2. As for what you say about the command to despoil you of your property: Make your sons merchants that they may despoil, little by little, the Christians of theirs.

"3. As for what you say about making attempts on your lives: Make your sons doctors and apothecaries, that they may take away Christian lives.

"4. As for what you say of their destroying your synagogues: Make your sons canons and clerics in order that they may destroy their churches.

"5. As for the many other vexations you complain of: arrange that your sons become advocates and lawyers, and see that they always mix in affairs of state, that by putting Christians under your yoke you may dominate the world and be avenged on them.

"6. Do not swerve from this order that we give you, because you will find by experience that humiliated as you are, you will reach the actuality of power.

"Signed: Prince of the Jews of Constantinople."

If you would like to read and circulate *Los Protocolos de los Sabios de Sion* in the Spanish language, just email me for a free MSWord or Adobe pdf e-book version, with my short introduction (also in Spanish). EagleRevisionist@aol.com. My newspaper and internet article entitled "The Ideology of National Revolution" also appears in English and Spanish. http://www.gnosticliberation front.com/ideology__of_national_revolution.htm and http://tsu namipolitico.com/ideologia706.htm.

In an April 20, 1943 Radio Roma broadcast, the eminent poet, philosopher and scholar Ezra Pound said these wise words:

"If or when one mentions the Protocols alleged to be of the Elders of Zion, one is frequently met with the reply: Oh, but they are a forgery. Certainly they are a forgery, and that is the one proof we have of their authenticity. The Jews have worked with forged documents for the past 2,400 years, namely ever since they have had any documents whatsoever. And no one can qualify as a historian of this half-century without having examined the Protocols. . . . What we know for certain is that they were published two decades ago. That Lord Sydenham wrote a preface to them. That their content has been traced to another sketch said to have appeared in the 1340s. The interest in them does not lie in [the] question of their having been, or not been concocted by a legislative assembly of rabbis, democratically elected, or secretly chosen by the Mysterious Order of Seven Branched Antlers or the Bowling Society of Milwaukee.

"Their interest lies in the type of mind, or the state of mind of their authors. . . . What is interesting, perhaps most, to the historian is their definite campaign against history altogether, their declared intention to blot out the classics, to blot out the record, and to dazzle men with talk of tomorrow."

While the Jews and their court historians, paid panderers all, love to rant on and on about the Protocols being a so-called forgery, they never, ever refer to the preceding information or the distinct implication that the Protocols, especially as they were manifested in the late 19th century, are but an overview, a portion of conspiracy plans that have been afoot for centuries. Read the Protocols again. Every point is either in full process or has already happened.

Will the self-deceived ones, of all races and nations, ever wake up? If this were to happen, truly cataclysmic events might occur, as they did in the not-so-distant past. In the present day, the Khazar AshkeNAZI Zionist Israeli apartheid Talmudic terrorist regime seems dangerously close to pushing the envelope a little too far. If people wake up and wise up around the world, this time around, the results could be profoundly different. The Dark Forces know this well, and that is why they fear the Protocols so much, and never cease in their mission to deter their circulation.

Many websites have them posted, so print out the material and pass it on. Take my word for it; you never really know where your copy might end up or who might eventually see it. Sometimes just the simple act of reading can have a profoundly spiritual and intuitive effect on some people. I've seen it happen. Stay clearly sighted on an informational ministry. Reach out and plant a seed, spread the word.

Khazarian Zionism and the dark forces now ride the ascendant wave, and the warriors of truth and light are few and far between. This will change, but we are in a very low phase of the cosmic cycle, when the thugs seem to have their way.

The Protocols have appeared in many languages over the years.

CHAPTER 20

Talmudism Today

A t the same time the author has had to take counsel of prudence in the selection of material, for the Jews have always counted on the fact that, if the whole truth were told in one comprehensive utterance, no one would believe it. Thus, bigots and minds bursting with discoveries they have made, have never been feared by the Jews. People are incapable of believing or receiving certain knowledge which runs counter to their habitual manner of thinking; facts are not accepted on proof, but on understanding." —Israel Moses Sieff as seen in Vol. 4, "Birthing the Phoenix," No. 225 of *The Phoenix Journals*

For those of you who have trekked this far with us, all the way to the end of our safari into the Judaic jungle called Talmud, one way or another you've made a decision. You've read the book and seen the resources and references I assembled. As I told you in the beginning, the most explosive revelations of all come from Judaic folk themselves. Regardless of what some might prefer to believe, when we unveil the actual origins, history and beliefs of Judaism, the results are strikingly revealing and, how shall we say, more than a little bit overwhelming and disconcerting. The old Indo-Aryan religions tell us that all we really see in life is Mahamaya, the Great Illusion, and that we shall not truly ascend to higher levels until we become personally willing to recognize and deal with the truth. Jesus said "you will know the truth, and the truth will set you free."

The Talmud and Zionism

"Zionism is Jewish nationalism." —Rabbi Stephen Wise, 1933

"When the lord thy god shall have brought thee into the land, which thou art going in to possess, and shall have destroyed many nations before thee. . . seven nations much more numerous than thou art, and stronger than thou. And the lord thy god shall have delivered them to thee, thou shalt utterly destroy them. Thou shalt make no league with them, nor show mercy to them." — Deuteronomy 7:1-2

"Every time we do something, you tell me America will do this and will do that. . . . I want to tell you something very clear: Don't worry about American pressure on Israel. We, the Jewish people, control America, and the Americans know it." —Israeli Prime Minister Ariel Sharon, October 3, 2001*

Especially after the Khazar conversion in the eighth century, Talmudism came to accentuate some of the most perverted and predatory elements of ancient Hebrew culture and religion, its worst traits and traditions. The geopolitical expansionist movement called Zionism, especially at the upper levels, is made up of many who are little more than psychopathic atheists and bolshevists. This cult of power seekers glommed on to Judaism and Old Testament ethnocentrism, not to mention the ugliest teachings of the Talmud, to create the current nuclear-armed menace to world peace and justice. In one way or another, Talmudism lies at its heart.

This is acutely and painfully obvious in how the apartheid ministate, so-called, self-styled and misnamed as Israel, practices ethnic cleansing against the Palestinians in the cruelest of ways. Are they "fighting terrorism"? Or doing it themselves? If you agree that Zionism is committing crimes against humanity, now you know from whence came the inspirations, aspirations, expectations, implications, falsifications, fabrications and justifications.

"I would much rather see reasonable agreement with the Arabs on the basis of living together in peace than the creation of a Jewish state. . . My awareness of the essential nature of Judaism resists the idea of a Jewish state with borders, an army and a measure of temporal power, no matter how modest. I am afraid of the inner damage Judaism will suffer—especially from the development of a narrow nationalism within our ranks." —Albert Einstein, in a 1938 press interview

Zionism is the uppermost and paramount demonstration of Talmudic terrorism today. Along with its many victims—including Palestinians as well as European and American taxpayers—are the Judaic people themselves. Pray for an eventual exorcism of this demon whose satanic spirit is Zionism and whose nefarious and noxious name is Talmud. Until then, Judaism (and Judeo-Christianity) is sadly and solidly linked to the Zionist death machine. More and more each day, this is becoming an untenable political and personal position.

Do Good and Be Well

Spiritual people of all faiths need this information, not to mention voters and lawmakers. Share this book. Help me launch a truth-seeking missile.

Well, fellow explorers and truth-trekkers, all journeys come to an end, so we must part for now. As we fold our tents, remember what Rabbi Wise told us at the beginning of our expedition trail:

"The modern Jew is the product of the Talmud."

"And they turned away, and kept not the covenant. Even like their fathers they turned aside as a crooked bow. They provoked him to anger on their hills and moved him to jealousy with their graven things. God heard, and despised them, and he reduced Israel exceedingly as it were to nothing." —Psalm 77:57-59, designated Psalm 78 in Protestant versions. *Douay-Rheims English translation of the Latin Vulgate Bible.*

*On October 3, 2001, I.A.P. News reported that according to Israel Radio (in Hebrew, Kol Yisrael) an acrimonious argument erupted during the Israeli Cabinet weekly session the previous week between Israeli Prime Minister Ariel Sharon and his foreign minister, Shimon Peres. Peres warned Sharon that refusing to heed incessant American requests for a cease-fire with the Palestinians would endanger Israeli interests and "turn the U.S. against us. "Sharon reportedly yelled at Peres: "Don't worry about American pressure. We, the Jewish people, control America." http://www.mediamonitors.net/khodr49.html

Resources for Study

BOOKS, ARTICLES AND INTERNET RESOURCES FOR FURTHER STUDY:

[Even though lengthy, this bibliography and resource list is incomplete.]

Artamonov, M.I., *Studies in Ancient Khazar History* (in Russian) (Leningrad: 1936).

Baratz, H., *Collection of Works on the Question of Hebrew Elements in Ancient Russian Literature* (in Russian) Vol. I, Paris, 1926-27, Vol. II, Berlin, 1924.

Baron, S.W., *A Social and Religious History of the Jews*, 1952.

Bloch, Talia, "Genetics: A Skeleton in the Jewish Family Closet?," August 20, 2004. http://www.forward.com/articles/1864. http://www.thewinds.org/library/khazars.html

Borleis, Christian, "Tay-Sachs Disease," *The Barnes Review*, July 1997.

Brook, Kevin A., *The Jews of Khazaria*, 2nd ed. (Rowman & Littlefield Publishers, Inc, 2006).

Brook, Kevin A. (2005) "Khazars and Judaism" (Article in *The Encyclopedia of Judaism*, Second Edition (Leiden: Brill), vol. 2, pp. 1510-21).

Brook, Kevin A. (2005) "Khazar Empire" (Article in *Encyclopedia of World Trade: From Ancient Times to the Present* (Armonk, N.Y., M.E. Sharpe).

Brook, Kevin A. (2003) "The Origins of East European Jews" (Article in *Russian History/Histoire Russe*, vol. 30, nos. 1-2, pp. 1-22)

Brook, Kevin A. (2002) "Khazar-Byzantine Relations" (Chapter in *The Turks* (Ankara: Yeni Turkiye), vol. 1, pp. 509-515)

Brook, Kevin A. (1999) *The Jews of Khazaria* (Northvale, N.J.: Jason Aronson, Inc.) Mr. Brook is also the founder of www.khazaria.com, the largest repository of information about the Khazars available on the Internet.

Brutzkus, J., Chaseren, *Jewish Encyclopedia* (NY: 1901-1906).

Dunlop, Douglas M., *The History of the Jewish Khazars* (Princeton, NJ: 1954,

1967). Recently (8/08), the only two available copies, a 1967 edition, were from a book dealer in Jerusalem and one in USA. Actually, the Israeli copy was the best buy at $100; the American one was $250. No digital versions were found.

Frazer, Sir James, "The Killing of the Khazar Kings" in *Folklore*, XXVII, 1917.

Freedman, Benjamin, "Facts Are Facts: The Truth About the Khazars" (Letters from Freedman to Dr. Goldstein), 1954.

Gabriel, Judith, "Among the Norse Tribes: The Remarkable Account of Ibn Fadlan," in *Aramco World*, Vol. 50, No. 6, Nov./Dec. 1999.

Golden, Peter B. (1980). *Khazar Studies: An Historico-Philological Inquiry into the Origins of the Khazars*, Vol. 1. Budapest: Akadémiai Kiadó.

Golden, Peter B. (1990). "The Peoples of the South Russian Steppe," in *The Cambridge History of Early Inner Asia*, ed. Denis Sinor. Cambridge, UK: Cambridge University Press.

Golden, Peter B. (1992). *An Introduction to the History of the Turkic Peoples*. Wiesbaden, Germany: Harrassowitz Verlag.

Grayzel, Solomon, *A History of the Jews* (Philadelphia: Jewish Pub. Soc., 1947).

Grigor-Scott, Anthony. *Bible Believers Newsletter*. This website has a wealth of material on this and many related topics. Various cases have been brought against him to force him to take down his site, but this has not happened at this point in time. Visit http://www.biblebelievers.org.au/.

Halevi, Judah, *Kitab al Khazari*, translated from the Arabic (London: 1931).

Higger, Prof. Martin, *The Jewish Utopia* (Baltimore: Lord Baltimore Press, 1932). The only known extant copy surfaced at the University of Texas Library.

Hoffman, Michael, *Judaism Discovered* (Independent History and Research, 2008).

Johnson, Paul, *A History of the Jews* (NY: Harper, 1987).

Koestler, Arthur, *The 13th Tribe: The Khazar Empire and Its Heritage* (New York: Random House, 1976).

Kutschera, Hugo Feiherr von, *Die Chaeren* (Vienna: 1910).

Landau, ?, *The Present Position of the Khazar Problem* (in Hebrew; Jerusalem: 1942).

Martillo, Joachim, *The Origins of Modern Jewry: Against the Rationalization of Zionist Crimes*, http://eaazi.blogspot.com/2007/10/origins-of-modern-jewry.html

Mullins, Eustace, *Mullins' New History of the Jews*, 1978.

Noonan, Thomas S., (1997). "The Khazar Economy." *Archivum Eurasiae Medii Aevi* 9:253-318.

Oliver, Revilo, "The Khazars," *Liberty Bell* magazine.

Phoenix Journals. Over 100 volumes of spiritual teachings, commentary, and the inside story on many things, including the Khazar conspiracy, Zionism and a great deal more. Some of these fascinating books may be preserved on the Internet, but I have lost touch with the original publishers.

Poliak, A.N., *Khazaria—A History of a Jewish Kingdom In Europe or Kazaraiyyah*, only available in Hebrew (Tel Aviv: 1944 and 1951).

Poliak, A.N., *The Khazar Conversion to Judaism.* In Hebrew (Jerusalem: Zion Pub., 1941).

Pope, Hugh, "Freed of Russian Yoke, Turkic Nations Find They Miss the Alphabet" in *The Wall Street Journal*, 10.24.00, and fax from the author in Istanbul, dated 10.27.00.

Qumsiyeh, Mazin, "Zionazi Racial Science," Yale University, addresses the flaws in Zionazi racial science in a letter to the Society of Histocompatibility and Immunology.

(More material can be found at THE AMBASSADORS—OPINIONS—Vol. 5, Issue 1 (January 2002). http://ambassadors.net/archives/ issue11/opinions2.htm).

Rosenthal, Harold Wallace, "Modern Jews Are Neither Shemites Nor Israelites," 1976 interview.

Roderich-Stoltheim, F. and translated by Pownall, Capel, *The Riddle of the Jew's Success*, (Leipzig: Hammer Verlag, 1927), (Michael Santomauro: 2005). This informative but rarely seen book, translated from German, speaks of the Chasaren; the Jews portrayed as a race; the real history of ancient Israel etc. See pp. 220-26.

Sharf, A., *Byzantine Jewry—From Justinian to the Fourth Crusade* (London: 1941).

Stang, Alan, "Khazars, Communists, Zionists and These United States," News With Views.com, July 31, 2008.

Tiffany, John, "The Khazars—Non-Semitic Jews," *The Barnes Review*, Vol. III, No. 7, July 1997.

Vernadsky, G., *Ancient Russia* (New Haven: 1943).

Vernadsky, G., *Kievan Russia* (New Haven: 1948).

Wade, Nicholas, "Gog, Magog and the Kingdom of the Khazars: Geneticists Report Finding Central Asian Link to Levites." http://www.nytimes.com/2003/09/27/science/27GENE.html?tntemail0

Wexler, Paul, "Khazars," on http://www.israelshamir.net/.

White, Arnold, *The Modern Jew* (London: Wm. Heinemann, 1899).
I have included this little-known book written by British Jews about other

Jews. It does not mention the Khazars specifically, but is a great read for those studying the Judaic mindset. Curiously, the copyright page following the title page says, "... and is not to be imported into the USA."

Zeki Validi Togan, A., *Volkerschaften des Chaserenreiches im Neunten Jahrhundert* (Korosi Csoma-Archivum, 1940).

Zjaczkowski, M., "The Problem of the Language of the Khazars," in *Proceedings of the Breslau Society of Sciences*, 1946.

Zuckerman, C. (1995). "On the Date of the Khazars' Conversion to Judaism and the Chronology of the Kings of the Rus Oleg and Igor: A Study of the Anonymous Khazar Letter from the Genizah of Cairo." *Revue des Études Byzantines* 53:237—270.

INTERNET LINKS TO A COMPENDIUM OF ARTICLES ON ZIONISM

Read and circulate all the stories, but for a well-researched reliable guide to the Zionist movement, see the title article by Judy Andreas. For a true WWII shocker and what the early Zionists tried to do, see the second and third items. And, don't miss what an Orthodox rabbi has to say, the last story.

ZIONISM IS NOBODY'S FRIEND
http://rense.com/general71/zzon.htm

WWII NAZI-ZIONIST COLLABORATION
http://rense.com/general82/nzzi.htm

ZIONISM & THE ESTABLISHMENT OF MODERN POLAND
http://gnosticliberationfront.com/zionism_and_the_establishment1.htm

ZIONISM—A CONSPIRACY AGAINST JEWS
http://rense.com/general82/zaag.htm

A REAL CASE AGAINST THE JEWS
http://rense.com/general82/case.htm

THE EVILS OF ZIONISM
http://www.realjewnews.com/?p=58

POLL—AMERICAN JEWS HATE NEOCONS, AIPAC
http://washingtonindependent.com/563/i-know-what-jews-like

CHURCHILL ON ZIONIST WORLDWIDE CONSPIRACY
http://rense.com/general82/zxow.htm

10 QUESTIONS TO ZIONISTS
http://www.nkusa.org/Historical_Documents/tenquestions.cfm

ADDITIONAL MATERIAL

As to the "holocaust" check out this article, and read a little bit more about Khazarian Zionism.

Deconstructing 6,000,000 Holo-Myths, Exploring the Occult Origin of a Crucial Holocaust Dogma. Download and save the pdf link as an Adobe file.
Help launch this "Truth Seeking Missile." Download as a free pdf e-book. http://www.rense.com/general82/decon.pdf
Also, just click and read it online www.gnosticliberationfront.com/deconstructing_six_million_holo_myth.htm

PROFILE

About the Author

Dr. Harrell Rhome lives on the Texas Gulf Coast, where he researches and writes about current events, overlooked and ignored history, true-crime stories, world religions and metaphysics. Among other things, he has been described as a Revisionist philosopher. Harrell's articles appear in print publications and online. He is a contributing editor for *The Barnes Review* historical maga-  zine (Washington, D.C.), columnist for the Jeff Rense Program (USA) and for the *Nationalist Times* newspaper (Las Vegas, NV), a contributor to *New Dawn* magazine (Melbourne, Australia), *Tsunami Politico* online magazine (*en Espanol y Ingles desde Buenos Aires, Argentina*), Gnostic Liberation Front (USA, www.gnosticliberationfront.com), and other venues.

From the Temple To the Talmud

Exploring Judaic Origins, History, Folklore and Tribal Traditions

In *From the Temple to the Talmud,* Dr. Harrell
Rhome offers a panoramic look at Jewish history,
culture and religion from a Revisionist perspective.
Not content to merely repeat the findings of previous
researchers, Rhome offers a new interpretation of
Jewish history, one that is sure to enrage some and
leave others standing in ovation.

Going back to primary and ancient sources,
while also including research from scholars (many
of whom are now considered too politically incorrect
to cite by mainstream academicians), Rhome covers
this expansive history in a lively and easy to read
style, accompanied by many illustrations and a
lengthy list of sources for future research. No doubt, after reading *From the Temple
to the Talmud,* you will be well-versed in this fascinating and vitally important
subject which Rhome refers to as "the curiously camouflaged and conveniently
convoluted chronicle of the people called the Jews."

Chapters include: What Was the Ancient Hebrew Religion?; Exploring the Origins and Evolution of the Hebrew Language; The Old Testament Is Theology, Not
History; Esther, The Queen of Purim—A Talmudic Tale of Terror; Purim and the
Whole Megillah; Rome Gave Birth to Judaism; The Khazarian Connection; Judaic
Origins and Genetic Testing; The Yiddish Language and Ashkenazi Tribal Traditions;
Demystifying the Talmud; Talmudic Mysticism and the Occult; Unveiling the Kabala
—A Saga of Sorcery and Psychopolitics; Halakha Law and Talmudic Legalism; Judaism and Christianity—A Dysfunctional Relationship; Judaism and Christianity—
A Focus on the Iberian Expulsions; Judaism and Christianity—Banning and Burning
the Talmud; The Real History of the Hexagram Called the Star of David; The Protocols of Zion—Forgeries or Fact?; and Talmudism Today.

In the maverick tradition of one of the great historians of the modern era . . .

A gutsy newspaper with some powerful enemies

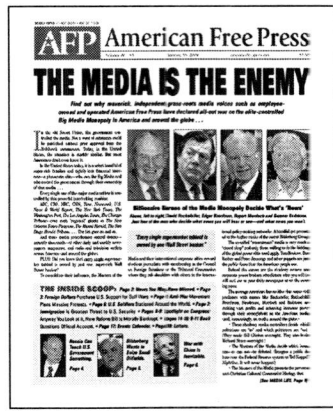

A no-nonsense independent weekly alternative to the "processed news" of the corporate Media Monopoly.

The one news outlet that dares to tackle the mainstream!

American Free Press (AFP) is the maverick national media voice that's been in the forefront reporting the uncensored news that the Controlled Media in America either ignores or suppresses.

You can count on AFP to bring the news that the major media either can not or will not report. Employee-owned-and-operated with no partisan axes to grind, AFP's reporters are committed to the truth, no matter whose ox gets gored.

AFP is the one national newspaper that's dared to tackle the Israeli lobby head on and challenge that clique of neo-conservative warmongers—that well-financed ring of arms dealers, lobbyists and "ex-Trotskyites"—who forced America into the no-win debacle in Iraq. AFP brings its readers the important stories consigned to the Orwellian Memory Hole by the self-styled "mainstream" media.

Each week—20 pages of uncensored news and information on a wide variety of topics, ranging from civil liberties and the fight against the police state to alternative health and wholistic therapies, taxes and finance, trade and foreign policy. You name it. AFP is on the cutting edge.

Big-name political figures and a host of powerful special interest groups have worked overtime to silence AFP's unswerving journalists whose track record is one that's unmatched by any other independent media voice today. If you have any doubts, why not take a look at AFP for yourself?

Isn't it time you subscribe?

American Free Press: $59 for ONE year (weekly issues) OR try out a 16-week introductory subscription for only $17.76.

Call 1-888-699-NEWS (6397) today and charge a subscription to major credit cards.

Or send your check, money order or credit card information (including expiration date) to:

American Free Press
645 Pennsylvania Avenue SE, Suite 100
Washington, D.C. 20003

Check us out at www.americanfreepress.net. Online subscriptions also available!

March of the Titans: A History of the White Race. Here it is: the complete and comprehensive history of the White race, spanning 500 centuries of tumultuous events from the steppes of Russia to the African continent, to Asia, the Americas and beyond. This is their inspirational story—of vast visions, empires, achievements, triumphs against staggering odds, reckless blunders, crushing defeats and stupendous struggles. Most importantly of all, revealed in this work is the one true cause of the rise and fall of the world's greatest empires—that all civilizations rise and fall according to their racial homogeneity and nothing else—a nation can survive wars, defeats, natural catastrophes, but not racial dissolution. This is a revolutionary new view of history and of the causes of the crisis facing modern Western Civilization, which will permanently change your understanding of history, race and society. Covering every continent, every White country both ancient and modern, and then stepping back to take a global view of modern racial realities, this book not only identifies the cause of the collapse of ancient civilizations, but also applies these lessons to modern Western society. The author, Arthur Kemp, spent more than 25 years traveling over four continents, doing primary research to compile this unique book. There is no other book like it in existence—a book to pass on from generation to generation, so that all will know the true history of the White race. New deluxe softcover, signature sewn, 8.25" x 11" format, 592 pages, hundreds of B&W pictures, four-page color section, indexed, appendices, bibliography, chapters on every conceivable White culture group and more. High-quality softcover, 592 pages, #464, *$42*.

The Dartmoor Massacre: A British Atrocity Against American POWs During the War of 1812. By Vivian Bird. Seven unarmed American prisoners were killed and more would die from the more than a score that were wounded. No members of the British garrison were killed or injured. The British garrison commander attempted to hide and bury the dead before the prison doctor could produce a body count. Also includes: a list of killed and wounded and how they died; the ships from which almost all were impressed by the Royal Navy; depositions from eyewitnesses on all sides; little-known details of the massacre; photos and diagrams. Softcover, 104 pages, #319, *$13. NOW JUST $8.*

War & Death of the American Dream. By Robert Thomas Raming. The two-party system in America is dysfunctional. It has degenerated into a group of career politicians corrupted by power. Once a beacon for liberty and justice, the U.S. has embarked on a course of war that threatens to destroy the American Dream. There is a small and secret group of power brokers intent on ending liberty as they establish a New World Order. Softcover, 205 pages, #450, *$12*.

Guilt by Association: How Deception and Self-Deceit Took America to War. Jeff Gates explains how the Israeli lobby endangers and discredits America by welding U.S. foreign policy to the colonial Zionism pursued by expansionist Israel. Shows how a transnational criminal syndicate staged the latest financial crisis. Softcover, 287 pages, #514, was *$25. Reduced price—$19.*

The New Babylon: A Panoramic Overview of the Historical, Religious and Economic Origins of the New World Order. Here are the facts on the Rothschild Empire-controlled "City of London" and its global reach—a "secret history" of the last 200 years and of the Talmudic origins of the New World Order in ancient Babylon. After writing *The New Jerusalem,* Michael Collins Piper realized there was more to the story of Zionist power in the world—there were hidden religious and economic reasons that explained why our republic had fallen into the hands of forces working to establish a New World Order. In this titanic volume—280 pages in length and relying on many hard-to-find historical documents and other materials—Piper explores the hidden history of the New World Order and explains how it all evolved: from the teachings of the Talmud to the rise of the International Money Power to the reign of the House of Rothschild. Softcover, 280 pages, #521, *$25.*

Judas Goats: The Infiltration & Subversion of the American Nationalist Movement. Here is Michael Collins Piper's nationalist blockbuster. This book—perhaps more than any other book ever written—exposes the Mossad, CIA, FBI and Southern Poverty Law Center sabotage of patriotic and nationalist groups in America throughout the last 75 years. Some real shockers in this uncensored exposé including: J. Edgar Hoover ran chapters of the KKK and Communist Party USA; federal agents in Oklahoma City at the time of the bombing; McCarthyism vindicated; FDR's Sedition Trial; the real Roy Bullock—ADL spy; Judas Goats still working in the movement. Much more. Softcover, 375 pages, #465, *$25.*

The Golem: Israel's Nuclear Hell Bomb and the Road to Global Armageddon. Veteran author Michael Collins Piper pulls no punches in asserting that Israel's nuclear "Hell Bomb" is pushing civilization toward global Armageddon and that the perpetration of this un-controlled weapons program has the world held hostage. Piper explains the danger the planet faces from American collaboration with a nuclear-armed Israel. Israel has worked relentlessly to construct an atomic arsenal—its Golem—as the foundation of its national security strategy. Outlining the whole shocking story, Piper demonstrates that America's international policy has been hijacked by supporters of Israel who—in combination with a mass media dominated by Zionists—have become the masters of America's destiny. Softcover, 198 pages, #571, *$25.*

Rebel Wisdom: A Collection of Confederate Quotations. Assembled by the TBR staff. History is written by the victors. The history of the War of Southern Secession was no different. But in this powerful 60-page booklet we hear from the vanquished—both well known and obscure. Quotes and speeches from Jefferson Davis, Robert E. Lee and Stonewall Jackson. Quotes from Longstreet, Forrest, Quantrill, Stuart and dozens more—from the generals to the privates. Also includes a list of top officers in the Southern military, leaders of the secessionist government, the Confederate Constitution, South Carolina's declaration of independence and more. Softcover, saddle stitched, 60 pages, #520, *$6.*

CALL 1-877-773-9077
TO CHARGE TOLL FREE

TBR ORDERING COUPON TBR subscribers take 10% off book prices

Item #	Description/Title	Qty	Cost Ea.	Total
		SUBTOTAL		
		Add S&H on books*		
	Send me a 1-year subscription to TBR for $46**			
	Send me a 2-year subscription to TBR for $78**			
		TOTAL		

*S&H ON BOOKS: Add $5 S&H on orders up to $50. Add $10 S&H on orders from $52.01 to $100. Add $15 S&H on orders over $100. Outside the U.S. double these S&H charges.

TBR SUBSCRIPTION PRICES: U.S.A: $46 one year; $78 two years. **Canada/Mexico: $65 per year. **ALL OTHER NATIONS:** $30 per year delivered via air mail.

PAYMENT OPTIONS: ❏ CHECK/MO ❏ VISA ❏ MC ❏ AMEX ❏ DISCOVER

Card # _____

Expiration Date _____ Signature _____

CUSTOMER INFORMATION:

Name _____

Address _____

City/State/Zip _____

RETURN WITH PAYMENT TO: THE BARNES REVIEW, P.O. Box 15877, Washington, D.C. 20003. Cal 1-877-773-9077 toll free to charge to major credit cards.

TTT911

CPSIA information can be obtained at www.ICGtesting.com
Printed in the USA
LVOW090531271111

256598LV00002B/1/P